Early Christianity

Examining sources and case studies, this fascinating book explores early Christianity, how it was studied, how it is studied now, and how Judaeo-Christian values came to form the ideological bedrock of modern western culture.

Looking at the diverse source materials available, from the earliest New Testament texts and the complex treatises of early Christian authors such as Lactantius and Eusebius, to archaeology, epigraphy, and papyrology, the book examines what is needed to study the subject, what materials are available, how useful they are, and how the study of the subject may be approached.

Case study chapters focus on important problems in the study of early Christianity including:

- the book of Acts as a source for the social dynamics of cities and the tensions inherent in Hellenistic Judaism
- orthodoxy and organization in early Christianity
- early Christianity and the Roman empire.

Also including a comprehensive guide for students that lists major collections of literary and non-literary sources, the chief journals and series, and important textbooks, *Early Christianity* is an excellent aid to the study of Christianity in history.

Mark Humphries is senior lecturer in Classics at the National University of Ireland, Maynooth. He is the author of *Communities of the Blessed* (OUP 1999) and a chapter in the *Cambridge Ancient History* XIV (2000). He is a general editor of the series *Translated Texts for Historians*.

Classical Foundations

The books in this series introduce students to the broad areas of study within classical studies and ancient history. They will be particularly helpful to students coming to the subject for the first time, or to those already familiar with an academic discipline who need orientation in a new field. The authors work to a common brief but not to a rigid structure: they set out to demonstrate the importance of the chosen subject and the lines of recent and continuing research and interpretation. Each book will provide a brief survey of the range of the subject, accompanied by some case studies demonstrating how one may go on deeper into it. Each will also include guidance of a practical kind on sources, resources and reference material, and how to pursue the subject further. When complete, the series will comprise a critical map of the whole field of ancient studies.

The series is planned to include:

Early Christianity
Greek History
Greek Literature
Greek Philosophy
Late Antiquity
Latin Literature
Roman Social History
The Roman Empire

Books currently available in the series:

Roman Social History
Susan Treggiari

Latin Literature
Susanna Morton Braund

Greek History
Robin Osborne

Early Christianity
Mark Humphries

Early Christianity

Mark Humphries

LONDON AND NEW YORK

First published 2006
by Routledge
2 Park Square, Milton Park, Abingdon, Oxon OX14 4RN

Simultaneously published in the USA and Canada
by Routledge
270 Madison Ave, New York, NY 10016

Transferred to Digital Printing 2007

Routledge is an imprint of the Taylor & Francis Group, an informa business

Typeset in Garamond by
Florence Production Ltd, Stoodleigh, Devon

Printed and bound in Great Britain by
TJI Digital, Padstow, Cornwall

British Library Cataloguing in Publication Data
A catalogue record for this book is available from the British Library

Library of Congress Cataloging in Publication Data
Humphries, Mark.
Early Christianity/by Mark Humphries. – 1st ed.
p. cm. – (Classical foundations)
Includes bibliographical references and index.
1. Church history – Primitive and early church, ca. 30–600 I. Title. II. Series.
BR165.H74 2006
270.1–dc22 2005023645

ISBN10: 0–415–20538–7 (hbk)
ISBN10: 0–415–20539–5 (pbk)

ISBN13: 9–78–0–415–20538–2 (hbk)
ISBN13: 9–78–0–415–20539–9 (pbk)

For Tim, Ash, Luke, and Joey

God shall have a starring role in my history of the world. How could it be otherwise? If He exists, then He is responsible for the whole marvellous appalling narrative. If He does not, then the very proposition that He might has killed more people and exercised more minds than anything else. He dominates the stage.

Penelope Lively, *Moon Tiger*

I do not know if you are one of those who look down on everything called religion and theology with disdain or indifference. And yet, no matter how one looks at Christianity, and possibly regards it as a mistake, is it not of real value to pursue the history of this mistake and discover the world shaking events and transformations this mistake had caused?

Adolf von Harnack, private letter, 1869
(cited in Frend 2003: 11)

Contents

Preface

It is quite a challenge, I have discovered, to write a book that explains not only what one does, but also how and even why one does it. That this book should have been written at all, and that the writing of it was a pleasurable task, should be attributed to the support of many friends and colleagues. First and foremost, I am grateful to Richard Stoneman for his invitation to contribute to the *Classical Foundations* series. In these days when university courses empower students to choose from a diverse range of modular units, and when, as a consequence, university teachers cannot assume that all students will have had the same basic training, it seems to me useful that there should be books that provide students with basic orientation in specific subjects and their methodologies. Richard is to be commended, therefore, for taking the initiative in editing a series of books that answers this need. More than that, I am grateful to him personally for his assistance and encouragement – not to mention his great patience – at various stages in the thinking through and writing of the volume, and for feeding me both his own thoughts and those of other contributors to the series. Also at Routledge, Amy Laurens and Annamarie Kino have seen the book through the press most efficiently. I have been saved from many errors and infelicities by the perceptive copy-editing of Frances Brown.

Others too have made their contributions to whatever virtues the book possesses. Much of the initial thinking that underpins this book was done while I was a doctoral student in St Andrews between 1993 and 1996. I should like to reiterate my gratitude to the many who were thanked in the published version of my doctorate (Humphries 1999), especially Gillian Clark and Mary Whitby, who have done much to shape my attitudes to early Christianity and late antiquity. Although the initial thoughts for the book were generated elsewhere, it was written entirely at the National University of Ireland, Maynooth. One could wish for no better colleagues than David Scourfield, Kieran McGroarty, Gordon Campbell, Michael Clarke, and Maeve O'Brien: they have provided an ideal environment in which to think and work, by turns supporting me and refusing to let me take myself too seriously. Like them, I have found that my research and teaching would be an immeasurably more taxing business (if not down-right impossible) were it not for the excellent organizational skills of Breege Lynch. Teaching and research are inextricably linked activities, so I am happy to thank those Maynooth students who have endured my courses touching on the Roman empire, early Christianity, and late antiquity for listening to my ideas, criticizing them, and, above all, insisting that my exposition *should be clearer*. Meanwhile, many friends in Ireland, Britain, and beyond have provided all manner of support, both academic and personal. In particular, Ann Marie Mealey sustained me in so many ways during completion of the book. As always, my family has been the touchstone of humanity against which I can judge the worth of my endeavours. I continue to be grateful to them for their love, support, and interest in what I do. My first book was dedicated to my parents; it is only right, therefore, that the second should be offered to my brother and his family. Needless to say, none of those mentioned above should be blamed for the eccentricities or shortcomings of what I have written.

Introduction: how to use this book

This book is designed for those beginning the study of early Christianity, particularly students at university pursuing courses on aspects of the ancient Greek and Roman world, and for those general readers for whom the subject holds some fascination. Like the other books in this series, it aims to map out the subject, providing novices with basic orientation on issues, methods, and sources; it is not, therefore, yet another history of the early Christian centuries (for examples, see chapter 7). In common with the guidelines offered by the publisher of the series, and suggestions made by the authors of other volumes, it is unashamedly a personal and idiosyncratic volume. Perhaps appropriately for a volume on the emergence of Christianity in the ancient world, my aim here is to preach, and not necessarily to the converted. I hope that, having read all or some of it, students and general readers will have some idea of what the study of early Christianity entails; how in various ways it might be approached; what problems are likely to be encountered when studying it; and why, perhaps, the subject might be exciting, worthwhile, and even important.

Methods of citation

All sources, ancient and modern, are cited in parentheses in the main text. This is intended to cut down on distracting scholarly apparatus such as footnotes. For ancient sources, see chapter 3 and the relevant section of chapter 7. Modern works are listed in the bibliography at the end of the book. All references have been kept to a minimum so as to reduce disruption of the flow of the text. Endnotes are used only to provide additional information that it would have been too cumbersome to include in the main text of the book. In general, I have tried to limit my citations to works that are available in English (hence translations of works in other languages). This is not to denigrate the massive achievements of non-Anglophone authors, but it recognizes an utterly lamentable reality of modern Anglophone society: the decline in the study of modern European languages. I remember well that, when I began my studies as an undergraduate, more than half of the first reading list I was given comprised works in French, German, Italian, and Spanish. Sadly, not many university teachers would feel confident enough to do this any more. Readers of this book who follow up references in the books and articles listed in my bibliography will soon discover, however, the riches to be gleaned from scholarship published in other languages.

Modern authors are cited by means of the 'Harvard system', that is, by the author's surname (sometimes preceded by an initial, or initials, in cases where two or more authors have the same surname) followed by the date of publication of the article or book to which I am referring, and then the page number. Such references may be followed up easily enough in the bibliography. Thus, for example, Pagels 1988: 56 refers to page 56 of E. Pagels (1988) *Adam, Eve, and the Serpent*, Harmondsworth: Penguin. Page numbers in lower case Roman numerals refer to citations from the preliminaries (preface, foreword, and so forth) of a book. Where a modern work has multiple volumes, the volume number is indicated by upper case Roman numerals (e.g. I, 172 = volume one, page 172).

The citation of ancient sources particularly must seem somewhat arcane to those unfamiliar with the study of the ancient world. The numbering of such references depends not on page numbers, as is the case with modern books, but on the manner in which ancient, medieval, or modern editors divided up the text. Generally speaking, such references are tripartite, with the separate elements divided by full stops. The first element alludes to the book (in ancient and medieval terms meaning not the whole work, but rather one of its larger constituent units); the second to the chapter; the third to a section or (in biblical texts) verse. Thus the reference Eusebius, *Ecclesiastical History* 6.7.3 refers to book 6, chapter 7, and section 3 of that work. A similar system is used when referring to books of the Bible, except that the names of the books are used instead of numbers. (Readers familiar with biblical texts may notice that I also put the names of biblical texts *in italics*, rather than leaving them in roman typeface, which is the more common practice; I do so in order to indicate that I am treating the books of the Bible as sources on an equal footing with the writings of other ancient authors, whether Christian, pagan, or Jewish.) Thus *Acts* 14.8–12 refers to chapter 14, sections (or verses) 8 to 12, of the *Acts of the Apostles* in the New Testament. While this basic principle holds for most ancient sources, some will have an idiosyncratic system of numbering; this will usually be described in editions and translations of the relevant work.

For ancient sources I have decided, for the most part, to eschew abbreviations. These too can often cause confusion for beginners. The only place where I have deviated from this is for books of Christian scripture, the New Testament. The shortened forms used in this book correspond to those commonly used at the tops of pages in modern bibles. The principles I have used can be elucidated quite briefly. Gospel accounts are referred to by the name of the author to whom they are commonly (but, as we will see in chapter 3, incorrectly) ascribed. Thus *Mark* is shorthand for *The Gospel according to Mark*. For the various epistles, I have used the shorthand of simply using the name of the addressee: thus *Philippians* for Paul's *Letter to the Philippians*.

Where there is more than one letter sent to the same addressee, or where a number of letters are ascribed to the one author, I have used the following format: *1 Corinthians* refers to Paul's *First Letter to the Corinthians*, and *1 Peter* refers to *The First Epistle of Peter*.

Non-literary sources, such as inscriptions and papyri, present particular problems of citation. Inscriptions have been cited by their number in particular collections: this is highlighted by the abbreviation 'no.' in the citation. For example, Smallwood 1967: no. 376 means inscription number 376 in E. M. Smallwood (1967) *Documents Illustrating the Principates of Caius, Claudius, and Nero*, Cambridge: Cambridge University Press. I have not cited many papyrus texts or similar materials, such as texts on leather, except for those from the Dead Sea Scrolls (chapter 3) and the Nag Hammadi library (chapter 5). Explanations of their systems of citation will be found in standard translations of them: for the Dead Sea Scrolls, see Vermes 1997; for Nag Hammadi see Robinson 1988.

Dates

I feel that beginners will require some explanation of the dating conventions I have used. The early Christians who are the subject of this book did not know the system of dating that allows us (or many of us at any rate) to fix ourselves at the beginning of the third millennium. On the contrary, they would have used a variety of dating techniques, defining the year (amongst other methods) according to who were the consuls (chief magistrates) in the city of Rome, how long an emperor had been in power, when the year fell in the taxation cycle, or how long it had been since the foundation of their local major city. Our system of dating owes its origins to the endeavours of the sixth-century monk Dionysius Exiguus, whose scheme originated as an offshoot of his efforts to regularize the date for the church's Easter celebrations. As part of his computations, Dionysius devised a system of dating years according to a sequence beginning with the birth of Jesus

Christ; events happened, therefore, 'in the year of the Lord', or, in Dionysius' Latin, *Anno Domini*. Unfortunately, and notoriously, Dionysius' calculations went awry, placing the birth of Christ some four or five years after it actually may have occurred. Nevertheless, this is the system we use today, with the term *Anno Domini* abbreviated as AD. The corresponding system of dating events prior to Christ's birth is altogether later, seeming not to have originated until the seventeenth century. From this we get the system of dating events according to years (counted backwards) 'Before Christ', or BC.

BC and AD dating is, then, an explicitly Christian reckoning of time, and as a consequence it has been the focus of much vigorous scholarly debate, however nit-picking and preposterous that may seem to those outside academic circles. Frequently BC and AD are replaced with BCE and CE, a convention that seems to have arisen, in a commendable spirit of religious inclusivity, among biblical scholars, and which is becoming common, even in books on aspects of non-biblical antiquity. BCE and CE stand for 'Before the Common Era' and 'Common Era', and thus divest the calculation of time of its Christian element. But it seems to me that making a Christian era a common one seems a surreptitious way of imposing a Christian conception of time on non-Christians. It strikes me, moreover, that this debate will not matter much to many readers of this book, for whom BC and AD are familiar and uncontroversial. In any case, most dates in this book are to be assumed to be AD: I have only appended the abbreviations AD and BC where there is ambiguity.

The structure of this book

Early Christianity is a complex subject, encompassing all areas of human endeavour, and too large to be covered by a single volume of modest proportions. The topics touched on in the following chapters could be (indeed, have been) the subject of numerous and lengthy books in their own right. For example, I could have written much more about the interpenetration between early Christian theology and classical philosophy, early Christian attitudes to gender, or questions of early Christian doctrine (more broadly than it is discussed in chapter 5). For the purposes of this book, however, I have chosen to limit my analysis of aspects of early Christianity in the ancient Mediterranean to three major topics: how the origins of Christianity were influenced by the social and cultural world of the early Roman empire (chapter 4); the problems of maintaining orthodoxy and unity as Christianity spread throughout the Mediterranean world (chapter 5); and the nature of the early Christians' dealings with the Roman authorities (chapter 6). The purpose of these chapters, however, is not to give a narrative of these particular aspects of early Christianity, but, by means of case studies and discussions of the sources, to suggest ways in which these topics might be approached. For that reason I have sometimes left discussions open-ended, rather than seek to reach definite conclusions. Indeed, it is my hope that those topics could form the basis of student discussions in a tutorial or seminar. It is hoped that readers interested in other topics may satisfy their curiosity by following up the leads provided in chapter 7's guide to study aids and in the bibliography. By way of establishing a context for the modern study of early Christianity, the first three chapters will deal with questions of how we approach the topic. The first chapter introduces the basic contours of the subject and discusses reasons why we might want to study it. Many generations of scholars have done so, of course, and my second chapter examines the ways in which early Christianity has been examined in the past. In this discussion I have sought to emphasize how the researches of earlier scholars were often driven by agendas particular to their own time, place, and religious beliefs (or lack of them). This is a useful reminder to readers of this book that they might want to ponder how their own approach is shaped by similar concerns. Next, chapter 3 outlines what source materials are at the disposal of anyone seeking to delve into the world of the early Christians, and what problems of interpretation those sources present.

For all its limitations, I hope that the book will touch on areas that are of interest to most students of early Christianity, and that it will give beginners some guidance on how the subject might be studied. I should stress, however, that this book is intended as a starting point, nothing more. If you are using it for your studies, then use it in conjunction with some of the other works suggested in chapter 7 and listed in the bibliography. You cannot learn everything from one book! Above all, try to immerse yourself in the ancient sources, either through the many excellent sourcebooks available or, preferably, by reading translations of complete texts. If you can read the texts in their original languages, then so much the better.

Finally, I do not think that it is out of place to say something of the perspective of the author, even if some may see this as pretentious. To study early Christianity is to touch on topics that have meant, and still mean, a great deal to many people. As chapter 2 shows, the manner in which early Christianity has been studied in the past was shaped by the agendas of scholars of the times. Moreover, attitudes to early Christianity have been inextricably linked to areas of debate where emotions run high and where, in some extreme cases (such as the relationship between Christianity and Judaism), there has been conflict and even the spilling of blood. These are sobering considerations for the historian of early Christianity. It is hardly possible to approach such a topic without bringing along one's own intellectual or emotional baggage. For my own part, I am not in any sense a committed Christian; nor did I experience a religious upbringing beyond a conventional trip to the baptismal font as an infant. Even so, I did grow up amid religious friends and relatives in a society saturated by Christian values. My early childhood was spent in Northern Ireland during a period when sectarian violence between Christians was rife, although I left before I was of an age when such sectarian differences would have had any serious impact on my life. (Indeed, it was only in my last weeks there that other pupils at my predominantly Presbyterian primary school surmised that, on account of my Roman Catholic baptism, I must therefore have been, in the language of derogatory sectarian name-calling, 'a Fenian'.) Nevertheless, I think this has influenced the framework in which I interpret religious history, Christian or non-Christian. It is all too easy to dismiss as ignorance the religious fervour that underpins sectarian hatred. To me, however, this background of bitter religious antagonism has served as a constant reminder that the historical religious beliefs and opinions that I study surely meant a great deal to those who professed them. The study of early Christianity entails not just an appreciation of culture, ideas, and social institutions, but a realization that one is dealing with the passions that have motivated people's souls. To treat these topics seriously seems to me not simply the academic duty of a historian, but the moral obligation of a human being.

Chapter 1

What is early Christianity and why does it deserve study?

The shape of early Christianity

It may be worth beginning with a definition of what is meant in this book by 'early Christianity'. Let me take 'early' first. I will be analysing Christianity between the life of Jesus Christ, in the early first century AD, and the conversion of the Roman emperor Constantine (306–37) to Christianity at the beginning of the fourth. By setting these limits and by describing the Christianity in this book as 'early' it will seem that I am imposing upon it the traditional approach of dividing the past up into distinct periods (e.g. 'ancient', 'medieval', 'early modern', etc.). Such periodization, as it is called, is rather out of fashion with historians these days. Of course, human activity does not neatly fall into such categories. They are devised, rather, by historians looking back on the past and trying to impose some 'structure' on a rather more chaotic reality. For that reason, therefore, such periods may be described better as *historians'* concepts rather than as *historical* ones (cf. K. Jenkins 1991: 16). It was not the case, after all, that Christians leaped out of bed one morning and exclaimed that early Christianity was at an end and that late antique or medieval Christianity had begun. Indeed, one recent study has shown that deciding where early Christianity ends is difficult to determine, and that the change to medieval Christianity was something that happened gradually and fitfully over a number of centuries (Markus 1990). Yet one has to begin somewhere and, pedagogically, periods provide manageable chunks that can be comprehended easily by students. Even so, I ought to offer some justification for the limits set on the particular period I have chosen if they are not to appear entirely arbitrary.

My choice is dictated by a happy coincidence of the practicalities of publishing and what I discern as ancient realities. It is anticipated that this series will contain another book on the period after Constantine's conversion, so it seemed appropriate for me to draw my study to an end at that point. But that decision imposed by the publisher reflects a real difference between the character of Christianity in the pre- and post-Constantinian periods. After Constantine's conversion, the Roman state generally accorded Christianity its support, and emperors (with the exception of the pagan convert Julian 'the Apostate', who ruled for about a year and a half between 361 and 363) were also vigorous in promoting the interests of the Christian community (E. D. Hunt 1998). In other words, the Christian church now began to be an important institution of – as opposed to just *in* – the Roman empire. As such, Constantine's conversion marks an important stage in the process by which the Christian church was to become the major political and social as well as religious institution of medieval Christendom.

Before Constantine's conversion the situation was rather different. Far from enjoying the adherence or support of the emperors, Christianity periodically experienced their wrath in the form of persecution (although, as we shall see in chapter 6, this was never a uniform process and defies easy generalizations). So what unifies the Christianity described here is that it existed within an intermittently hostile environment whose form it could not determine and whose destiny it could not dictate, for all its aspirations to do so. This political circumstance was reflected in a variety of other social realities that influenced the development of Christianity before Constantine. Limited resources, wedded perhaps to a fear of intermittent persecution, meant that prior to Constantine's conversion early Christianity was unable, except at a local or regional level, to construct public administrative institutions (by which we might mean – in modern terms – a hierarchy of bishops) that could oversee the affairs of all Christian communities throughout the whole of the Roman empire.[1] As a result, individual Christian groups often developed in isolation from each other. This meant that when, under Constantine, they were at last able to engage in free communication with each other, they often found that their approaches to certain aspects of ritual, organization, and the articulation of belief threw up numerous opportunities for debate (see chapter 5). In short, during the period between Christ and Constantine, Christianity evolved as a religion within the society of the ancient Mediterranean, heavily influenced by, but with very little capacity to shape, that society. It is this that gives unity to the subject of this book.

Of course, the conversion of Constantine, while it represents an important landmark, does not mark a complete break in the development of Christianity. Christians and their leaders did not immediately start behaving in radically different ways, except, perhaps, in their attitude to the Roman emperor and imperial institutions (such as the city).[2] Rather, the history of Christianity is marked by significant continuities between the periods before and after Constantine. The support of the Roman empire and its personnel was not given to the church unconditionally: some Christians continued to experience harassment from the imperial authorities even after Constantine's conversion (see chapter 6). Similarly, the world into which Christianity was born did not change immediately with the birth of Jesus, however much some Christians, both now and in the past, might wish to believe that this was so (see chapters 3 and 6). Nor did the development of Christianity occur in a vacuum, unaffected by the society in which it evolved. If we are to understand the particular circumstances that influenced the origins and development of Christianity, then, we will need to look back in time before Jesus' career and the activities of his followers. Hence, while the focus of this book is the period between Christ and Constantine, it will sometimes be necessary to range beyond these limits to explain particular aspects of early Christianity.

At the risk of seeming facetious, I should also say something on what the word 'Christianity' means in this book. As various chapters below will argue, early Christianity possessed certain characteristics that distinguish it from modern Christianity. We would be making a serious error if we wished to make early Christianity fit in every respect expectations derived from study or experience of its modern descendant. For example, any debate as to whether or not the emperor Constantine was 'really a Christian' (a hoary question favoured by a certain style of scholar) would go seriously awry if the emperor's Christianity was expected to conform neatly with modern definitions of what a Christian is. To assess Constantine's Christianity, we need to comprehend what Christianity meant generally in the early fourth century and, altogether more specifically, we should attempt to determine what it might have meant to Constantine himself.

More importantly, I wish to distinguish between my approach to 'early Christianity' and more traditional accounts of 'the early church'. To talk in terms of 'the early church' is to give priority to institutional manifestations of Christianity. What is worse, perhaps, is that treatments of 'the early church' risk becoming partisan. Sometimes they privilege one particular definition of 'the church', emphasizing continuities that may be discerned in its development as an organization and in its definitions of belief. Such approaches tend to focus on the affairs of bishops, theologians, and their opponents, and thus to marginalize (or even omit) other groups, such as women and the laity at large (cf. Rousseau 2002: 5). A significant repercussion of this approach is that traditional histories of 'the church' often stress how throughout history it had a monopoly on 'orthodox' or 'correct' doctrine (see chapters 2 and 5 below). Groups that deviated from this 'church' are dismissed as 'heretical' and portrayed as temporary aberrations from what came to be identified with 'the church'. Such partisanship, it should be noted, reveals the extent to which modern scholars of early Christianity can be regarded as prisoners of the sources upon which they rely: many early Christian writings – from the first-century texts that make up the New Testament to Eusebius of Caesarea's early fourth-century *Ecclesiastical History* – are concerned (in part at least) with precisely such questions of authority and correct belief within the Christian community. As I will argue later in this book (especially in chapter 5), however, such a perspective represents only one particular view of what early Christianity should be; there were other views and they are as much a part of the early Christian story as 'the church'. Indeed, some modern scholars have argued that the diversity of practice and belief apparent in early Christian writings makes it difficult to identify a single, easily defined phenomenon that can be called 'Christianity' in this period. For that reason, it has become fashionable in some circles to talk in terms not of a single early Christianity but of plural early Christianities.[3] In sum, then, the Christianity described in this book may seem surprisingly strange and diverse to readers expecting it to be little different from, say, modern Presbyterianism or Catholicism. That, however, is part of its fascination.

A further factor influencing the scope of this book on early Christianity is that it is published in a series called *Classical Foundations*. It therefore approaches early Christianity as a topic for study within the classical world, the ancient civilizations of Greece and Rome. But such civilizations were diverse, and even within a university Classics department you might receive very different definitions of what is 'important' in the study of classical antiquity if you were to ask, on the one hand, a scholar of fifth-century BC Greek literature or, on the other, an archaeologist working on the Roman army. In other words, the shape and contents of a book on early Christianity for *Classical Foundations* will be influenced by the author's own view of the Classical world. Before proceeding further, therefore, it will be worthwhile to explain what that authorial perspective is.

I am writing this book as someone trained and employed as a Roman historian, with interests primarily in social and cultural history. For the period between Christ and Constantine this means that I am concerned with the society of the Roman empire which, for most of that time, stretched from Britain in the north to the Sahara desert in the south, from the Atlantic coast of Spain and Portugal in the west to Syria and Jordan in the east. At the heart of this enormous expanse of territory lay the Mediterranean Sea which, for many Greeks and Romans, was viewed as the centre of the inhabited world. As a Roman historian approaching the topic of early Christianity, it is the Mediterranean and the lands bordering it that will form the focus of my study. From this perspective, early Christianity was a phenomenon that was born in the Middle East, that spread out from there through the eastern Mediterranean to Asia Minor and Greece, and which from there made its way to the west, to Africa, Gaul, and, at the centre of the empire, to Italy and Rome itself. Of course, this perspective is not the only one possible. A classicist who works on philosophy rather than social history, for example, would take a very different view of what is important in the study of early Christianity (e.g. Jaeger 1962; Pelikan 1993). Similarly, Christianity did not only spread from the Middle East to the west, but in other directions too: east to Armenia and central Asia, and south to Ethiopia, Arabia, and beyond. This last topic, however important it certainly is, lies outside the interests of most scholars working on early Christianity from the perspective of the classical world, and so is not considered here. Let us return, therefore, to the Mediterranean.

It is only fair to advise readers that I consider the Mediterranean background crucial to understanding the evolution of early Christianity. This is hardly an original insight; attempts have been made, for example, to appraise the career of Jesus as that of 'a Mediterranean Jewish peasant' (Crossan 1991). But not everyone who studies the ancient Mediterranean interprets it in the same way, and what they mean by 'the Mediterranean background' will depend on the criteria they use to define it. Some, for example, talk about Mediterranean culture in terms of its unity, emphasizing characteristics that may be found throughout its length and breadth (e.g. Esler 1994: 19–36). I must confess that, while I have some sympathy with this approach, my overall view is somewhat different. Although there are certainly some features – both now and in antiquity – that unite the Mediterranean, the region as a whole is equally a mosaic of smaller cultural units. My thinking here is influenced by Fernand Braudel (1902–85), the great twentieth-century French historian who did so much to emphasize the unity of the Mediterranean but also highlighted its diversity. He wrote:

> The Mediterranean is not a single sea but a succession of small seas that communicate by means of wider or narrower entrances . . . [T]here is a series of highly individual narrow seas between the land masses, each with its own character, types of boat, and its own laws of history . . . Even within these seas smaller areas can be distinguished, for there is hardly a bay in the Mediterranean that is not a miniature community, a complex world itself.
>
> (Braudel 1972: I, 108–10)

Braudel's analysis, although it drew on data from all periods, concentrated on the sixteenth century. Late in life, he turned his attention to the Mediterranean in antiquity (and prehistory); but the results were not published until after his death (Braudel 2001). Even so, Braudel's influence on historians of the Mediterranean in the classical world has been considerable, particularly where modern historians of the ancient world have chosen to study developments over the long term (what Braudel called the *longue durée*) rather than focus on the events of traditional political history. Indeed, recent studies have similarly emphasized for antiquity and the middle ages that the unity of the Mediterranean can be only loosely defined. Moreover, such unity is held in tension by the diversity of the region's constituent environments and cultures (Hordern and Purcell 2000: 9–49, 485–523).

It is to this view of the ancient Mediterranean that I tend, and it is important to stress this at the outset since I see it as the canvas upon which early Christianity was painted. This canvas comprises not just unifying elements, such as those characteristics that we may identify as 'Greek' or 'Roman', but also the diverse patchwork of myriad local cultures. For example, the New Testament *Acts of the Apostles*, when describing the visit of the apostle Paul and his assistant Barnabas to the city of Lystra in Lycaonia in the middle of Asia Minor, notes that locals, when reacting to Paul's activities, spoke in their local Lycaonian language (*Acts* 14.11; cf. Mitchell 1993: I, 172–3). From such accounts we get a taste of the diverse cultural landscape that confronted the early Christians.

Amid all this cultural diversity it is important to stress the religious diversity of the ancient Mediterranean. The world inhabited by early Christianity was, to quote the title of a recent and important book on this subject, 'a world full of gods' (K. Hopkins 1999). Christianity competed with other gods – the Jewish God and the multifarious deities of Mediterranean paganism – and the way in which the Christian message was received was heavily conditioned by the religious expectations of the inhabitants of this cultural milieu (chapter 4). In some cases, this could lead to confusion and mistakes. A famous example comes from the aforementioned visit of Paul and Barnabas to Lystra in Lycaonia. Paul, in one of his efforts to display the power of Jesus Christ, effected a miraculous cure on a man crippled from birth. Needless to say, the locals were impressed, but they did not at first attribute the miracle to what Paul himself would have deemed to be the correct source. 'The gods have come down to us in the likeness of men!' they exclaimed, before identifying Barnabas with Zeus and Paul, because he talked so much, with Hermes, the messenger of the gods (*Acts* 14.8–12).

Such misapprehensions could afflict Christians too. I always feel rather sorry for Hermas, the second-century author of a work on penance and forgiveness called *The Shepherd*, whose own sins and errors were typified by his misunderstanding of the Christian visions he experienced. Hermas recounts how, in the days when he was a rather lapsed Christian, he was travelling to Cumae on the Bay of Naples when he had a vision of an old woman who presented him with a book of mysterious prophecy. At first poor Hermas failed to realize that the old woman was a personification of the church, and that the books she had given him were full of teachings about Christian virtues. Instead, he thought that the woman was the Sibyl, a pagan prophetess, and that the books were full of pagan prophecy (*The Shepherd of Hermas*, vision 2.1.3–4; 2.4.1). It is hard to blame him for interpreting his vision this way: after all, in antiquity Cumae was reputed to have been the home of a particularly famous Sibyl, whose prophecies were contained, moreover, in books (Parke 1988: 77–99, 152–6).

From its origins, then, Christianity was a religion that, in both its action and its self-representation, was deeply embedded in the Mediterranean contexts within which it developed. Wherever we look in early Christian literature, we see the activities of Jesus, his followers, and their successors touched by the diverse experiences of life in the Mediterranean world of the Roman empire. Its social, political, economic, and cultural rhythms permeate the writings of the New Testament and later Christian authors. Such were the frameworks within which early Christians defined themselves, their aspirations, and their expectations. Yet it is not simply the case that early Christianity conformed supinely to the constraints presented by this Mediterranean context. On the contrary, Christianity sought to overcome such obstacles. That it did not fragment entirely, but endeavoured to maintain its integrity and identity, indicates the measure of its success in meeting these challenges.

Approaching early Christianity in the twenty-first century

Why do we study early Christianity? Why do the lives of early Christians still matter to us as we begin the third millennium? Twenty years ago, the Oxford historian Robin Lane Fox, beginning his own study of the rise of Christianity and its eclipse of paganism, felt that the answers to such questions were obvious. 'The subjects of this book', he remarked, 'need no apology for their importance' (Lane Fox 1986: 7). Not everyone today would share this confidence, as we shall soon see. There can be no straightforward answers to the questions set out above, and any answers will be contingent on when, where, and by whom the questions are asked, and who gives the response. Indeed, even Lane Fox knew that his own approach to the subject was peculiarly personal, the product of his upbringing and education (Lane Fox 1986: 8). I have no doubt that this is as true for the answers that I am about to give as for those offered by others who have approached the subject.

Today, I feel, we cannot dispense with the apology that Lane Fox deemed unnecessary. The religious contours of our society have changed considerably since the early 1980s, when Lane Fox was writing. In many parts of the modern industrialized world, especially in its Anglophone regions, religion in general – and, some might feel, Christianity in particular – seems to have been on the retreat in the face of growing secularization. This phenomenon embraces the effects (not necessarily coextensive) of more widespread education, greater popular awareness of science, political disengagement from or suppression of religion, and the rise of materialist consumerism (Park 1994: 48–54; cf. J. Taylor 1990). In such circumstances, religion, having once occupied a central place in society and its debates, moves to a more marginal position. Writing this book against an Irish backdrop has thrown these trends into sharp relief. In the late 1980s, when I became a university student, the Roman Catholic church was still a very powerful force in Irish politics and society. Since then, however, its influence has waned precipitously. A succession of scandals has undermined the church's moral eminence, while the economic prosperity associated with the rise of the Celtic Tiger has enabled Irish people to pursue their personal goals independent of religious precepts. Hand in hand with this have come wide-ranging changes in public morality, such as in attitudes to marriage (and divorce), contraception, and the place of women in Irish society.

In such circumstances, the intrinsic importance of studying religious traditions, early Christianity among them, would seem to have declined correspondingly. The rest of this chapter aims, therefore, to justify the study of early Christianity in this context. Of course, there can be no single argument in support of this field of study: different people will approach the subject for different reasons. As such, then, I aim to appeal here to a wide constituency of opinions. Not everyone will find each of the various reasons given below equally convincing; indeed, they may even reject some of them. I do not see this as a problem, however: we humans are a varied and individualistic bunch, and our reasons for studying or being interested in a particular subject are correspondingly diverse.

Modern Christians and early Christianity

It may be as well to begin with those for whom the study of early Christianity would appear to be least controversial. There are many modern Christians for whom the study of early Christianity does not need justification, being perfectly explicable as a search for their religious roots. For them this chapter – and even this book – might seem an unnecessary exercise (thus J. Kelly 1991; contrast R. Williams 2005). Many will seek affirmation of their own beliefs and lifestyles in the lives of early Christians. Depending on what sort of affirmation they are looking for, and how they are looking for it, some of them will find it. The next chapter will show how, historically, the study of early Christianity has often been driven by the Christian agendas of later ages. Here I want to suggest that this is still the case today.

Among the more controversial of modern Christian groups are the Jehovah's Witnesses, who frequently hit the headlines because of their strong rejection of the modern medical practice of blood transfusion, even in cases where its administration might mean the difference between life and death. Of course, their rejection – which encompasses (some might even say conflates) both oral ingestion and transfusion into the veins – is based primarily on an appeal to bans on the consumption of blood in both the Old and New Testaments (e.g. *Deuteronomy* 12.23–5; *Leviticus* 7.26–7; *Acts* 15.20). But they have also appealed to early Christianity as part of their effort to show that this biblical rejection of consuming blood has been obeyed also throughout history by 'true Christians' (Jehovah's Witnesses 1990/2000). Among the evidence they cite for this view is the account in Eusebius of Caesarea's *Ecclesiastical History* (see pp. 35–40) of the persecution of Christians that broke out in 177, during the reign of the emperor Marcus Aurelius, at Lyons and Vienne in southern Gaul. Among the Christian martyrs was a woman named Biblis, who rejected the notorious pagan accusation that the Christians ate children with the retort: 'How could children be eaten by people who are not even allowed to eat the blood of brute beasts?' (*Ecclesiastical History* 5.1.26). Similarly, they cite the third-century north African author Tertullian who, in his *Apology*, a work of Christian self-defence against various pagan accusations, remarked that Christians on trial were offered blood sausages by pagan prosecutors who knew that such food was anathema to them (*Apology* 9.14). By invoking such early Christian evidence, the Jehovah's Witnesses contend that their prohibition on blood transfusions means that they too are 'true Christians', keeping alive biblical teachings on the matter. Yet their interpretation of these texts is not uncontroversial. It might be objected that the injunctions mentioned in Scripture or in Eusebius and Tertullian (and other early Christian authors: cf. Minucius Felix, *Octavius* 30) are culturally specific, reflecting assumptions peculiar to the historical contexts in which they were made. It seems that in the early Christian period, for example, such objections might have been raised because of the origin of the blood and meat: it came from animals sacrificed to the pagan gods and was tainted for this very reason. Indeed, the consumption of sacrificial meat and blood was one of the demands made in some trials of the early Christians (Lane Fox 1986: 455).

If for some modern Christians the study of early Christianity provides justification for their current practices, for others the results can be rather disconcerting. Investigations into early Christianity might seem to promise a vista onto a purer vision of Christian life, uncontaminated by centuries of theological wrangling, ecclesiastical politics, and the pursuit of worldly wealth and power. Such is the frustrated assumption confessed by Elaine Pagels, a scholar who has devoted her career to examining the various brands of early Christian belief and practice that were later condemned as heresy (see chapter 5), when she reflects on why she took up the study of early Christianity:

> [W]hen I was a graduate student at Harvard and dissatisfied with the representatives of Christianity I saw around me, I wanted to find the 'real Christianity' – and I assumed that I could find it by going back to the earliest Christians. Later I saw that my search was hardly unique: no doubt most people who have sought out the origins of Christianity have really been looking for the 'real Christianity', assuming that when the Christian movement was new, it was also simpler and purer . . . What I found out was the opposite of what I'd expected . . . What I did *not* find in the process of this research was what I had started out to find – a 'golden age' or purer and simpler early Christianity.
>
> (Pagels 1988: 151–2)

However much the results might confound the expectations, many modern Christians, whatever their confessional allegiances, will agree nevertheless that the study of early Christianity is an essential element in their quest to define who they are (e.g. Lyman 1999: 1–15).

A similarly disconcerting experience might be felt also by those who, although they were brought up in a Christian environment, have abandoned their religious attachments. There are some respects in which many western countries might be defined as 'post-Christian', in that they have gone through a period in their history when institutional Christianity occupied a central place in their culture, but subsequently has been marginalized by the forces of secular humanism and liberalism (Park 1994: 144). In such societies, those who have turned away from Christianity might also study early Christians in some sense as a way of justifying their rejection of religion, particularly in its organized, more doctrinaire incarnations. Even so, they often find that their attitudes to early Christianity are still profoundly informed by their experiences of its modern counterpart. The late Keith Hopkins, author of a study of Christianity that sought to place it firmly in the context of the religious milieu of the Roman empire, freely admitted that, in researching his book, he became aware of the residual religious biases that seemed to confound his professed atheism. Reflecting on his engagement with scholars from a range of religious traditions, he discovered something disquieting about what he had believed were his attitudes to Christianity: 'Beneath the liberal veneer, there was a reluctance, a deep resistance to be open minded, to unlearn the half-conscious absorptions of childhood and adolescence. Put another way, my atheism was indelibly Protestant' (K. Hopkins 1999: 2). Regardless, then, of whether or not one considers oneself a Christian, engagement with early Christianity involves some element of confrontation of one's own identity and system of beliefs, be they religious or secular.

The secular challenge

At the opposite extreme are those who might argue that any study of religion, and not just early Christianity, should be consigned to the dustbin of history. For them the processes of secularization outlined above demonstrate loudly the bankruptcy of religion in general. To many, religion seems to represent all that is backward and primitive, from which humanity has been emancipated by the triumph of 'rational scientific' explanations over 'superstitious' ones. I cite as evidence (albeit anecdotal) a radio interview I heard at the point when I was first formulating the ideas for this book. The atheist interviewee called for the replacement of religious education in schools with the teaching of science, citing as support for this view the evidence (also anecdotal) that pupils at a Protestant school in Northern Ireland had been taught that the defeat of the Spanish Armada showed God's favour for Protestant England against Catholic Spain. The rhetoric of this might seem persuasive at a superficial level: sectarianism, it could be argued, fuels murderous hatred, thus proving that religion is a source of social evil. But looked at more closely, the argument seems glib and myopic, based primarily on an emotive rather than a rational response to a particular situation.

In the first place, it is extremely doubtful that the eradication of religious education in schools would actually achieve the result that the interviewee desired. Religious ideas are inculcated by means of a wide variety of media, among them teachings within the context of religious institutions (in churches, synagogues, and mosques), wayside preachers, and billboard posters. Stamping out religious education, then, would require clamping down on a wide range of activities, raising questions of the morality of such action since it might reasonably be interpreted as persecution. Suppression runs the risk, therefore, of replacing one form of intolerance with another. Even then it might not be effective. In spite of all efforts to restrict or even suppress religious activity in the former Communist countries of eastern Europe, many religious groups have maintained their vitality and emerged with renewed vigour in the aftermath of the collapse of the Eastern Bloc during the 1990s.[4]

The argument is also flawed in its uncritical assumption that scientific education will be effective. There are surely numerous obstacles to this. Can it be assumed that all school students will be able to understand the extraordinary complexities of, say, quantum mechanics or biological evolution? Any process of education requires at some level the arrangement of material into chunks that students can manage (as noted above in terms of periodization); this often demands some degree of simplification in the early stages of the learning process, with greater sophistication being introduced later on. This might lead to imperfect understanding of the scientific theories under discussion. For example, the popular visual image of human evolution emphasizes a linear development, where the various stages between an ape-like creature and modern humans are shown as following one another in strict succession. Yet this image of a single linear progression is actually very misleading, failing to account, for example, for the coexistence for many centuries of humans belonging to the Neanderthal and *Homo sapiens* lineages. Such popular misunderstandings of scientific theory are indicative of the reality that, while there certainly exists an objective body of scientific data, its interpretation is prone to human misunderstanding (Fortey 1997: 180). This may lead to wilful and dangerous distortion: for example, the racist doctrines of Nazism and white supremacist movements have often justified themselves on the basis of what they have claimed to be scientific data (see Peukert 1994 on the Nazis). Anyone who argued that science should be banned from schools for these and other pernicious misapplications would be subject to ridicule, and rightly so. It seems to me equally mistaken to argue that the study of religions should be suppressed because their tenets too have been used to fan the flames of hatred.

Attempts to eradicate religion from the educational system are indicative also of a particular cultural bias. The perceived decline of religion outlined earlier in this chapter appears to have been most precipitous in the modern industrialized nations, especially in western Europe and north America (although generalizations are risky, and there are important differences between – and within – these two regions: B. Wilson 1990: 572–80). In these cultural contexts, it may be much easier to take the view that religion is an increasingly marginal phenomenon. Yet such a view ignores the demonstrable reality that in many parts of the world religion is not on the retreat at all, but remains an important facet of people's lives and identities.

Studies of religious demographics suggest that while the twentieth century certainly saw an extraordinary rise in the number of people who, for various reasons, might be termed 'non-religious', it has also seen most religions continue to flourish – and even enjoy a resurgence (Geertz 2000: 172–8). Hinduism and Islam in particular have increased, largely through population explosions in Africa and Asia (J. Taylor 1990: 633–4; Park 1994: 129–30). Meanwhile Christianity, while it has been marginalized in many industrialized nations, continues to be the world's largest religion thanks to missionary successes and increasing populations in Africa, Asia, and Latin America. Indeed, since 1900, the distribution of Christians throughout the world has changed from a situation where Europe accounted for about half of the world's Christians to one where it now contains less than a quarter (J. Taylor 1990: 635–7). It is projected, moreover, that by the middle of the twenty-first century, Christianity will be overwhelmingly a religion of what is now termed the Third World; furthermore, the brands of Christianity that will be espoused there will be predominantly of a conservative hue, however much that might surprise or even dismay 'liberals' in the west (P. Jenkins 2002).

Even in Europe the picture defies glib generalizations. In the struggle for nationhood that has characterized European history in the nineteenth and twentieth centuries, religion has often been a central element in the definition of national identity (Hobsbawm 1992: 67–73, 123–4). Ireland and Poland, for example, have made great play of their Roman Catholicism. More recently, religion – and not just Christianity of course – has been one of the categories by which the ethnic groups of the former Yugoslavia have sought to assert their identity. Thus Serbs and Croats have stressed their adherence to the Eastern Orthodox and Roman Catholic traditions respectively. Neither statement of religious identity should be seen in isolation. For the Serbs, Eastern Orthodoxy, like their use of the Cyrillic script, emphasizes their kinship with the Slavic peoples of much of eastern Europe, especially Russia, while for the Croats, Roman Catholicism, like their use of the Roman alphabet, is emblematic of their aspirations to be admitted to the western European community of nations.[5]

It might still be objected that the resurgence of religious fervour in south-eastern Europe is anomalous, out of step with what is happening elsewhere in the modern industrialized world. Yet there is evidence to suggest that the widely heralded collapse of religion in the modern west has been overstated. While it seems true that in many such countries institutional Christianity is on the retreat, with declining numbers of those practising religious observance regularly, there are signs that religion is reasserting its role in society in a reconfigured shape. In terms of Christianity, there has been a remarkable flourishing of various evangelical groups, many of which espouse fundamentalist brands of belief (Kepel 1994: 100–34). Other successes have been in the domain of esoteric cults, such as the increased adherence of western Europeans or north Americans to eastern religions like Buddhism, or the revival of what are variously termed indigenous religions, nature religions, or neo-paganism.[6] Such developments in the west seem to evidence the desire among some to return to religious basics. They might be seen as mirroring trends in the Islamic world, for example, where various movements dubbed 'fundamentalist' have attracted considerable support, sometimes in the face of stiff state-sponsored opposition (Kepel 1994: 13–46). Objections that western industrialized nations are somehow immune to such fundamentalism do not convince. In recent times the United States has seen the powerful political alliance of conservative Republican politicians and the evangelical, fundamentalist Christians of the self-proclaimed 'moral majority' (Kepel 1994: 117–23). Indeed, even institutional Christianity may not be as terminally ill as is widely assumed. While attendance at church services may be in decline, other areas of church activity are flourishing. In recent years in Britain, for example, there has been vigorous competition for places in schools run by, particularly, the churches. Many of those competing to send their children to such institutions do not profess any religious beliefs themselves – indeed, this has been part of the problem – but they see in religious schools a bastion of educational standards that they perceive to be in decline in secular state-run schools. More recently, the phenomenal success of Mel Gibson's film *The Passion of the Christ* (2004) and the huge crowds that gathered in Rome after the death of pope John Paul II and for the election of Benedict XVI (April 2005) have shown that there remains a lively interest in Christianity even in supposedly secular societies in the industrialized world.[7] Against such a background some scholars have been talking about a process of 'desecularization', as religions reassert themselves in various arenas, not least politics. It has been argued – even before the events of 11 September 2001 suddenly put religion back at the centre of political debate – that '[t]hose who neglect religion in their analyses of contemporary affairs do so at great peril' (Berger 1999: 18).

Religion, then, is by no means as defunct as its detractors would have us believe, and remains a vital force in both western and global society. There can be no denying that it presents modern humanity with many problems, but refusing to understand it is not an effective means of answering such challenges: that is simply to follow the example of an endangered ostrich and stick one's head in the sand. To return to a point of contention raised earlier, it is not an adequate response to the Jehovah's Witnesses to ridicule their views on blood transfusion as backward and superstitious. Those who wish to argue against them may find that countering them on their own ground may be as effective a response as seeking to impose on them scientific reasoning. Indeed, the Witnesses have proved themselves adept at countering such scientific attacks: part of their strategy for dealing with criticism of their opposition to blood transfusion has been to present medical evidence which they believe supports their case (Jehovah's Witnesses 1990/2000). Anyone seeking to debate with the Witnesses would be best advised to do so on all levels, not just one. To argue, then, for the suppression of religious education and study is based on misleading assumptions about the place of religion in modern global society and the ability of scientific explanations to displace religious ones. Thus the study of early Christianity belongs as much to the repertoire of modern intellectual disciplines as any scientific subject. But enough of this negative, defensive posture! What are the positive arguments that can be advanced for the study of religion in general and early Christianity in particular?

Anthropology, culture, and early Christian studies

There are various levels at which the study of early Christianity may be recommended. As we have just seen, religion is thriving across the globe, and therefore, our understandings of other societies need to take account of the role that religion plays in them. This is something that has long been understood by anthropologists, who are concerned with the study of human culture. In speaking of 'culture' they do not mean, in terms of the rather narrow élitist definition of the word, the best (literature, painting, music, whatever) that humans have produced. Rather, they take the term more broadly, to indicate something like collective patterns of meaning, often expressed in symbolic terms, which allow people to communicate – between each other and from one generation to the next – their understanding of the universe and their attitudes to life. In these terms, culture is an essential part of what makes us what we are as human beings: social animals who use these patterns of meaning to interact with each other (Geertz 1973: 33–54). Such patterns of meaning may be expressed in various sorts of symbols, such as words, gestures, or pictures; but they may also be expressed in terms of belief. As such, then, belief, including the organized form that we call 'religion', is a central element in our humanity.

Moreover, anthropologists have argued that religion often provides a key to understanding a particular culture, above all in terms of that culture's efforts to impose order on the cosmos (Geertz 1973: 87–125). Indeed, much of their work has been focused on elucidating the 'belief-systems' (a bit of anthropological jargon meaning something like religion) of various societies, not only in the traditional milieu of anthropological fieldwork, among 'other peoples' living in the non-industrialized world, but also increasingly in regions such as western Europe (e.g. L. Taylor 1995). If anthropology can claim that in helping us to understand both 'alien' or foreign cultures and our own it has an important role to play in our modern pluralist society (whether local, regional, or global), then the study of various cultures' religions – as of their social structures or attitudes to gender – must necessarily form an important part of anthropology's contribution. Yet understanding a culture requires more than examining what it is like right here and now; it also demands that we comprehend how that culture sees and interacts with its traditions, religious as well as historical, as part of its self-definition. For example, comprehending how Shi'a Muslims differ from Sunnis will require some understanding of their view of their Islamic heritage. Likewise, our understanding of Christian societies, or even of post-Christian ones, demands an effort to comprehend their Christian heritage and how they interact with it.

Where, however, does the study of early Christianity fit into this scheme? At one level, of course, early Christianity is an important element in modern Christianity's heritage. We have already seen, for example, how the Jehovah's Witnesses marshal early Christian testimonies as part of their defence against blood transfusion. In other parts of the world too the early Christian past is used to articulate notions of identity. Every Easter, for example, Filipino Catholics re-enact the Way of the Cross (Jesus' carrying of the cross to the site of his crucifixion), where those participants dressed as the Roman soldiers harassing Jesus may, in a delicious paradox, represent the Spanish conquerors who brought Christianity to the Philippines in the first place (Ballhatchet and Ballhatchet 1990: 501). Yet there is another level at which early Christianity may be of anthropological interest, and that is within the confines of the study of the ancient world itself.

Although modern anthropology is largely concerned with the study of contemporary cultures, it has provided methodologies that have proved useful to those studying past societies. In particular, the explicit problems that anthropology realizes exist in attempting to describe an alien culture have proved useful to modern historians seeking to understand ancient society, which might equally be described as an alien culture. One of the pitfalls in studying Graeco-Roman antiquity comes from the assumption that ancient culture and society was not much different from our own. At an innocuous level, this can lead to amusing answers from students to examination questions. More seriously, however, it can lead to spurious lessons being drawn from history. Anthropological approaches to the study of antiquity have reminded us, however, that in many respects the ancient world is an incredibly strange and confusing place, and our efforts to understand it are often hampered by the modern preconceptions that, intentionally or otherwise, we bring to it.

In addition to anthropology, studies of the Graeco-Roman world influenced by modern literary theory have underlined the extent to which ancient texts present subjective interpretations of events and experiences, not transparently objective ones. This is not to deny, of course, that things actually happened in the past (to put it bluntly: real people dying, suffering, or killing), but that is not the same as claiming that there is a single indisputable version of the truth that can be discovered. What we need to recognize is that when we study historical documents or write our own accounts of the past we are dealing with various layers of interpretation, with different tellings and retellings (by ancient authors and modern interpreters) of what happened – or, to put it another way, with different versions of the past.

Moreover, what we choose to study about the ancient world and the ways in which we choose to study it often reflect the particular priorities and perspectives of our society. Different generations of historians – indeed, different *individual* historians – will place emphasis on different things, and in many cases this will reflect not only the varying personal tastes and interests of individual scholars, but also something of the culture and society in which they work (for some examples, see chapter 2). Study of the ancient world (indeed, of any period in history) reflects the priorities of the society in which that study is undertaken. Traditionally, that has meant the deeds (mainly military and political) of 'great men', or 'great works' of literature (usually produced by or for those same 'great men'): precisely the sorts of things that you would expect to be of interest to members of a male social élite. In recent decades, however, there has been an erosion of the traditional hierarchies of social and political power and the giving of a voice to those traditionally excluded from its structures on account of gender, race or class. In turn, this has led to the emergence of different ways of studying the past, reflecting the interests of these newly empowered groups in society, and resulting, for example, in the growing importance of the history of social underclasses or gender in the ancient world. Hence the study of the ancient world acts as an intriguing mirror of the society in which we live and our efforts to understand it.

Within the discipline of classical studies, religion has been one of the beneficiaries of this shift in emphasis from the traditional focus on the grand narratives of war and politics, and of the rise of approaches to the study of antiquity informed by anthropology and literary theory. Studies of religion in the Roman world into which Christianity was born have made enormous advances in recent decades, particularly in terms of sensitivity to the cultural differences between the ancient world and our own. At one stage, pagan religion was considered to be of marginal importance to ancient society and, moreover, was thought to be clearly in decline by the early centuries of the Christian era, thereby making inevitable the eventual triumph of Christianity. This view was taken largely because scholars felt that ancient paganism failed to match the criteria they set for a successful religion. As recent studies have emphasized, however, these criteria were based on a set of assumptions largely influenced by modern Christianity. In other words, the various pagan religions of the ancient Mediterranean were judged in terms of whether or not they satisfied the needs that modern Christianity was deemed to satisfy. By these standards, ancient religion, which did not boast an organized clergy and did not emphasize the *personal* nature of the relationship with the divinity (articulated through private prayer and the influence of religion on private morality), was considered inadequate. More recent studies of ancient religion, many of them informed by anthropological studies of non-Christian religions, have rejected this traditional approach, seeing its interpretations of Roman paganism as clouded by what are termed 'Christianizing assumptions', and therefore as anachronistic (e.g. Price 1984: 10–19; Beard and Crawford 1985: 26–7; Feeney 1998: 12–14). Furthermore, it is now considered wholly erroneous to assert that pagan religion was in decline in the early Christian centuries, and that any account of the triumph of Christianity must account for its success in the face of the robust vitality of paganism (e.g. MacMullen 1981 and 1997; Lane Fox 1986; K. Hopkins 1999).

The upshot of all this recent scholarly activity is that religion is now understood as a vibrant phenomenon permeating every aspect of life in antiquity, thus making its study central to our understanding of ancient society and culture. Moreover, within the field of ancient religion, early Christianity occupies a particularly important position, in that it permits us a unique opportunity to study the dynamics of cult in exquisite detail. This is because of the extensive range of primary sources that have survived about Christianity from antiquity, a factor that sets Christianity apart from other religions in the ancient world. With the exception of Judaism, no other ancient religion generated so much surviving documentation. That said, however, we must be aware of the limits of early Christianity as a test case for the study of ancient religion (cf. Elsner 2003). Christianity was fundamentally different from many of the other religions found in the ancient Mediterranean region. Christianity was a monotheistic cult, with room only for its own god, in stark contrast to the polytheism of Graeco-Roman paganism, which could accommodate belief simultaneously in many gods. Indeed, that exclusivity of Christianity was to cause the fledgling religion serious problems in its encounter with the Roman empire (see chapter 6). Yet for all that, as I hope this book will show, the massive range of sources for early Christianity allows us to study many aspects of life in the Mediterranean world of the Roman empire in all its diversity. That in itself makes the subject interesting and important for those fascinated by the ancient world. Moreover, the sorts of paradigm shifts in the study of the Greek and Roman worlds that I have outlined above have also had an impact on the study of early Christianity. As we will see in chapters 2 and 3, this is not only because of the discovery of new evidence, but because of the application of new approaches to the subject.

Early Christianity, then, is a subject that deserves study for a variety of reasons, ranging from its intrinsic interest, to its importance for understanding how modern humanity arrived at its present condition, to its utility for comprehending certain dimensions of the lived experience of the people of the ancient world. It commands our attention whether we define ourselves as Christian, non-Christian, or even post-Christian.

Chapter 2

Tradition and revelation: the historical quest for early Christianity

The study of early Christianity is not a new subject. Its origins go back to the very earliest days of the church, when, for example, the authors of the books of the New Testament sought to articulate their views about the origins of the movement to which they belonged, either through accounts of Jesus Christ's life and the activities of his followers (thus the gospels and the *Acts of the Apostles*), or through works of spiritual advice or apocalyptic prophecy (the New Testament epistles and the book of *Revelation*). Some of these writings will be discussed later in this book, and in this chapter I want to examine how the topic has been approached by those who have looked back on the period from Christ to Constantine as a unit. Even with this restriction, we are still dealing with an area of research boasting a long pedigree, with efforts to narrate the history of early Christianity and excavate its material remains both beginning under Constantine himself.

In what follows, I aim to survey how the study of early Christianity has developed over the last seventeen centuries. It will emerge that interest in early Christianity has often been channelled in such a way as to reflect the concerns of later ages.

Investigations frequently were driven, more or less explicitly, by confessional agendas, as Christians of various persuasions, as well as members of other religions and those who profess atheism, have hotly contested early Christianity, seeking in it some validation of their own actions and beliefs or rejections of such beliefs. As we saw in the last chapter, many later generations of Christians have sought to claim early Christian traditions as their own. Similarly, many non-believers have sought, by means of their investigations into early and other periods of Christian history, 'to expose the fraudulent or inadequate bases of Christian belief and to reveal the shortcomings of ecclesiastical practice in their lurid detail' (Robbins 1975: 357). For each of the chronological segments that I delineate (periodization again, I am afraid), I will set historical and archaeological analyses side-by-side, since they were often undertaken to achieve identical goals. Within each chronological chunk, however, I will begin with efforts to write down the early Christian story before proceeding to archaeology. This is not because I subscribe to the notion that archaeology is the servant of written history, but because this is traditionally how it has been regarded by those who have studied early Christianity (cf. Snyder 1985: 8–9). That in itself is revealing: much research into early Christianity has been driven by theological agendas, as a quest for the truth lying behind texts, and for the most part archaeological material has been deployed as a 'handmaiden' to that endeavour.

Discovering early Christianity in the age of Constantine

The first attempt to write an account of the rise of Christianity was the *Ecclesiastical History* penned in Greek by Eusebius of Caesarea, who died in 339. Eusebius was a Christian bishop (of the capital of Roman Palestine, Caesarea: hence his sobriquet) and had been acquainted with the emperor Constantine – although Eusebius, keen to win prestige, may have exaggerated the closeness of their friendship (Barnes 1981: 265–6). In its surviving form, the *Ecclesiastical History* reaches its climax with

Constantine's conversion to Christianity, which is welcomed as the realization of biblical prophecies of God's ultimate triumph. Constantine's enjoyment of God's favour, for example during his war with Licinius, his rival as emperor, in 324, is described in language redolent of the praise heaped on the pious kings of the Old Testament:

> On him, as the reward for his piety, God bestowed from Heaven above the trophies of victory over the impious; but the guilty one [i.e. the unfortunate Licinius] he cast down, with all his councillors and friends, prone beneath Constantine's feet.
>
> (*Ecclesiastical History* 10.9.1)

Now Eusebius' history went though a number of editions, the dates of which have been vigorously debated (Barnes 1981: 126–47). Although this triumphant outcome of a Roman emperor converting to Christianity may only have appeared in the latest versions, it seems that all editions of the *Ecclesiastical History* were characterized by a theological interpretation of the history of the church. Indeed, taken as a whole, Eusebius' theological efforts were of a decidedly historical bent, in that he sought to demonstrate the truth of God's power through instances of divine intervention in human history (Barnes 1981; Hollerich 1999).

This framework was to have an important impact on Eusebius' account of early Christian history. Moreover, as a bishop, he identified Christianity firmly with the institution of the church, and his account focused on the church's efforts to maintain its integrity, both spiritual and institutional. Thus the *Ecclesiastical History* was no disinterested narrative, but an argued, even polemical, account. Like many early Christian writers, Eusebius sought to demonstrate the unique claims of the church, as the earthly embodiment of the true Christian religion, to biblical tradition and divine revelation (cf. K. Hopkins 1999: 89–92). To do this Eusebius had to undermine rival claimants to what he deemed to be the church's own heritage, and at the outset of his narrative, as he enumerated the major themes of his work, he highlighted a number of areas where his defence of the church's integrity would loom large.

Prominent among these themes were 'the lines of succession from the holy apostles' juxtaposed with 'the names and dates of those who, through a passion for innovation, have wandered as far as possible from the truth' (*Ecclesiastical History* 1.1.1). Here Eusebius was concerned with the cohesion of the church and those internal dissensions that threatened to tear it apart. A bishop himself, Eusebius was a staunch believer in and defender of the authority of the institution of a church led by bishops to act as mediator between God and humankind. Hence the *Ecclesiastical History* sought to justify not only the church's unique claim to propagate God's message, but also its right to crack down on those who challenged its authority. His approach to this issue, as the lines quoted above demonstrate, was twofold. In the first place, he was a determined advocate of tradition, by which he sought to shore up the integrity of the church by showing how the bishops of his own day were the direct successors of the apostles who had followed Jesus Christ. Second, and in opposition to the bishops, he portrayed as upstarts and revolutionaries, with no claims to this tradition, those who challenged the church's authority and teaching: in other words, those whom he castigated as heretics (see chapter 5). Side by side, these narratives of episcopal succession and heretical opposition served to validate the church's claims that it was the unique mediator, in an unbroken line from the time of Jesus, of the Christian message to humankind.

In addition to asserting the integrity of the church and attacking those who sought to undermine it from within, Eusebius emphasized as a third major theme in the *Ecclesiastical History* Christianity's struggles with those external forces that rivalled its claim to be the true religion. The biblical traditions that the church had claimed for its own could also be regarded as the property of another religious group: the Jews. This rivalry between Jews and Christians over the heritage of scripture had been exploited by some pagan critics who had sought to undermine Christianity's credibility by casting it as a deviant form of Judaism (Wilken 2003: 112–17). This made it imperative for Christians to prove the validity of their claims over and against the Jews, to show that it was Christianity (and the church), and not Judaism, that represented God's true plan for humankind. In the second and third centuries, Christians had responded to this conundrum by claiming that the Jews, by not recognizing Jesus as God's Messiah, had shown themselves incapable of interpreting their own scriptures, a failure that provoked their abandonment by God, who now favoured the Christians. Eusebius elaborated on this theme, and he devoted a large part of his narrative to demonstrating that the traditions of scripture belonged to the Christians, not the Jews. He asserted, for example, that although the Old Testament's Hebrew patriarchs (Abraham, Isaac, and Jacob) together with Moses and the prophets had lived before the Incarnation of Christ, they none the less followed lifestyles that were Christian in everything but name (Barnes 1981: 184–6). To drive the point home, Eusebius promised that he would devote considerable space in the *Ecclesiastical History* to 'the calamities that overwhelmed the Jewish nation immediately after their conspiracy against our Saviour' (*Ecclesiastical History* 1.1.2), thus demonstrating that Judaism had been rendered obsolete by the birth of Jesus.

The final theme to which Eusebius drew special attention at the start of his narrative was 'the widespread, bitter, and recurrent campaigns launched against the divine message, and the heroism with which, when the occasion demanded it, men faced torture and death to maintain the fight in its defence' (*Ecclesiastical History* 1.1.2): in other words, persecution and martyrdom. Their prominence in Eusebius' narrative might seem to imply a hostile attitude to the Roman empire, but this was not the case. The blame for persecutions is placed not on the institutions of the empire, but on the individual emperors who instigated action against the Christians (see chapter 6). Generally Eusebius presented the empire as an institution that accorded the church the respect it deserved. It thus contrasted sharply, in Eusebius' view, with the Jews, whom he blamed collectively for initiating persecution, which he saw as compounding their perfidious failure to acknowledge Christ as the true Messiah (*Ecclesiastical History* 3.5.1–2). Indeed, Eusebius saw the empire as the instrument through which God displayed his displeasure against the Jews. The Roman conquest of Jerusalem and the destruction of the Jewish temple in AD 70 were interpreted by Eusebius as the Abomination of Desolation foretold by the Old Testament prophet Daniel (*Ecclesiastical History* 3.5.4–5; cf. *Daniel* 11.31). Furthermore, and in spite of the persecutions, Eusebius saw the Roman empire as an institution ordained by God as part of his scheme for the propagation of the Christian faith. As one of the proofs of this, Eusebius noted the coincidence between the birth of Christ and the establishment of peace in the Roman world under the emperor Augustus (27 BC–AD 14). It was a point he emphasized in various other works, including an oration delivered before the emperor Constantine himself:

> At the same time, one empire – the Roman – flourished everywhere, and the eternally implacable and irreconcilable enmity of nations was completely resolved. And as the knowledge of One God and one manner of piety – the salutary teaching of Christ – was imparted to all men, in the same way and at the same time a single sovereign arose for the entire Roman empire and a deep peace took hold of the totality. Together, at the same critical moment, as if from a single divine will, two beneficial shoots were produced for humankind: the empire of the Romans and the teachings of true worship.
>
> (Eusebius, *Tricennial Oration* 16.4, adapted from Drake 1976)

Taken as a whole, then, Eusebius' examination of early Christianity validated his belief in the central role of an orthodox church in a divinely ordained history of humankind. The themes he chose to emphasize became, moreover, fundamental areas of study for those who investigated early Christianity in later ages, right down to our own time.

Eusebius' lifetime coincided with the development of another interest in Christian antiquity. No sooner than the Roman province of Palestine, along with the rest of the eastern empire, came under Constantine's jurisdiction in 324, an intense fascination with the material heritage of early Christianity began to develop. The whole process received the blessing and active encouragement of Constantine himself. Under his guidance, Roman Palestine began its transformation into Christendom's Holy Land: a goal for pilgrim journeys and a source of sacred relics (E. D. Hunt 1982). This led to the first excavations of early Christianity's physical remains. Indeed, perhaps the first contender for the title of 'early Christian archaeologist' is no less a personage than the emperor's mother, the dowager empress Helena (E. D. Hunt 1982: 28–49; Frend 1996: 1–6). Her methods, however, would surely make all modern archaeologists faint.

In 325, the same year in which he tried to achieve Christian theological unity at the council of Nicaea (see chapter 5), Constantine embarked on an ambitious building programme in Palestine (Walker 1990). He ordered the construction of churches at the sites of Christ's birth in Bethlehem, and of his death, resurrection, and ascension into heaven at Jerusalem and the Mount of Olives. A year later, his mother embarked on her journey to Palestine, and it may have been under her supervision that many of the discoveries of the holy places were made. Eusebius' account of the discovery of Christ's tomb is instructive of the sort of methods used:

> It appeared suddenly and contrary to all expectation: the revered and hallowed monument (*martyrion*) of the Saviour's resurrection. This most holy cave presented a faithful representation of the Saviour's return to life, in that, after lying buried in darkness, it again emerged into the light and afforded all who came to witness the sight a clear and visible

> proof of the wonders that had once taken place there, a testimony to the resurrection of the Saviour louder than any voice.
>
> (Eusebius, *Life of Constantine* 3.28)

It was not a case of the excavators finding the tomb as much as the tomb finding them. No books were consulted, no historical specialists called to the scene: this was identification by faith in miracles. The manner in which Christ's tomb was held to have revealed itself was a demonstration of the divine favour that Constantine's schemes seemed to enjoy. By archaeology and by history, then, the triumphant coming together of church and empire had been demonstrated. In terms of historiographical and archaeological approaches to early Christianity, the age of Constantine proved to be pivotal, and provided a model for later research into the early Christian past.

Early Christianity from late antiquity to the middle ages

Eusebius of Caesarea's *Ecclesiastical History* was destined to enjoy considerable acclaim, to the extent that Eusebius' basic view of early Christian history came to be perpetuated throughout late antiquity and into the middle ages. In the fifth century, particularly at Constantinople under the emperor Theodosius II (408–50), the *Ecclesiastical History* found numerous continuators – Socrates, Sozomen, Theodoret, and Philostorgius – who appended to Eusebius' narrative accounts covering the period from Constantine up to their own day. In time, their histories were also continued by the sixth-century lawyer Evagrius, or edited together into a synthesis, such as those compiled in the late fifth century by Gelasius of Cyzicus or in the sixth by the Italian aristocratic monk Cassiodorus (Momigliano 1990: 142–5). As a result, Eusebius' account was woven into a seamless narrative of Christian history from the time of Christ up to the early middle ages. Although these later authors made various innovations in how ecclesiastical history was written, not least because many of them were not bishops but laymen, they generally preserved Eusebius' positive appraisal of the role of the empire in God's plan for humanity. Similarly, they continued to emphasize the importance of the episcopate to the smooth running of the church (Harries 1991; Urbainczyk 1997).

Several of Eusebius' works were also translated into Latin for readers in the western provinces of the Roman empire, the *Ecclesiastical History* among them. The circumstances in which its translation was produced indicate that Eusebius' positive portrayal of God's intervention in human history was part of its appeal. In the first decade of the fifth century, groups of Gothic warriors spilled through Alpine passes into northern Italy. The first major city they encountered was Aquileia, a great trading emporium at the head of the Adriatic (a sort of ancient equivalent to Venice) and the seat of a thriving Christian community (Humphries 1999: 191–6). These were worrying times for Aquileia's Christians who, fearing that the Goths might suddenly attack them, looked to their bishop Chromatius to provide spiritual inspiration. As part of his response, Chromatius commissioned his friend the monk Rufinus, who had spent much of his life in the Greek east of the Mediterranean, to translate Eusebius' *Ecclesiastical History* into Latin for his flock. Rufinus was also asked to provide a continuation of Eusebius' narrative, covering events down to recent times. In his preface to the completed work, Rufinus recounted how Eusebius' positive account of Christian history could provide inspiration to its readers. By contemplating the earlier trials and tribulations of the faith, then, the inhabitants of Aquileia might take heart that God would look after them in their time of tribulation. Thus Eusebius' positive appraisal of early Christian history was disseminated to the west.

The years between Eusebius and Rufinus also saw continued investigation into the material heritage of early Christianity. Persecution by the Roman state had stopped, in general, with Constantine's conversion, but accounts of martyrdoms continued to be used as a source of spiritual and ethical inspiration for Christians enjoying the new-found peace of the church (Brown

1981). As part of this interest, church leaders – and, indeed, those seeking to challenge their authority (Cooper 1999) – sponsored efforts to recover physical remains connected with these early Christian heroes. One of the most concerted efforts occurred at Rome under the guidance of bishops like Damasus I (366–84), who oversaw the widespread refurbishment of Christian burial chambers in the Roman catacombs, particularly those associated with the burial of earlier bishops of Rome (Stevenson 1978: 24–44). As Damasus' contemporary and friend Jerome recorded, such burial places became popular attractions for Christians to visit on Sundays (Jerome, *Commentary on Ezekiel* 40.5). Much as had been the case with the narratives of Eusebius and his successors, this material record of earliest Christianity was used to validate the practices and beliefs of later generations of Christians. Most famously, the bishops of Rome fostered the cult of martyrs and the veneration of their relics as a means to buttress the spiritual authority of the Roman church (Humphries 1999: 53–6). Other Christian leaders used similar tactics. During his struggle with the imperial court in 386, for example, bishop Ambrose of Milan (bishop from 374 to 397) saw the miraculous discovery of relics of the martyrs Gervasius and Protasius as a sign from heaven that his cause was right (McLynn 1994: 209–19).

In archaeology as in history, then, the attitudes of the age of Constantine and Eusebius continued to flourish throughout the fourth century and into the fifth. Yet there soon occurred an event that threatened to undermine fatally this optimistic vision of Christian history championed by Eusebius and his successors. On 24 August 410, the city of Rome was sacked by those same Gothic warriors whose appearance in Italy had prompted Rufinus' Latin edition of the *Ecclesiastical History*. It was the first time that the Eternal City had been captured by a foreign enemy in 800 years, and the event sent a seismic wave of shock and horror throughout the Roman empire: 'if Rome can perish', wrote Jerome soon afterwards, 'then what can be safe?' (Jerome, *Letter* 123.16). Worse than this, however, the Gothic sack seemed to add grist to the mill of pagans who had long argued that abandonment of Rome's old gods could only bring disaster upon the empire (Croke and Harries 1982: 28–51). There was plainly a need for a reassessment of the role of God in human history.

The most systematic response came from perhaps the finest mind that Latin Christianity ever produced, the north African bishop Augustine of Hippo (354–430). His response to the catastrophe of 410 was to result in his *City of God*, a massive meditation on human history and the nature of God's role in it (O'Daly 1999). In it, Augustine thoroughly rejected the positive model, evinced by Eusebius amongst others, that the successes of the Roman empire were easily comprehensible as part of God's grand scheme for humanity (see chapter 6). For all that, positive views along the Eusebian model continued to assert that the Roman empire had an important place in God's plan for human history. Emblematic of these was the *Seven Books of Histories Against the Pagans* by the Spanish priest Paulus Orosius. It was composed in the immediate aftermath of the sack of Rome, in order to refute pagan complaints that blame for the event should be laid at the door of Christian 'atheism'.

Orosius' extraordinary contention was that, far from demonstrating that the positive Christian view of Roman history was misconceived, the sack of Rome had actually reinforced its validity. In Orosius' version, the gloomy reaction to the sack of Rome was entirely misplaced. What this event had actually shown was that faith in the Christian God had guaranteed survival. In addition to contending that the sack had been no cataclysm, Orosius argued that the Goths had been particularly scrupulous not to harm any Romans who had sought refuge in the city's churches (*Seven Books of Histories Against the Pagans* 7.39–40). Orosius thus maintained Eusebius' positive view of the Roman empire in God's plan for humankind. He agreed with Eusebius, for example, that the peaceful conditions obtaining in the Roman empire at the time of the Incarnation had been part of God's plan. But he went further (*much* further) than Eusebius (or anyone else for that matter) when he made the erroneous assumption, on the basis of the *Gospel of Luke*'s account of Mary and Joseph travelling to Bethlehem at the time of a Roman census, that Jesus had been enrolled as a Roman citizen soon after his birth (*Seven Books of Histories Against the Pagans* 6.22)! Orosius' account of early Christianity in the period before Constantine concentrated on persecutions, but much more than Eusebius he interpreted these persecutions in terms of biblical analogies. The ten persecutions that he identified in this period had in turn prompted divine retribution on sinful Romans that Orosius equated with the ten plagues visited on Egypt when Pharaoh refused to let Moses and the Israelites return to the promised land (*Seven Books of Histories Against the Pagans* 7.26–7; cf. *Exodus* 7–12).

It is not hard to see why Orosius' history should cause modern historians of the ancient world to throw up their hands in despair at his lack of rigour. Yet in spite of these objections, Orosius' view of history was to enjoy enormous success, even more so than Augustine's (Hay 1977: 22–3). For much of the middle ages it provided the standard history of the ancient world, and thus of early Christianity. It was endlessly quoted and excerpted, and so frequently copied that there are some two hundred known manuscripts of the work. It was even translated into Anglo-Saxon – an endeavour once thought to have been undertaken by none other than king Alfred the Great himself (Bately 1980: lxxiii–lxxxi).

Although in many respects the middle ages depended on late antique accounts – Eusebius, Rufinus, Orosius – for its knowledge of the early Christian period, this is not to say that medieval Christendom produced no scholarship of its own on the subject. Far from it: early Christianity continued to exercise fascination throughout the middle ages, above all as an era of heroic martyrs whose fortitude was held up to ordinary Christians as a paragon of exemplary piety. Under the guidance of church leaders, martyrs remained the focus of cult activities: their shrines were destinations of pilgrimages and the anniversaries of their martyrdoms became important feast days (Brown 1981). As part of the elaboration of such cults, there was great demand for stories about the sufferings and miracles of the martyrs, to the extent that medieval authors lacking any reliable information about particular martyrs would indulge audiences with pious fictions. For example, whereas all the contemporary accounts of the excavation of the relics of the martyrs Gervasius and Protasius by Ambrose of Milan in 386 (see p. 43) agree that these saints were hitherto completely unknown, this did not stop someone in the middle ages from compiling an entirely fanciful account of their trial and execution (Humphries 1999: 223).

Another area in which the middle ages perpetuated the view of early Christianity that had evolved in the fourth and fifth centuries was the fascination with the foundation and early history of bishoprics. We saw that this was one of the ways in which Eusebius sought to demonstrate that the church had maintained its integrity since the earliest times. Throughout the middle ages, lists of bishops for various cities were compiled, maintained, and sometimes shamelessly concocted. Such records were not the stuff of dry scholarship, but were incorporated into the life of the church. Bizarre (and unimaginably boring) though it may seem to us, lists of bishops were actually read out on major feast days, thereby affirming the links of a particular congregation with the very earliest days of Christianity (Humphries 1999: 1–4).

The chief virtuosi of this practice were, of course, the bishops of Rome. It was on the basis of such lists, going back to Peter, the chief of Christ's apostles, that during the middle ages (and indeed beyond) the church of Rome claimed supremacy throughout Christendom. Moreover, accounts of the succession of Roman bishops were often adopted as a chronological framework by historians writing in other parts of western Europe (Momigliano 1990: 148–9). Yet Rome's authority did not go unchallenged, and one of the tactics adopted by its rivals was to claim an apostolic foundation of their own. Thus, for example, in the eleventh century, when the pope Gregory VII (1075–83) sought to assert his authority over the church of Milan on the basis of his position as the successor of the apostle Peter, the Milanese responded that their church had also been founded by an apostle, and fostered a tradition in which Barnabas, the assistant of Paul in *Acts*, had come to Italy and become Milan's first bishop. The papacy and its supporters were understandably outraged, and rejected the Milanese claim out of hand (Humphries 1999: 56–65). Yet not even the Roman church was immune to such inventive recreations of the early Christian past, especially when papal authority was at stake, and there is surely no more famous medieval forgery than the *Donation of Constantine*. This text, written in the eighth century, told how the primacy of the Roman church had been decreed by Constantine himself shortly after his conversion (Edwards 2003).

Early Christianity was also the subject of investigation in the middle ages as a quarry for theological ideas. The great medieval compendia of Christian doctrine and theology, such as the *Decretum* by the twelfth-century canon lawyer Gratian or the *Summa Theologiae* of Thomas Aquinas (*c*. 1225–74), depended in no small measure on extracts from early Christian authors. For the most part, primacy was accorded to Christians of the fourth and later centuries: western Christendom regarded as ancient Christianity's greatest teachers, or 'doctors', bishop Ambrose of Milan (*c*. 339–97), Jerome (*c*. 345–420), bishop Augustine of Hippo (354–430), and pope Gregory the Great (*c*. 540–604). That said, some earlier Christians did receive attention. The third-century Alexandrian theologian Origen, for example, enjoyed some vogue in the intellectual circles of Cistercian monasticism in the twelfth century, where he was read not in Greek but in the Latin translations of his works produced during the fourth- and fifth-century controversy over his orthodoxy. Origen's fate in eastern Christendom, however, was altogether less happy: he was repeatedly condemned for heresy during the three centuries after his death, with the result that the original Greek texts of most of his theological treatises have disappeared, through either neglect or deliberate suppression (Trigg 1983: 254–5).

Any activity in the middle ages that might be termed 'early Christian archaeology' was largely confined to the hunt for relics, either of Jesus himself and his apostles or of the early martyrs. The circulation of fragments of martyrs' bones and clothing, which had begun in the fourth century, continued to flourish throughout the medieval period. From the eleventh century onwards, moreover, the relic trade in western Europe was supplemented by an influx of material from the eastern Mediterranean. Crusades to bring the Holy Land under Christain control were accompanied by a scramble for relics, particularly those associated, often on spurious or legendary grounds, with Jesus and his disciples: hence the many fragments of the True Cross and the quest for the Holy Grail. Moreover, western Christians were not averse to plundering the relic collections of their Eastern Orthodox brethren. In particular, the thuggish vandalism of 1204, when the armies of the Fourth Crusade ransacked Constantinople rather than push on to Jerusalem, led to a veritable deluge of early Christian artefacts making their way west (Geary 1994: 194–256).

In sum we can see that throughout the middle ages early Christianity continued to be viewed, much as it had been in Eusebius of Caesarea's time, as part of the living tradition of the church, a source of inspiration to later generations of Christians. Throughout the middle ages, the early Christian past had been conceived of within biblical traditions that divided the history of the world into seven ages. The first five – marked by pivotal events such as the Creation of the world, the Flood, the birth of the patriarch Abraham, the reign of king David, and the captivity of Israel in Babylon – culminated with the birth of Christ. Thereafter came the sixth age, in which scholars in the middle ages believed they were living, and which would endure until Christ's Second Coming, at which juncture the seventh age would begin (Hay 1977: 27–9). Early Christianity, then, was not a remote, discrete period in the minds of medieval scholars; rather, it was part of this sixth age in which they themselves also lived. But from the fifteenth century onwards there occurred a revolution in European intellectual behaviour that brought about significant changes in how early Christianity was regarded.

Renewal, reform, and the origins of critical scholarship

The origins of a more rigorous approach to the study of early Christianity can be traced to the fifteenth and sixteenth centuries, when a chain of seemingly unrelated events made knowledge of the subject suddenly easier and more desirable. The stirrings of the European Renaissance; the development of printing; the collapse of the Byzantine empire in the eastern Mediterranean, culminating with the Turkish conquest of Constantinople in May 1453; and the fallout after Martin Luther nailed his ninety-five theses to the door of the castle church in Wittenberg on the last day of October 1517: all played a role.

From the fourteenth and fifteenth centuries, for a wide variety of reasons, intellectuals, at first in Italy but soon elsewhere in Europe, began to look at the heritage of the ancient world with renewed interest. This movement, known to us as the early modern Renaissance, was to have a fundamental impact on the way in which Christianity impinged on the European self-consciousness, and was to have a wide-ranging impact on the development of scholarship. The revived interest in all things ancient brought with it a concern to try to recover as much as was possible of the writings of ancient Greek and Roman authors. This encouraged scholars to develop rigorous standards for assessing the content of ancient texts, often through the close study of their linguistic content, giving rise to the discipline known as philology. These trends marked the turning of intellectual efforts more generally away from an exclusive concentration on the pursuit of sacred knowledge, much as had been the case in the middle ages, towards investigation of areas of primarily human achievement: hence the emergence of the scholarly movement called humanism.

In addition to searching for ancient texts in local libraries, the intellectuals of western Europe were soon indulged with a deluge of manuscripts from the Greek east of the Mediterranean. As the rising power of the Ottoman Turks began to encroach on the Byzantine empire based on Constantinople, Byzantine grandees began to send books from their libraries to the west, either out of concern for the preservation of their manuscripts or simply because they hoped to sell them for money. Among the intellectual loot that accrued to the west in this way were works that had hitherto been almost unknown by western readers. By happy coincidence, this rediscovery of the classical past occurred just as, in the mid-fifteenth century, Europeans began to command the technology of the printing press. This enabled many new editions (and translations) of ancient authors to be mass-produced, and thus reach wider audiences than would have been possible under the medieval system of copying manuscripts (Bolgar 1954: 276–80).

With the Renaissance, moreover, a new view of history came to predominate, sounding the death knell of the Christian 'seven ages' model that had predominated throughout the middle ages. As the European intelligentsia began to see themselves as participating in a rebirth of classical culture, they began to see the period between the fall of the Roman empire and their own time as belonging to some sort of interlude, falling as a middle age between two apogees of human development. From this emerged the division of history into ancient, medieval, and modern epochs, and with it new humanist, secularized standards of historical research (Hay 1977: 27–9, 90–1). Pagan antiquity, in all its aspects, came to be considered as a respectable area of intellectual endeavour, and with it flourished a new tradition of painstaking research into antiquity known as 'antiquarianism' (Momigliano 1990: 54–79). At the forefront of such antiquarian endeavours was the classification not just of the literary remains of classical antiquity, but of its physical artefacts too. Indeed, it is with the Renaissance that we get the first stirrings of modern archaeological method (Schnapp 1996: 122–38).

Yet it would be wrong to imagine that these trends resulted in the intellectual marginalization of Christianity. Quite the contrary: the scholars involved in humanist endeavours were themselves Christians, and their revived interest in the ancient world was extended to Christian antiquity also. Their rediscovery of the early Christian world shared many of the features and trends that had characterized the renewed study of the pagan classics. The pressure exerted on Byzantium by the Turks, for example, was crucial. Relations between the Byzantine and western churches in the later middle ages had been hampered by the unfortunate reciprocal excommunication of the Roman pope and the Constantinopolitan patriarch in 1054. In a last, desperate, and ultimately futile effort to rally western support against the Ottoman onslaught, however, Byzantine emperors had sought a rapprochement with Latin Christendom. As Byzantine and papal legates met at inconclusive councils, certain individual Greek Orthodox churchmen turned to Latin Christianity with gusto. Prominent among them was Bessarion of Trebizond, who was made cardinal by pope Eugenius IV in 1439 and settled in Italy a year later. Like many others, Bessarion brought the contents of his library with him to the west, and while he may be best remembered today for his efforts to introduce classical Greek texts to western audiences, no less significant was his collection of early Christian writers. Such texts became the focus of editorial activity by humanists who began to publish both editions and translations of these newly discovered works by the fathers of the Greek church (Geanakoplos 1976: 265–80; Backus 1991: 296–9).

Given the extraordinary diversity of early Christianity that we will investigate later in this book, it was perhaps inevitable that the application of scholarly activity to its literary output would produce some unsettling results in a society dominated by a church that insisted on the essential unity of Christendom and its faith. Among the pioneers of the new philological approach to ancient texts was Lorenzo Valla (*c.* 1406–57), whose classical interests led him to produce Latin translations of Homer, Herodotus, and Thucydides. It was to be philology that prompted Valla's most famous work, and one that was emblematic of the extension of scientific antiquarian research to early Christianity. In 1440 he produced his enquiry into the document known as the *Donation of Constantine* (see p. 47), which had been exploited since the eleventh century as a fundamental buttress of papal claims to temporal authority throughout western Christendom.

Valla, however, examined the language of the *Donation*, found that it simply could not have been composed in the fourth century, and denounced it as a forgery. Valla's work provided a template for the more rigorous study of early Christian documents that was soon to take off in a radically new direction. In northern Europe, a revolt against the authority of the bishops of Rome was to have a significant impact on the study of early Christianity.

Confronted by the challenges to its authority issued first by Martin Luther (1483–1546) and other Protestant reformers, the church of Rome appealed, as it had always appealed, not only to scripture, but also to tradition. Above all, the popes asserted that as the successors of the apostle Peter they were the supreme spiritual authorities in Christendom. In turn, this compelled the emerging voices of Protestantism to counter the Roman arguments. Although the Protestants were keen to justify their actions on the basis of biblical precepts, they nevertheless saw the strength of arguments informed by appeals to Christian tradition (Meyendorff 1991: 782). Thus, for example, Luther defended his controversial liturgical innovations by citing support from Cyprian, a third-century bishop of Carthage, and Athanasius, bishop of Alexandria for much of the fourth century. In the process, early Christianity became one of the battlefields on which the forces of Protestant reform and Roman Catholic revival fought out their ideological campaigns (Backus 1991: 292–5, 301–2).

As part of their challenge to the Roman church's claims to represent the true traditions of Christianity, the Lutherans sponsored a massive historical enterprise, coordinated by the extraordinary Croatian biblical scholar Matthias Francowitz, known as Flacius Illyricus (1520–75). The result was *Historia Ecclesiae Christi* (*History of the Church of Christ*), published at Basel between 1562 and 1574, and better known, perhaps, as the *Magdeburg Centuries*. It was a highly polemical work, which sought to show how the 'pure' church of the early Christians was gradually brought under the 'demonic' influence of Rome (Ditchfield 1995: 273–8). The Roman response was swift and, in the end, more sustained. Under the guidance of Cesare Baronio

(1538–1607) – better known by the Latin version of his name, Caesar Baronius, and one of the leading lights of Counter-Reformation Rome – a team of scholars compiled the *Annales Ecclesiastici* (*Ecclesiastical Annals*). As its title suggests, this was a year-by-year account of the history of the church from its origins designed to prove, against the *Magdeburg Centuries*, that it was the church of Rome that was the true inheritor of early Christian traditions. It had been Jesus Christ himself who had established the church, and he had then entrusted its care to Peter, whose successors were, of course, the popes (Ditchfield 1995: 278–85). Baronio's *Annales* were to be immensely successful: editions of varying completeness were reprinted endlessly until the nineteenth century, in stark contrast to the mere three printings enjoyed by the *Magdeburg Centuries*. As such, they hint at an important division that had arisen in the attitudes of Protestantism and Roman Catholicism to early Christianity. For the Protestants it was *biblical* Christianity, the early church as presented in the books of the New Testament, that was to become of greatest importance (Duffy 1977: 287–92). Roman Catholics, by contrast, continued to emphasize their continuity with the traditions of the early Christian centuries even after the times of the apostles (Ditchfield 1995: 277–8).

It might seem incredible to us at the beginning of the third millennium that early Christianity should have evoked such passions. To us it seems a remote period, separated from us by a gulf of centuries, but to many in the period of the Reformation the early Christians were a vibrant, living presence among them. We have noted already that, throughout the middle ages, Christians continued to celebrate the suffering of early Christian martyrs. The phenomenon continued into the early modern period (Ditchfield 1995: 36–42), but at the same time there was an effort to place knowledge of these early saints on a much surer footing. A guiding light for this enterprise shone forth from various Flemish Jesuit priests, the most prominent of whom was John van Bolland (1596–1665). With his colleagues Bolland (also known by the Latin form of his name, Bollandus) collected and edited writings about the saints (known generically as 'hagiography'), publishing the texts as the *Acta Sanctorum* (*The Deeds of the Saints*) from 1643. Once again, there was an obvious link between scholarly enterprise and the spirit of Catholic renewal: the volumes of the *Acta Sanctorum* presented texts relating to saints according to their place in the liturgical year: thus the volumes were devoted to months (or parts of months), listing the saints in the order of their feast days (Hay 1977: 159–61). A similar enterprise, albeit proceeding chronologically through the centuries and focusing on monastic saints, was initiated by the Maurists, a French congregation of Benedictine monks. Members of the order also undertook to prepare editions, based on the best possible manuscripts, of various early Christian authors such as Ambrose of Milan (Knowles 1959).

Just as the study of martyrs was given new impetus in the Catholic reaction to the Protestant Reformation, so too was the investigation of the early histories of individual Christian communities. As a result, the lists of bishops that had been carefully recorded in the middle ages were now the subject of detailed antiquarian review. Thus in Italy Ferdinando Ughelli (1596–1670) oversaw production of the *Italia Sacra* (Ditchfield 1995: 331–51), while in France the Assembly of Clergy, made up of bishops and abbots, was responsible for coordinating compilation of the *Gallia Christiana*. Such works, which narrated the history of the church by focusing on its constituent local congregations, risked pointing up divisions in the church.[1] In deference to such concerns, it was no accident therefore that Ughelli's *Italia Sacra* began with 'Rome, that first of all churches, the mother of sane dogma, the pinnacle of apostolic honour, the most noble seat of the supreme pontiff' (quoted in Humphries 1999: 3). The force of tradition, then, remained strong.

Such excursions into the history of early Christianity were accompanied by efforts to collect and collate its archaeological remains. The antiquarian investigations into the surviving artefacts of pagan antiquity gave rise to a similar interest in the material record of the early Christians, and the centre for much of this activity, as in so much else, was Rome. Throughout the middle ages, a number of catacombs continued to be visited, much in the way that Jerome records they were in the fourth century (see p. 43). In the late sixteenth century, however, new discoveries began to be made, which excited the minds of the historical scholars of Counter-Reformation Rome, Cesare Baronio among them. Systematic exploration had to wait two decades, however, until the task was taken up with great energy by Antonio Bosio (*c.* 1575–1629), dubbed by a later generation of Christian archaeologists as 'the Columbus of the catacombs'. Bosio's investigations were meticulous: for twenty years he explored the vast maze of underground passages beneath Rome, taking notes, making drawings, and seeking out every possible literary reference to the catacombs. The results were published, posthumously, in 1634 in four great volumes entitled *Roma Sotterranea* (*Subterranean Rome*). With Bosio, it might be claimed that the modern study of early Christian archaeology had its origins (Stevenson 1978: 47–52; Frend 1996: 13–16).

The rise of modern scholarship

Bosio's work on the catacombs was published just over a decade before the treaty of Westphalia (1648) brought decades of bitter and brutal warfare between Roman Catholics and Protestants to an end. But if the struggle now turned away from physical violence, debates between the two sides over early Christianity lost nothing of their vigour. Many of the trends that we have seen emerge in the wake of the Lutheran Reformation now settled into customary practice. Among Roman Catholics, energetic scholarly efforts were focused on investigating and codifying the traditions that they believed linked them to the early Christians. Such traditions were not merely the stuff of dry scholarship, but had consequences for how the church saw itself and its rivals in its own day. Thus the various forms of emerging Protestantism could be condemned as revivals of the heresies of the ancient church (cf. Wiles 1996: 52–61). At the same time, Roman Catholicism was engaged also in campaigns of militant evangelization in the newly conquered territories of central and south America. In the confrontation with native American religions, it was believed that lessons could be drawn from early Christianity's encounter with Graeco-Roman paganism (MacCormack 1991; Reff 2005).

Throughout the seventeenth and eighteenth centuries, Roman Catholic scholars produced new editions and additions to works that preserved and propagated their traditions, such as Baronius' *Annales Ecclesiastici*, the *Acta Sanctorum*, and the Maurist editions of early Christian texts. Such enterprises laid the foundations of much later Roman Catholic scholarship on early Christianity. In the nineteenth century, for example, many of the Maurist editions were republished under the guidance of the French cleric Jacques-Paul Migne (1800–75). This was a massive undertaking, yielding 221 volumes of the *Patrologia Latina* and 162 of the *Patrologia Graeca*. Likewise the investigations into the lives of the saints undertaken by the followers of John van Bolland have proved to be even more enduring: the Bollandists, an organization founded in his memory, still flourishes, publishing its scholarly journal *Analecta Bollandiana* twice each year.

Protestant interest in early Christianity was largely confined to the time of Jesus and the apostles. Even so, their reactions to Roman Catholic scholarship on the early Christian period could be harsh and scoffing. When, for instance, Gilbert Burnet (1643–1715), later bishop of Salisbury and himself a historian, travelled in Italy in 1685–6, he rejected the enthusiastic Catholic view that the catacombs were evidence of a sizeable and flourishing Christian community at Rome in the first centuries AD, and suggested instead that many of the catacombs had been dug not by Christians but by pagans (Stevenson 1978: 52; Frend 1996: 17). Such views were informed by prejudice as much as scholarship. Protestant polemics disputed the Roman Church's claims that it represented the traditions of early Christianity, and, as part of their attack, sought to demonstrate how post-apostolic Christianity had become contaminated by the Graeco-Roman culture (and therefore the paganism) in which it developed. Some forty years after Burnet visited Rome, the same journey was made by one Conyers Middleton. On returning to England, he wrote an account of what he had seen. The title of his book, published in 1729, leaves nothing about its polemical purpose to the imagination: *A Letter from Rome Shewing an Exact Conformity between Popery and Paganism: Or, The Religion of the Present Romans to be derived entirely from that of their Heathen Ancestors*! For Protestants, then, the early Christian traditions to which Rome laid claim were utterly corrupt. Purity was to be found instead in the Christian movement described in the New Testament, and it was from this that Protestantism claimed to be descended (Smith 1990: 14–25).

Such polarizations of opinion about early Christianity became all the more acute in the eighteenth century with the application to other areas of historical enquiry of the processes of analytical, secular reason associated with the European Enlightenment. History writing increasingly moved away from the ecclesiastical focus that had dominated in the middle ages and early modern period. Endeavours by non-clerical historians were now largely directed to satisfying the well-known precept of David Hume (1711–76) that it was the duty of cultivated people to know their own country's history and that of Greece and Rome (Hay 1977: 184). In turn, however, the techniques of historical analysis associated with secular reason were applied also to Christian history in a manner that was frequently highly critical of Christian traditions. In the anti-clerical atmosphere of revolutionary France, for example, Charles François Dupuis (1753–1809) published an account of comparative religious history that argued that all religions were, essentially, variations on the same basic pattern: in one swift blow, the special status of Christianity was swept away (Smith 1990: 26–33). In the English-speaking world, this rational scepticism of Christianity is perhaps best represented by Edward Gibbon (1737–94), who encapsulated the themes of his *History of the Decline and Fall of the Roman Empire* as 'the triumph of barbarism and religion' (Gibbon 1776–88 [1994]: III, 1068).

However much we may disagree with Gibbon's bleak assessment of late Roman, Byzantine, and medieval history, there can be no denying that he sought to write history in the modern sense, based on a thorough assessment of primary sources. And crucially, he had no qualms in extending to the history of Christianity the same analytical skills of secular reason that might be applied to any other province of human endeavour (Gibbon 1776–88 [1994]: I, 482–3). Gibbon's narrative included, in chapters 15 and 16 of its first volume, a notoriously critical and ironic account of early Christianity (cf. Womersley 1988: 99–133). At its outset, Gibbon explicitly contrasts the theological and historical approaches to religion:

> The theologian may indulge the pleasing task of describing Religion as she descended from Heaven, arrayed in her native purity. A more melancholy duty is imposed on the historian. He must discover the inevitable mixture of error and corruption, which she contracted in a long residence upon earth, among a weak and degenerate race of beings.
> (Gibbon 1776–88 [1994]: I, 446)

In Gibbon's view, the history of early Christianity ceased to be in any way a source of moral edification. For all its faults, his analysis emancipated early Christianity from the constraints of ecclesiastical debate and considered it as a part of human history. As such, he provided a model for later generations of historians to approach the topic with academic rigour. Gibbon's reassessment was part of a broader reassessment of the heritage of the ancient world. He lived in the age of the grand tour, when travel to the lands of classical antiquity became fashionable. In addition, with the increasing cordiality of relations between western Europe and the Ottoman empire in the eighteenth century, this opened up not just Italy to such travellers, but also Greece and the eastern Mediterranean. Of course, interest in classical antiquities remained paramount, but early Christian remains also attracted interest (Frend 1996: 23–37).

Towards modernity: early Christianity in the nineteenth and twentieth centuries

The nineteenth and twentieth centuries saw remarkable advances in the study of early Christianity. These developments are inextricably bound up with changes in the structure of knowledge over the last two hundred years. The publication of Charles Darwin's *The Origin of Species* in 1859, whatever the personal views of its author, irrevocably challenged the notion of a divinely created universe; the centrality of religious institutions suddenly became precarious; the forces of secularization gained new impetus. A major influence has come from changes in the structure of universities and the professionalization of academic disciplines. New methodologies have emerged in the study of early Christianity and, at the same time, many of the resources that form the basis for modern research. In short, the last two centuries have been characterized as witnessing a shift 'from dogma to history' as 'the study of the early Church [moved] from the study of the history of the development of doctrinal orthodoxy to the history of Christianity in all its many forms and ideals' (Frend 2003: 1).

A crucial influence was exerted by the German scholar Adolf von Harnack (1851–1930). A Lutheran who initially pursued the study of theology, Harnack found himself uninspired by the abstractions of philosophy but fired by the study of church history. He served as professor of ecclesiastical history at various German universities, culminating in an appointment (secured by the personal intervention of Kaiser Wilhelm II) at the Humboldt University in Berlin. Throughout his career, Harnack was a zealous advocate of the study of early church history, arguing that it could be used to correct uncritical dogmatic opinion. He published widely on various aspects of early Christianity, but perhaps his most lasting contribution was in the area of textual criticism. Harnack's energy in this field was instrumental in launching two important series of publications: *Texte und Untersuchungen zur Geschichte der altchristlichen Literatur* (*Texts and Studies on the*

History of Early Christian Literature), founded in 1882, and *Die griechischen christlichen Schriftsteller der ersten drei Jahrhunderte* (*The Greek Christian Authors of the First Three Centuries*), begun in 1897 (Frend 2003: 9–31). Other important series were initiated around the same time. In 1886 the first volume of *Corpus Scriptorum Ecclesiasticorum Latinorum* (*Corpus of Latin Ecclesiastical Writers*) was published in Vienna; the series is still in progress today. By this time comprehensive editions of early Christian inscriptions from Rome and France were already in progress. The tools for the modern study of early Christianity were coming together.

Harnack's critical approach to early Christian texts provoked some opposition from the Lutheran church. His contemporary, Louis Duchesne (1843–1922) also found himself criticized, this time by the Roman Catholic hierarchy. Duchesne's work – on early Christian liturgy and on the *Liber Pontificalis*, a chronicle of the early popes – threw into doubt many of the central tenets of the Catholic view of history, such as the foundation of the church at Rome by St Peter. For similar assaults on time-honoured traditions, Duchesne found his *L'Histoire ancienne de l'Église* (1906–10; published in English as *The Early History of the Church*, 1909–24) placed on the Roman Catholic Index of Prohibited Books in 1912. This came in the midst of the campaign against 'Modernism' under pope Pius X (1903–14) and other historians besides Duchesne were condemned (O. Chadwick 1998: 346–59). It was a sign that, for all the progress 'from dogma to history', ecclesiastical concerns had not disappeared. Indeed, as recently as 1929 the Roman archaeologist Orazio Marucchi (1852–1931) published a volume that aimed to show 'that in the catacombs . . . we find the most ancient monuments confirming the present Catholic faith' (1929: 25).[2]

Marucchi's work built on the researches of Giovanni Battista de Rossi (1822–94), who undertook the first really thorough work in the Roman catacombs since Bosio in the early seventeenth century. Others too were beginning to explore the archaeological heritage of early Christianity. By now, of course, archaeology had advanced considerably from the antiquarian endeavours of the Renaissance and Enlightenment. More scientific approaches, first developed in northern Europe and Scandinavia, were applied to the Mediterranean world, and the study of early Christianity was one of the beneficiaries. A fine example of the new fieldwork being done is provided by the efforts of Scotsman W. M. Ramsay (1851–1939), who tirelessly traversed Asia Minor in search of classical and Christian antiquities.

Indeed, in many respects the fields of Graeco-Roman antiquity and early Christianity were beginning to coalesce. This was evident, for example, in the excavations conducted by French and American archaeologists at the Hellenistic and Roman frontier outpost of Dura Europos, perched above the river Euphrates in what is now Syria. The finds at Dura Europos caused a sensation. In 1931–2 the excavators explored a building decorated with frescos that had clearly been a church. The remains were far from spectacular, and Dura certainly yielded more dazzling finds, such as the Jewish synagogue unearthed in 1932–3. What really mattered about the Dura church, however, was that it could be dated very precisely: the city had been destroyed in a war between Rome and Persia in AD 256, thus making the building the earliest securely datable church known. A memoir of the excavations shows the excavators' excitement:

> Our camp was awestruck by the extraordinary preservation of Christian murals dated more than three-quarters of a century before Constantine recognised Christianity in 312. The scenes were small, but they were unmistakable. It is true that compared with the paintings in the Temple of the Palmyrene Gods [another building excavated at Dura] they were sketchy and amateurish, but that mattered little, for they were Christian!
>
> (C. Hopkins 1979: 91)

Awestruck the excavators may have been, but they published and discussed the Dura church in the broader context of the other remains found at the city. Early Christianity was now more than ever being considered as an aspect of Roman imperial civilization.

From the mid-twentieth century onwards the study of early Christianity has undergone radical change. A topic that had once been the preserve of churchmen, who studied it to illuminate theological concerns, now increasingly became a field of endeavour for scholars drawn from the laity, or even from entirely different religious backgrounds, such as Judaism. The study of early Christianity has been affected also by the various trends that have come to shape late twentieth-century secular scholarship of the ancient world more generally. At the same time, new sources for early Christian history began to be gleaned from archaeological excavations: not only physical remains such as the Dura church, but also new documents such as the papyrus books found at Nag Hammadi in Egypt (see chapter 5). By this point of my narrative of early Christian studies I am beginning to encroach on topics that will crop up in later chapters of this book. I will limit my final remarks here, therefore, to outlining some of the more striking features of the study of early Christianity as we enter the third millennium.

Among the major transformations of recent decades in scholarship of the ancient world – among English-speaking scholars particularly – has been a flourishing interest in the period known as late antiquity. This term, roughly speaking, designates the period from the political upheavals that enveloped the Roman empire in the third century AD to the era of the first Arab invasions in the seventh. Edward Gibbon's judgement that this era represented nothing more than a depressing narrative of 'decline and fall', characterized by the 'triumph of barbarism and religion' (see p. 57), was overthrown by the work of scholars such as Peter Brown (born in 1935), who himself was building on the scholarship of an earlier generation of brave and lonely Byzantine historians such as Norman Baynes (1877–1961). Late antiquity has come to be regarded as a period of dynamic transformation, as the classical culture of Greek and Roman antiquity fused with emerging Christianity (and, later, Islam) to forge the contours of an entirely new civilization. In this context, early Christianity has come to assume a new importance as one of the chief forces in the metamorphosis that saw the ancient world become the middle ages (Brakke 2002: 475–80).

The result of this new scholarly activity has been that the study of early Christianity has become decoupled from the study of 'pure' church history and its quest for the origins of dogma. Scholars trained as classicists and historians have brought to early Christianity questions and methodologies fashionable in their own disciplines: gender, literary discourse, and sociological theory have all been brought to bear on the early Christian world. None of this is to say that early Christianity is no longer studied by theologians, or that such theologians continue to pursue old-fashioned studies as if sealed off in a bubble from other scholarly developments. Nor does it mean that contemporary lay or non-Christian scholars are any less prone to interpret early Christianity in ways that reflect personal preconceptions or agendas. As was the case in the days of Eusebius, Cesare Baronio, or Adolf von Harnack, studies of early Christianity continue to reflect the concerns of the age in which they were written.

Chapter 3

The search for early Christianity: sources and their interpretation

This chapter will explore the astonishingly diverse range of ancient source materials available to those studying early Christianity. I should say at the outset that this will not be in the form of a catalogue: further guidance on accessing the sources will be provided in chapter 7. Rather, my aim here is to point out the character of the available evidence, to highlight problems of interpretation that it presents, and to indicate the sorts of questions that can be most usefully asked of the different sorts of sources. This will provide background to the topics investigated in chapters 4–6. It makes sense to begin with what Christians themselves wrote about the origins and development of their movement. Next I will consider what information can be gleaned from sources written by contemporary pagan and Jewish observers. Then I will turn to various categories of artefacts, ranging from archaeological remains to papyrus texts, that also shed light on the early history of Christianity. At the end of the chapter, I will reflect briefly on some questions of methodology.

Christian literature

The New Testament

Most modern Christians – and many non-Christians – will naturally commence their search for early Christianity with the books contained in the New Testament. This collection contains twenty-seven works: four accounts of Jesus' ministry and death (the gospels); a narrative of the deeds of Jesus' immediate successors (the *Acts of Apostles*); twenty-one letters, thirteen of which are ascribed to the apostle Paul; and *Revelation*, an apocalyptic vision of the future. In terms of their contents, these various books can answer different sorts of questions about the nature of the Christian movement at its earliest stages. The gospels and *Acts* present, on the face of it, something like a narrative of Christian origins. The letters are concerned with the lifestyle and faith to which early Christians were expected to adhere. *Revelation*, with its coded allusions to Rome as ancient Israel's great foe Babylon, seems to present a mental portrait of early Christians suffering in this world, perhaps because of persecution, but hopeful that good would vanquish evil in the end.

Some modern historians of the ancient Roman world have engaged with the New Testament texts in ways that differ little from their approach to other ancient sources. They have sought to integrate them with other ancient evidence to yield a portrait of the earliest followers of Jesus that is firmly embedded in the social and cultural world of the Roman empire (e.g. Sherwin-White 1963; Mitchell 1993: II, 1–10). Such an approach has been particularly pronounced in the study of the *Acts of the Apostles*, a text that seems to present an account of the earliest expansion of the Christian movement in a narrative form with which modern historians of the ancient world are familiar. A. N. Sherwin-White (1911–94), one of the leading Roman historians of the twentieth century, gave a neat summation of what is so attractive about this text for the modern scholar of the Roman world:

> In Acts or in that part of Acts which is concerned with the adventures of Paul in Asia Minor and Greece, one is aware all the time of the Hellenistic and Roman shading. *The historical framework is exact. In terms of time and place the details are precise and correct.* One walks the streets and market-places, the theatres and assemblies of first-century Ephesus or Thessalonica, Corinth or Philippi, with the author of Acts. The great men of the cities, the magistrates, the mob, the mob-leaders, all are there. The feel and tone of city life is the same as in the descriptions of [the geographer] Strabo and [the orator] Dio of Prusa. The difference lies only in the Jewish shading.
>
> (Sherwin-White 1963: 120 [emphasis added])

In some respects, an attempt to reconcile data from the New Testament writings with those drawn from classical sources can be a fruitful approach. Indeed, the case study in chapter 4 of this book will examine how far this style of investigation can get us in understanding the world of the apostle Paul. Nevertheless, there are serious problems that must always be borne in mind. Even those books of the New Testament that appear to give straightforward historical information can mislead. Thus the *Gospel of Luke* presents Jesus' human parents Joseph and Mary travelling to Bethlehem to comply with the census conducted by the Roman governor Quirinius (2.2). The miraculous conception of Jesus happens only a short time (1.26) after that of John the Baptist, which this gospel says occurred 'in the days of Herod, king of Judaea' (1.5). But this historical verisimilitude collapses when we discover that Herod died in 4 BC and that Quirinius' census only occurred in AD 6.[1] There is a further risk that modern Roman historians are becoming isolated from current trends in New Testament studies undertaken by biblical scholars. In particular, by treating certain New Testament writings little differently from classical sources, Roman historians risk losing sight of the special problems that biblical texts present. In what follows, I will concentrate on what is perhaps the major problem that will concern anyone trying to reconstruct the origins of Christianity from the New Testament texts: their 'historical reliability'. This topic has been much discussed, but it is worth reiterating here a few salient points on a number of interrelated questions about these texts: their authorship and date and how their theological significance has a bearing on their utility as historical sources.

It is important to appreciate how the New Testament came into existence and why it contains specific texts and not others. The New Testament was not put together in the immediate aftermath of the events that much of it seems to describe: the activities of Jesus and early Christian leaders such as Paul. Instead, the texts that make up what is called the New Testament canon were only agreed upon gradually over a number of centuries. Indeed, the first securely datable list of the twenty-seven books that modern Christians regard as scripture was not set down until the mid-fourth century;[2] up until that time (and afterwards too) there circulated many other gospels, acts, letters, and apocalypses (see chapter 5). Why were they excluded from the canon while other texts made it into the New Testament? The reason was that the New Testament texts were deemed – after much debate – to represent certain truths. But their truthfulness was not dictated on grounds of historical reliability, even if it is now generally agreed that most of the texts included in the New Testament were, in fact, written earlier than those other writings that were excluded. Rather, the decision as to what was true or not was made according to judgements of the emerging institution of the church. Determining the truthfulness of a text partly depended on how widely it was used by Christian communities as scripture. Much more important, however, were theological considerations, where a text's truth was judged according to the extent that it was an 'orthodox' (literally 'right belief') representation of those Christian teachings that were regarded as normative by the early Church (Metzger 1987: 251–4). That the books deemed to be canonical were filled with orthodox teaching was attributed by early Christians to one factor above all: the biblical authors' writings were believed to have been inspired by God through the action of the Holy Spirit (Metzger 1987: 255). In other words, the reasons for a text's inclusion in the New Testament was its doctrinal soundness, not its historical reliability.

As divinely inspired sources of orthodox teaching, the texts in the New Testament possessed considerable authority (as they still do for modern Christians). One reflection of this can be seen in the names ascribed to various of the writings. We talk, for example, about the gospels of Matthew, Mark, Luke, and John, or the letters of Paul, or the *Revelation* of John. But this does not mean the same thing as when we talk about, for example, the *Annals* of Tacitus or the *Twelve Caesars* of Suetonius. That Tacitus and Suetonius wrote those works is universally accepted by modern ancient historians. This is not always the case with the books of the New Testament.

Let us take the gospels first. None of them includes, within its narrative, the name of the person who wrote it. The closest we get to this is in the final chapter of the *Gospel of John*. After a description of 'the disciple whom Jesus loved . . . who had reclined next to Jesus at the last supper' (*John* 21.20), the text states: 'This is the disciple who is testifying these things and has written them, and we know that this testimony is true' (21.24). At no point, however, is the name of this especially beloved disciple divulged. Indeed, there is a further problem: many scholars regard the last chapter of the *Gospel of John* as a later addition to the text, meaning that any information it gives pertaining to the work's authorship is entirely spurious. In spite of this absence of precise identifications of authorship, the gospels were ascribed to named writers already by the end of the second century. The *Gospel of John* was attributed to one of Jesus' disciples, John the son of Zebedee (*Mark* 10.35); the others were ascribed to Mark, who had been Peter's companion in Rome (*1 Peter* 5.13; cf. Eusebius, *Ecclesiastical History* 2.15); to Jesus' disciple Matthew (Eusebius, *Ecclesiastical History* 3.24.5–6); and to Luke, one of the apostle Paul's travelling companions (*Philemon* 24; Irenaeus, *Against Heresies* 3.1.1). Thus the doctrinal authority of the gospels was reinforced by the fact that they were believed to have been written by persons who were either Jesus' own disciples or companions of his earliest apostles.

We encounter a slightly different problem with *Revelation* and the letters of John and Paul. *Revelation* opens with a clear statement of the author's name: 'The revelation of Jesus Christ, which God gave him to show his servants what must soon take place; he made it known by sending his angel to his servant John' (*Revelation* 1.1). Shortly afterwards, the main account of *Revelation* is cast as an address from 'John to the seven churches that were in Asia' (1.4). Other than that, the author says nothing about himself. From the second century, however, Christians identified this John with the disciple, the son of Zebedee, and so with the author of the fourth gospel and three letters also in the New Testament. Examination of the style and content of these various texts by modern scholars suggests, however, that this ancient identification is wrong (Schnelle 1998: 519–23). As for the three New Testament letters ascribed to John, whereas the *Second* and *Third Epistles of John* state clearly that they were written by 'the elder [*presbuteros* in Greek] John', the *First Epistle of John* contains no such claim. Although early Christians saw all three letters as having the same author, modern scholars are divided on the issue: some see the three letters as the work of one author (e.g. Johnson 1999: 561–2); others argue that the author of the first letter is different from the author of the other two (e.g. Schnelle 1998: 454–5).

When we turn to Paul's letters, the author's identity seems at first glance to be more securely established. All of the New Testament letters attributed to him begin by identifying the author as 'Paul, a servant of Jesus Christ, called to be an apostle' (thus *Romans* 1.1), or by some similar form of words. And yet, of the thirteen letters that begin this way, six (*Colossians*, *Ephesians*, *2 Thessalonians*, and the pastoral letters, *Titus* and *1* and *2 Timothy*) are regarded by most New Testament scholars to be forgeries written at a slightly later time by other authors who saw themselves as Paul's successors and wrote under his name. They did so in an effort (ultimately successful, as the letters' inclusion in the New Testament shows) to give their writings the authority associated with Paul's name (Schnelle 1998: 276–348). These forgeries are usually referred to as the deutero-Pauline (that is, 'secondary Pauline') letters to distinguish them from the other seven Pauline letters believed to be the apostle's genuine compositions. Indeed, some scholars make a further distinction marking out the Pastoral Epistles as a group separate from the other deutero-Pauline letters (Ehrman 1997: 242–3, 320–39).

The authenticity of the genuine Pauline letters is judged by a variety of means: their written style and vocabulary are regarded as consistent; their theological content is coherent; and they address matters that historians regard as plausible concerns for Christian communities in the 50s when Paul was active (e.g. Ehrman 1997: 242–310). By contrast, the inauthentic letters differ in terms of style, structure, and content. At times, they even contradict statements in the genuine letters. For example, whereas the genuine letters talk of salvation and the resurrection of Christ's followers in the *future* tense, as experiences to which Christians can look forward (*Romans* 5.9–10 and 6.4; *1 Corinthians* 3.15 and 5.5), the deutero-Pauline epistles speak about such matters in the *past* tense, and therefore as experiences which Christians feel they have already achieved (*Colossians* 2.12; *Ephesians* 2.5).[3] Similar problems attach themselves to the ascriptions of the remaining five letters in the New Testament (one each by James and Jude, one addressed to the Hebrews, and two by Peter).[4] Of course, many of these arguments about authorship are subjective. They depend in large measure upon the extent to which scholars agree that specific characteristics (such as style, vocabulary, and content) are sufficient to establish the authorship of a particular document. Not all scholars agree with the verdicts I have set out above. As a consequence there is much debate about the attribution of many of the letters contained in the New Testament.[5]

Further problems arise when we begin to consider the dates of the various books in the New Testament. In modern bibles, the books are so arranged that the gospels come first, followed by

Acts and the various epistles, and with *Revelation* at the end. This order makes sense in terms of how the contents of the various books contribute to a portrait of the emergence of Christianity. Thus the New Testament begins with the events of Jesus' life, before assembling the deeds and writings of his earliest apostles, and concluding with *Revelation*'s glance towards the future. But this was not the order in which they were written. This is clearest if we consider the relationship between the seven genuine letters of Paul and the book of *Acts*. The last datable event in *Acts* is the arrival of Festus as the governor of Judaea (*Acts* 25.1), an event which seems to have occurred at the very end of the 50s, after which Paul himself was dispatched to Rome as a prisoner (*Acts* 27–8). Paul's genuine letters, however, seem to date earlier than this, from the period of his missionary journeys. Any references they contain to his imprisonment (e.g. *Philippians* 1.14, 17; *Philemon* 10) most likely refer not to his incarceration in Rome, but to his various spells in prison during his missionary journeys (*2 Corinthians* 11.23–7). In other words, the genuine Pauline letters are *earlier* than *Acts*, even though *Acts* precedes them in the order of books set out in the New Testament.

There are similar difficulties concerning the historical reliability and dating of the gospels. I cannot possibly review here in detail the myriad arguments that have been set forth on this most vexed issue. However, a few basic (and, to the extent that such a thing is ever possible, uncontroversial) statements about them may be made:

(1) As we have seen, none of the gospels can be confidently ascribed to the individual authors under whose names they appear in the New Testament.

(2) The gospels were written in Greek. But Jesus' ministry in Galilee took place in a society that mainly spoke the Semitic language Aramaic. Hence the gospels were written for a very different audience than the one which heard Jesus' actual teachings. This is reflected, for instance, in the need felt by the author of the *Gospel*

of Mark to explain the meaning of terms in Aramaic (5.41), and even certain Jewish customs (7.3–4).

(3) The gospels represent not a single version of Jesus' career, but rather diverging traditions about and representations of it. They stress slightly different aspects of his career and teachings. Such discrepancies are most obvious in the case of the *Gospel of John*. They include a different presentation of the geographical scope of Jesus' ministry (which is said to encompass Judaea and Samaria as well as Galilee) and different chronological structures (*Matthew*, *Mark*, and *Luke* present the Last Supper as a Passover meal; *John* sets it a few days earlier than the Jewish festival). Such historical divergences are matched also by theological ones: *John* is much more heavily influenced by Greek philosophical thought than the other canonical gospels.[6]

(4) The fact that *Matthew*, *Mark*, and *Luke* are so different from *John* means that they are often regarded as belonging to a category that New Testament scholars call the 'synoptic' tradition: this literally means that they can be 'seen together'. This is manifested above all by striking verbal similarities between them. As a result, scholars have sought to uncover the origins of such similar materials. They have hypothesized various oral traditions about Jesus that influenced the gospels. Some have also speculated that there were lost written sources upon which some of the gospel authors depended. The best known of these is the one referred to as Q, from the German word *Quelle* meaning 'source'. It is argued to lie behind material that is in *Matthew* and *Luke*, but which is not found in *Mark*.

(5) Such considerations have led scholars to ascribe different dates to the gospels. Most agree that *John* is the latest, and *Luke* the third to be written. It is commonly assumed that *Mark* was written earlier than *Matthew*, despite their order in the New Testament canon. Even

so, not all scholars agree on this sequence of *Mark*, *Matthew*, *Luke*, and *John*: some suggest, for example, that *Matthew* and *Mark* were written much closer to each other in time, perhaps even at the same time; others contend that *Matthew* might even have been written before *Mark*.

(6) If the relative dating of the gospels is hotly debated, then any attempt to date them precisely is even more perilous. Much depends, for example, on the assumption that prophecies about future events ascribed to Jesus in the gospels are nothing of the sort, and are actually references to events *that had already happened* by the time a particular gospel was written. Thus Jesus' prophecy in *Matthew* that the Jewish temple in Jerusalem would be destroyed and that the city's population would be scattered to the mountains (24.15–16) could be a reference written *after* just such circumstances had come to pass with the sack of Jerusalem by the Romans in 70.

I have barely touched on the complex debates here, but I hope to have said enough to show that there are serious problems in any attempt to use the gospels as 'historical' texts. Most modern scholars would agree that they are not transparent narratives, through which we can access the events of Jesus' life and times. Instead they present carefully crafted accounts of Jesus' life, death, and miraculous resurrection. Jesus was regarded by the authors of the gospels as the Messiah ('the anointed one' in Hebrew, rendered in Greek as *Christos*, from which we get the English term 'Christ') whose coming had been foretold in the prophecies contained in the Hebrew scriptures that came to constitute the Christian Old Testament. Hence the authors of the gospels are concerned at every turn to show how Jesus' ministry complied with Old Testament prophecy.

In short, the gospels are not so much narratives as arguments in support of particular images of Jesus. Similar features, moreover, can be seen in the other texts in the New Testament. Thus *Acts of the Apostles* presents a debate between those who thought Jesus' message was only for the Jews, and those who argued that it should be preached also to the gentiles (non-Jews). Moreover, *Acts* presents this debate from the perspective of those who agreed with the second point of view. Such issues are even more explicit in the various New Testament letters, all of which were written to suggest solutions to particular problems confronting the emerging Christian communities (see chapter 4). In their various ways, then, the New Testament writings share a common thread: all of them are concerned with the nature of the nascent Christian movement's relationship to contemporary Judaism.

To sum up: none of the texts that make up the New Testament can be taken at face value as a transparent window onto earliest history of Christianity. Only a few of them were written by authors whom we can identify with any certainty. The narratives they contain or the arguments they communicate, whether about Jesus himself or about the actions and beliefs of his immediate followers, sought to articulate particular points of view. As a starting place for a study of the origins of Christianity, then, they are perhaps better regarded as a guide to problems than a source of solutions.

Apocryphal texts outside the New Testament

It has been noted above that the canon of the New Testament came into being only gradually, over the course of three centuries. While Christians debated what texts should be included, they also argued about what should be left out. There survive, for instance, gospels attributed to the disciples Thomas, Philip, and Peter, some of which contain materials (especially sayings of Jesus) that are found also in the canonical gospels in a different form. A number of infancy gospels also recount episodes from Jesus' childhood. Analogous to the biblical *Acts of the Apostles*, we possess other books recounting the careers (and sometimes violent deaths) of the apostles Andrew, John, Paul, Peter, and Thomas. There are apocryphal epistles too, including an alleged correspondence between Paul and Seneca, the Roman philosopher who was one of the luminaries of the court of the emperor Nero. Finally, there are apocalyptic texts, sometimes surviving in multiple versions, ascribed to Paul, Peter, and Thomas that resemble the New Testament book of *Revelation*. Some of these texts will be the focus of the case study in chapter 5. Here, however, I want to outline the basic features of these texts which have come to be regarded as apocryphal.

It is perhaps useful to begin with the very term 'apocrypha', which is a Greek word meaning 'secret things', in this context specifically 'secret writings'. This means that the apocryphal writings are sometimes viewed as containing secret teachings that were suppressed for some reason; some sort of foul play, or even power struggle, is sometimes suspected (see chapter 5). But this is an erroneous view. Texts came to be regarded as scripture only after protracted debates about their use and doctrinal integrity. As a result, some texts were included in the canon while others were excluded. It is nothing more sinister than that. Furthermore, it should be noted that the existence of apocryphal literature is not a uniquely Christian phenomenon. As we will see, Jewish authors also produced a large body of non-canonical scripture.

What light can such texts shed on the early history of Christianity? One popular view – often peddled in sensationalist works of tabloid history – is that some of them, particularly the apocryphal gospels, present a 'true' version of Christian origins that has been wilfully suppressed by the church. We have already seen, however, that the accounts contained in the canonical texts of the New Testament are far from being transparently true in terms of historicity. The idea that the apocryphal works are any more true is, I am afraid, sheer fantasy. Rather, these texts are useful not for the actual events surrounding the birth of Christianity, but for the development of early Christian speculations about Jesus and his significance. To put it another way, the various non-canonical works bear witness to particular early Christian traditions that flourished in the Roman world, but which then disappeared, and whose writings did not match up to the standard of doctrinal truth adduced by those authorities who assembled the New Testament canon. They provide clues to the ways in which Christianity might have developed – but did not (Ehrman 2003).

The writings of the 'church fathers'

In the tradition of scholarship on early Christianity, a dividing line is usually drawn between Christianity as it appears in the New Testament and that which appears in other writers from the early centuries. This distinction in scholarship is marked in various ways, such as different academic journals, conferences, and shelving arrangements in university libraries. It is also signalled by terminology: the early Christianity of the New Testament is often described as 'apostolic', whereas that described by authors writing after *c*. 100 is termed 'patristic'. The word 'patristic' (and also 'patrology', meaning the study of patristic writings) derives from the Greek word *patēr*, meaning father. It is used because early Christian writings outside the New Testament are attributed to individuals known collectively as the 'fathers of the church', in other words the figures through whose teachings and books the Christian tradition has been handed down to subsequent generations.

In many ways, such a designation is quite arbitrary and unsubtle. Hence there have been efforts to distinguish between different groups of fathers according to various criteria. They can be divided chronologically: thus 'early' and 'later' fathers. Or they may be categorized according to the language in which they wrote or their geographical context: thus Greek, Latin, and Syriac fathers; sometimes desert fathers; also (in a term that smacks of western cultural bias) Oriental fathers (from Egypt, Ethiopia, the Middle East, and the Caucasus – not China or Japan!). There are problems, however, with the very term father (and hence with patristic), not least because it gives priority to men over women.

Furthermore, traditional definitions of the term father have tended to award it only to those writers whose work was deemed to be orthodox; anyone else was simply a heretic.

At its heart, the concept of an age of the church fathers is based on the assumption that the apostolic period can be firmly located within the world described in the New Testament, and that the authors who wrote its books were exact contemporaries of either Jesus or his immediate successors. As we saw earlier, the reality is starkly different. Both canonical and non-canonical scriptures continued to be written for some generations after Jesus' death, while the problem of what actually constituted the New Testament was still being debated in the fourth century. As a result, there is some vagueness about where the apostolic period ends and the patristic age dawns. Indeed, texts that are classified today as works of church fathers – such as the *First Epistle of Clement* and the *Shepherd* of Hermas – were once regarded as having a similar authority to scripture and were included in manuscripts of the Bible (Metzger 1987: 187–9). An attempted solution has been to refine the basic definitions. Since the seventeenth century, the hybrid term 'apostolic fathers' has been used to designate those earliest Christian authors who wrote at the same time as, or very shortly after, the New Testament itself was being written. Even this term, however, excludes those writings of the period later condemned as apocryphal or heretical.

The works of early Christian writers present a great variety. There are many letters, which, like those in the New Testament, were written to advise Christian communities on issues of doctrine and discipline. For example, the late first-century *First Epistle of Clement* conveys the opinions of Christians at Rome to their brethren at Corinth about a dispute over leadership. Similarly, Ignatius of Antioch sent letters to various Christian communities while *en route* to Rome to face trial *c.* 110. From the mid-third century, we possess the voluminous correspondence of bishop Cyprian of Carthage, which is revealing of a wide range of issues confronting the early church, such as the impact of persecution and conflicts between bishops.

A large body of early Christian literature was concerned specifically with matters of church practice, discipline, and doctrine. Among Cyprian's other writings are treatises *On the Unity of the Catholic Church* and *On Baptism*. Many early Christians wrote works condemning as heretics those individuals and groups who subscribed to doctrines that the church came to regard as unorthodox. Important examples include Irenaeus of Lyons' tract against the Gnostics from the late second century, various writings produced a little later by the north African Tertullian, and a work *Against Heresies* written in the early third century by Hippolytus of Rome. Disputes about the nature of true doctrine also prompted works of biblical interpretation: the third-century Alexandrian scholar Origen was responsible for an extensive output of commentaries on books of scripture, covering both the Old Testament and the New.

Numerous other works reflect further internal concerns of individual Christians and their communities. Prophecy and revelation were not limited to the New Testament and the apocrypha: from early second-century Rome survives the *Shepherd* of Hermas which recounts the visions experienced by its author. The celebration of Christian worship is reflected in texts such as the *Didache* [*Teaching*] *of the Twelve Apostles* and Melito of Sardis' *On the Pasch*, both works of the second century. Since many Christians placed considerable store by tradition and the handing down of 'true' teachings from Jesus' time to their own day, there soon developed an interest in tracing the history of the church. Irenaeus of Lyons' polemic against the Gnostics included an account of the succession of bishops at Rome (see chapter 5). In the third century, Hippolytus of Rome and Sextus Julius Africanus (a native of Palestine, in spite of his name) composed chronicles recounting Christian views of history. The climax of early Christian historical scholarship came in the age of the emperors Diocletian and Constantine with the *Chronicle* and *Ecclesiastical History* of Eusebius of Caesarea.

As Christianity expanded into the Roman empire, Christians were compelled to assess the nature of their engagement with the society in which they lived. Such concerns prompted writings such as Tertullian's works on the moral dangers posed by the worship of pagan images, games in the arena, and extravagant fashions of female dress (see chapter 6). The public visibility of Christian communities also increased, meaning that sometimes they attracted hostile attention from outsiders. Hence various authors produced 'apologetic' works designed to explain Christianity (and its superiority to other religions) to Jews (such as Justin Martyr's second-century *Dialogue with Trypho*) and pagans (which Justin also wrote, as did Tertullian and many others) (see chapter 6). Actual conflict between Christianity and Roman society led to the production of accounts of martyrs who died for their faith. Such accounts were often derived from the transcripts of court proceedings during trials of Christians, but it is clear that they were often embellished with specifically Christian elements, such as miracles (Bowersock 1995: 23–39).

Early Christian literature also reveals much about the emerging religion's cultural profile. At first, all Christian writings (scripture and non-scripture, orthodox and heretical) were produced in Greek, not only in the eastern Mediterranean, but also in the Latin-speaking west of the Roman empire. A Latin Christian literature does not appear until the end of the second century with Tertullian in north Africa. Even after this, some western authors, such as Hippolytus, still wrote in Greek, and there was no standard Latin translation of the Bible until the end of the fourth century. Such factors suggest that Christianity in the western empire was initially a religion of immigrants (see chapter 4).

Content just as much as language is revealing about the culture of the early Christians. One of Irenaeus of Lyons' criticisms of the Gnostics was that they perverted Christian truth by importing ideas from Greek philosophy (*Against Heresies* 2.14.2). Yet Greek philosophical ideas can be seen permeating Christian writings as early as the *Gospel of John*. In the second and third centuries, authors such as Clement of Alexandria and Origen were adapting the language of Stoic and Platonic philosophy to

Christian theological speculations (Jaeger 1962; H. Chadwick 1966). Indeed, the accommodation of Christianity and philosophy became a central theme of apologetic literature, as Christians sought to defend the sophistication of their religion against its detractors.

The summary presented here presents nothing like a complete catalogue of early Christian writers and their works, but then we possess nothing like the full range of writings that once existed. The survival of early Christian literature has been susceptible to the vicissitudes of time just as much as the works of classical Greek and Latin authors. In addition, many early Christian works were actively suppressed (and destroyed) because they came to be regarded as heretical. This was the fate suffered by many works of Origen, perhaps the most brilliant early Christian interpreter of scripture. In addition, many of his writings survive not in their original Greek, but in Latin translations produced in the fourth century at a time when the orthodoxy of Origen's views was the subject of vigorous debate.

More conventionally orthodox works have also had a chequered history of preservation. The letter known as the *Epistle to Diognetus*, which provides interesting observations on what it was like to live as a Christian among Jews and pagans, would have disappeared forever had the sole surviving manuscript not been rescued from a pile of wrapping paper in a fishmonger's shop in Constantinople in the fifteenth century. (This charming story has a sad sequel: that unique manuscript was destroyed at Strasbourg in 1870 during the Franco-Prussian war.) Even so important a work as Irenaeus of Lyons' five-book polemic against the Gnostics does not survive complete in the Greek version he wrote. For a complete text, we are compelled to rely on a Latin translation probably prepared *c*. 300. For the fourth and fifth books, we can check this Latin version against a translation into Armenian. The only passages of Irenaeus' Greek to survive are extracts from the first and third books quoted by the fourth-century authors Eusebius of Caesarea and Epiphanius of Salamis (like Irenaeus, a writer against heresies).

Indeed, Eusebius' scholarly method, which developed out of his researches into biblical texts, led him to quote extracts from earlier writers that supported the arguments he himself sought to advance (Barnes 1981). As a result, his works contain extensive extracts not only from scripture but also from early Christian literature that would otherwise be irretrievably lost. His *Ecclesiastical History* in particular is a mine of such fragments: from it, for example, we have samples (not all of them complete) of letters written by Irenaeus (*Ecclesiastical History* 5.20, 23, 24).

Even where works do survive there are problems of authenticity similar to those that confront interpreters of the New Testament. We have already noted the existence of the *First Epistle of Clement*, but its text nowhere gives its author's name, which appears only in titles in the manuscripts. There exists, moreover, a *Second Epistle of Clement* – but it is a homily, not a letter, and its style is so wholly different from that of the *First Epistle* that it must surely have been written by another author. Other works too have come down to us under Clement's name, but none of them seems to be authentic either. The reason for this circumstance is not difficult to fathom. In the centuries before the canon of Christian scripture was closed, the *First Epistle of Clement* was read to Christian gatherings (Eusebius, *Ecclesiastical History* 3.16; 4.23.11). Within the church, then, the name of Clement was associated with a certain authority, and any work that had his name attached to it could share in that authority, much in the same way that the deutero-Pauline letters were regarded as important texts because they were believed to have been written by Paul.

Like the New Testament and the apocrypha, the writings of subsequent generations of Christians were produced in contexts of lively debate. Any effort to interpret them as historical sources must be mindful of this factor. Indeed, the very fact that many modern histories of early Christianity are for the most part accounts of disputes over doctrine and practice neatly reflects the character of the surviving ancient Christian literature.

Jewish and pagan literature

Once we move away from writings by and about the Christians themselves to look at what non-Christians wrote about them, we enter a realm of evidence that presents a whole range of different difficulties. One problem is definition. If we want to understand the sort of world in which Christianity developed, then it could be argued that *any* text written in the ancient Mediterranean world after about 200 BC is relevant. To an extent, that is true: texts that tell us something about Jewish and pagan religion, for example, will provide us with hints as to the possible responses that Christianity might have provoked among the inhabitants of the Roman world. Throughout the rest of this book I will cite a range of non-Christian sources, but for the purposes of the present chapter I want to limit my remarks to a number of specific problems relating to their interpretation.

Jewish writings

Since Christianity developed from within Judaism (see chapter 4) it might be expected that Jewish writings of the period will provide insights. Indeed, many modern authors concerned with Christian origins have sifted through Jewish sources looking for material that might help to 'explain' the careers of Jesus, Paul, and those who came after them. The results of such a quest will often depend on the nature of the questions being asked of the Jewish sources. A good example can be provided by the texts known as the Dead Sea Scrolls. These documents, which first came to public attention in 1947, were discovered quite by accident in a number of caves located near the remains of an ancient religious community at Qumran by the north-western shores of the Dead Sea.[7] They were written mainly in Hebrew (there are a few in Aramaic and Greek) on leather scrolls (with the obvious exception of the document called the Copper Scroll) and dated to the years between *c.* 225 BC and AD 70, with the majority belonging towards the end of that period. Their contents are diverse:

all books of the Hebrew Bible, with the possible exception of the book of *Esther*; works of biblical interpretation; rules for (presumably) the nearby religious community; works of poetry, prayer, and liturgy; and texts concerned with God's wisdom.

From the moment of their discovery, these texts provoked great excitement because they dated more or less from the time of Jesus. Furthermore, as the Scrolls began to be deciphered, they presented readers with texts that echoed the writings of the New Testament in significant ways. For example, the text known as the Messianic Rule, from cave 1 at Qumran, concludes with the following instruction for a gathering of the community:

> And [when] they shall gather for the common [tab]le, to eat and [to drink] new wine, when the common table shall be set out for eating and the new wine [poured] for drinking, let no man extend his hand over the firstfruits of bread and wine before the Priest, for [it is he] who shall bless the firstfruits of bread and wine, and shall be the first [to extend] his hand over the bread. Thereafter the Messiah of Israel shall extend his hand over the bread, [and] all the congregation of the community [shall utter a] blessing, [each man in the order of] his dignity.
>
> (*The Messianic Rule*, trans. Vermes 1997: 159–60)

There are obviously similarities between the ritual described here and the gospel accounts of the Last Supper (cf. Fredriksen 2000: 115). What are we to make of them? One reaction has been to postulate very close links indeed between the Qumran community and the earliest Christians. Such efforts have produced some rather sensational theories. For example, the texts say much about a leadership figure called the Teacher of Righteousness and his enemy the Wicked Priest. Some readers of the Scrolls have seized upon these figures and sought to identify them with the founders of Christianity: thus we have been presented with James, the brother of Jesus, as the Teacher of Righteousness and Paul as the Wicked Priest; even more eccentric has been the identification of the Teacher of Righteousness with John the Baptist and Jesus as the Wicked Priest (who was married, divorced, and remarried, and the father of four children!). There are obvious affinities between this approach and that which has been taken to some of the apocryphal gospels: both assume that the version of the events in the New Testament is a deliberate falsification and that the 'true' story was altogether racier and subsequently suppressed. Yet such attempts to see John the Baptist, or Jesus, or James, or Paul in the Scrolls are bad history. As the distinguished Dead Sea Scrolls scholar Geza Vermes puts it, 'all these theories fail the basic credibility test: they do not spring from, but are foisted on, the texts' (Vermes 1997: 22). Indeed, no appeal to early Christianity is necessary to explain the contents of the Scrolls: there are perfectly reasonable identifications of the various figures mentioned in them that can be made from Jewish history. It is better to view the Scrolls more neutrally, as a source of information that sheds light on certain trends in Palestinian Judaism at the time of the birth of Christianity (see chapter 4).

Another category of literature similarly attests to the fecundity of the Jewish religious imagination in this period. In the same way that many early Christians produced accounts of Jesus and his followers that failed to make the canon, so too many Jews of the Hellenistic and Roman periods produced texts on biblical themes that were not included in the canon of Hebrew scriptures (the texts that make up the Christian Old Testament). Here we encounter a slight problem of definition, since some of these Jewish texts are called 'apocrypha' and others 'pseudepigrapha'. The Old Testament apocrypha (as it is called by Christians) consists of certain books that had been included in Greek manuscripts of the Septuagint (the Greek translation of the Hebrew scriptures) and consequently were included also in early codices of the Christian Bible. In the fourth century, however, when the monk Jerome came to produce an authoritative Latin translation of the Bible, he limited his efforts to those texts included in the Hebrew canon; the remaining works (all of them in Greek) he regarded as 'apocrypha'. This term now encompasses historical works, such as the first and second books of *Maccabees*, that recount the Jewish revolt against the Hellenistic king of Syria in the mid-second century BC, and texts written in the style of scripture, such as the books called *Tobit*, *Judith*, and the *Wisdom of Solomon*. In addition to these works there exists a large corpus of literature that modern scholars have termed the 'pseudepigrapha', a word that means 'falsely ascribed'. In some cases, these works seem to have been written pseudonymously, in that their authors passed them off as works by one of the authors of the books of the Hebrew Bible. In other cases, however, the attribution developed more accidentally in the course of the copying and transmission of the texts in the manuscript tradition. The texts that make up the pseudepigrapha were composed by Jewish authors between *c.* 200 BC and *c.* AD 200. Apart from a few fragments preserved among the Dead Sea Scrolls, however, they have come down to us mainly from Christian collections (Jonge 1985).

Efforts to identify New Testament personalities in Jewish writings such as the Dead Sea Scrolls are built on the assumption that Jesus and his followers were so important that they *must* have made an impact upon contemporaries, both Jewish and Roman. The reality, at least for the first century AD, seems to have been more ambiguous. To stay with Jewish sources for the moment, consider the debate that has raged about references to Jesus in the works of the Jewish historian Josephus. He was writing after the Roman sack of Jerusalem in 70 and thus at the same time as the traditions about Jesus were beginning to take shape as the synoptic gospels. There is a notorious passage in his *Jewish Antiquities* (18.3.3) that summarizes the career, death, and resurrection of Jesus, and which even states explicitly that 'he was the Christ [i.e. the Messiah]'. This passage – known as the *Testimonium Flavianum* (the *Flavian Testimony*, after Josephus' adopted Roman forename, Flavius) – has provoked much scholarly argument. Some historians have accepted it as entirely genuine, although this opinion has fallen out of favour almost completely. Others have seen here – and in another passage that talks of 'Jesus who was called the Christ' (*Jewish Antiquities*

20.9.1) – the hand of a later Christian interpolator who either inserted the whole passage or added specific phrases about Jesus' messianic status to an account that had simply noted his existence as a historical figure (Schürer 1973–87: I, 428–41 reviews the question in detail). Whatever solution we accept for Jesus' appearance in the *Jewish Antiquities*, it is clear that Josephus *did* mention other figures who appear in the New Testament: apart from Roman governors such as Pontius Pilate and Jewish leaders such as king Herod, he noted in passing John the Baptist (*Jewish Antiquities* 18.5.1) and James the brother of Jesus (20.9.1). From Josephus' writings, then, we can attempt to place the emergence of the Christian movement against some sort of Palestinian milieu (see chapter 4). Indeed, by looking at a range of Jewish literature from the late Hellenistic and Roman periods we can gain insights into the sorts of religious debates that early Christianity shared with contemporary Judaism (Nickelsburg 2003). Such literature would include, in addition to Josephus and the texts from Qumran, the writings of the first-century AD Alexandrian Jew Philo, the writings of the pseudepigrapha, and the sayings by Jewish rabbis from the period after AD 70 that make up the collections known as the Mishnah and the Talmud.

Pagan writings

If we turn our attention to pagan sources, we find that they offer no references to Christianity until the beginning of the second century, at which point we find it mentioned by the historian Tacitus, by the biographer Suetonius, and in the letters of Pliny the Younger. Both Tactius (*Annals* 15.44) and Suetonius (*Life of Nero* 16.2) recounted how the Christians were oppressed by the emperor Nero (54–68). Both authors clearly agreed that while the Christians certainly deserved to be punished because of their impiety in terms of traditional Roman religious behaviour, their sufferings under Nero were a manifestation of the emperor's tyrannical behaviour. Of the two authors, Tacitus is most revealing. He (unlike Suetonius) linked the emperor's anti-Christian pogrom to events in the aftermath of the great fire that had destroyed much of Rome in 64. Tacitus also noted that the Christians were followers of a certain 'Christus', who had been executed by Pontius Pilate, and that the movement originated in Judaea. Beyond that, he said nothing, which suggests that this was the limit of his knowledge. Such apparent ignorance was not unique: even his contemporary Pliny the Younger, who personally presided over trials of Christians in Asia Minor, came to know very little about the new religion (see chapter 6's case study).

Meagre knowledge might also have given rise to confusion. Suetonius noted how the emperor Claudius (41–54) once expelled from Rome 'the Jews who were constantly causing disturbances at the instigation of Chrestus' (*Life of the Deified Claudius* 25.4). Scholars have suggested that the name 'Chrestus' was a colloquial (or garbled) reference to Jesus and have linked Suetonius' remark to the account in the *Acts of the Apostles* of Paul's encounter at Corinth with 'a Jew named Aquila, a native of Pontus, lately come from Italy with this wife Prisca, because Claudius had commanded all the Jews to leave Rome' (*Acts* 18.2; cf. Witherington 1998: 539–44). If this identification is correct, it suggests some element of confusion between Judaism and emergent Christianity, either by Suetonius himself or in his sources.

It was only as Christians became a more sizeable proportion of the Roman empire's population after the mid-second century that pagan authors took more notice of them and began to write about them at length (Wilken 2003). Christianity (like so much else) attracted the barbed tongue of Lucian of Samosata (*c.* AD 125–90) in his satirical works on the pagan prophet Alexander of Abonuteichos and the Cynic philosopher Peregrinus Proteus. Other authors took the Christians more seriously, however, and produced a series of well-informed attacks on Christianity. Among them were the philosophers Celsus, who wrote a work entitled *True Doctrine* some time around AD 170, and Porphyry, who penned a critique probably called simply *Against the Christians* at the end of the third century. Impressive though these pagan assaults on Christianity seem to have been, knowledge of their contents is limited. We are reliant on extracts of them quoted by Christians who replied to them. Celsus' *True Doctrine* is known only through quotations in Origen's response, the *Against Celsus*. Similarly, Porphyry's *Against the Christians* (which Christian Roman emperors of the fifth century ordered to be burned) is known only via fragments quoted by Christian authors. Hence we only know about these anti-Christian polemics from Christian responses that are themselves polemical: the opportunities for distortion of what Celsus and Porphyry actually wrote are considerable.

The fate of Celsus' and Porphyry's works is indicative more broadly of problems that we encounter in looking for pagan sources on early Christianity. We rely almost exclusively on Christian reports of pagan writings for what the pagans said. This is particularly the case with legislation against the Christians. Any modern account of Roman persecutions of the early Christians will depend for the most part on citations of anti-Christian laws found in Christian works, especially Eusebius' *Ecclesiastical History*. The number of pagan sources that survive independently is small (see chapter 6). Such circumstances provide us with a salutary warning. If we are to make anything of the few pagan sources that survive, then we need to try to reconstruct, as much as possible, a context for them that depends not on what Christians like Eusebius would have wanted us to believe, but on other texts penned by pagans.

Documentary sources and material remains

Peter Brown, one of the foremost scholars of the transformation from pagan to Christian in late antiquity, once began a book with the remark: 'I wish I had been one of the Seven Sleepers of Ephesus' (Brown 1978: 1). I sympathize with him. The story of the Seven Sleepers, preserved by the sixth-century Gallic bishop Gregory of Tours, tells of seven pious Christians who were walled up in a cave outside the city of Ephesus in Asia Minor during a persecution in the third century. They did not die, but miraculously fell into a deep sleep from which they were reawakened (equally miraculously, of course: an angel was involved) some two hundred years later, in the reign of the pious Christian emperor Theodosius II (408–50). One of them undertook a quick reconnaissance mission to Ephesus where he could scarcely believe his eyes at the changes that had taken place: the city that he had left had been a pagan one; the city to which he returned was thoroughly Christian.

The transformation of the cities of the Roman empire between the mid-third and mid-fifth centuries is one that is well known from archaeology. Across the Mediterranean world, buildings associated with the urban culture of pagan classical antiquity began to be neglected and their central place in the civic landscape was taken by Christian ones: to put it succinctly, where once cities had been dominated by temples, now there were large Christian churches. Of course, the rate of change varied from region to region, and it is by no means true that all classical buildings were abandoned or that all changes in urban life were wrought by Christianity (Ward-Perkins 1998). Nevertheless, it is clear that, at a fundamental level, urban topography underwent major changes in the century or so after Constantine's conversion. These changes are all the more impressive given the paltry material record for Christianity in the three centuries between Christ and Constantine. If it is generally desirable that studies of the ancient world should take account of archaeological evidence wherever possible, the simple truth is that the non-literary record for pre-Constantinian Christianity is meagre indeed. Consider the example just cited of church buildings. From the fourth and fifth centuries we have dozens of churches, many of which were renovated, rebuilt, and enlarged throughout that period. Thus we have a large body of material from which to deduce conclusions about late antique Christian architecture, liturgy, and society. For the previous three hundred years, however, our sample of Christian churches that can be studied in any detail is pitifully small: in fact, there is only one, the third-century church at Dura Europos in Syria.

This does not mean, of course, that there is no material evidence at all for Christianity before Constantine, but we must be circumspect about what it can tell us. I noted above that in order to understand the context within which Christianity developed, practically any contemporary non-Christian texts could be exploited. The same is true of the material record, whether archaeological, epigraphic, or papyrological. Nevertheless, there is a risk that such materials will be used to provide nothing more than pretty pictures for publications on the world of the early Christians.[8] There are, of course, archaeological artefacts that have a more direct relevance to the study of Christian origins: the heel bones (complete with iron nail) of a crucifixion victim called Yehohanan found in an ossuary (burial chest) from Jerusalem and an inscription recording Pontius Pilate unearthed at Caesarea are celebrated examples (Charlesworth 1988). For the first two centuries, however, archaeology provides no direct testimony to early Christianity. Its utility is limited to telling us about the broader context within which Christianity developed, providing insights, for example, into the Galilean world of Jesus (Reed 2000).

What material evidence do we have for Christianity in the period before Constantine? In terms of architectural structures, there is, as has been noted, only one church, that at Dura Europos. In spite of that, we can perhaps surmise something of the buildings in which Christians met before the construction of church buildings. The Pauline epistles refer constantly to assemblies of Christians in houses, while an apocryphal account of the career of Paul describes him hiring a property outside Rome for the purpose of holding Christian gatherings (*Acts of Paul* 11.1, in Schneemelcher 1992: II, 260–1). Many of the earliest surviving Christian churches were built over, or into, earlier structures, as was the case at Dura Europos. It is possible that they represent renovations of existing structures that had been used previously for gatherings of Christians for communal worship.

Among the early churches in Rome, for example, are a number called *tituli*, from the Latin term *titulus* for a plaque indicating ownership of a property. It has been speculated that these churches may have originated as private buildings whose owners gave over some space inside them for Christian gatherings. In most cases, it is difficult (if not impossible) to identify which rooms might have been used by Christians, but in the remains of an *insula* (apartment building) lying beneath the later church of SS. Giovanni e Paolo, there is a room in which a fresco was painted, perhaps at the very beginning of the fourth century, showing a praying figure. Around the same time, major renovations of the building were undertaken, perhaps to provide for an enlarged meeting area for Christians. Similar renovations can be found also in the remains of buildings underlying the later church of S. Crisogono. Meanwhile, at Aquileia in northern Italy, a huge church, consisting of two large halls, was built very early in the fourth century: it can be dated from inscriptions recording its construction under the city's bishop, Theodore, whose name also appears in a list of clergy attending a church council at Arles in 314. The size of his church, together with the sumptuous quality of the mosaics with which it was decorated, suggest a large Christian community in the city already by the end of the third century (Snyder 1985).

Apart from buildings, the most extensive material remains for pre-Constantinian Christianity are burial sites. Christians (along with Jews and pagans) constructed subterranean complexes of burial chambers called catacombs. There is extensive evidence for these at Rome, and in several other cities too (Stevenson 1978; Rutgers 2000). It is clear that catacombs continued to be used throughout late antiquity, meaning that the earliest burials are often difficult to date precisely. It seems most likely that the earliest Christian catacombs are no earlier than the third century. Certain cemeteries acquired special status through their association with the burials of martyrs: at Rome, for example, the burial ground on the Vatican hill was regarded as the resting place of the apostle Peter already by the time Constantine ordered the construction of a church there in the early fourth century.

The catacombs and the church from Dura Europos have also yielded some of the earliest examples of Christian art. Frescos from both locations show the development of a Christian iconography that owes much to both Jewish and pagan precursors. For example, depictions of the Magi adoring the infant Jesus show them wearing Phrygian caps (conical hats of which the point has fallen forward towards the brow): this was the typical iconographic device for indicating easterners and thus was deemed appropriate for the portrayal of wise men from the east.

From the third century also we have our earliest Christian inscriptions. Many come from burial contexts, such as sarcophagi and the plaques placed over burial places in catacombs. Some carry dates (in the form of the names of a year's consuls), which allow them to be dated from the early third century onwards. Many of these early inscriptions come from Rome, but there are also many of third-century date from the upper valley of the river Tembris in Asia Minor. A number of these bear the formula 'Christians for the Christians' (*Chreistianoi Chreistianois*, in Greek): such a blatant statement suggests that the people who commissioned these inscriptions were far from reluctant to state their Christian identity openly (Snyder 1985: 133–40; Mitchell 1993: II, 37–43).

Finally, we possess numerous papyri from Egypt that are revealing of different aspects of early Christian life. There are many examples of biblical texts in Greek from both the Old and New Testaments. Some are mere fragments, but there are also portions of a number of codices – that is, from bound volumes like modern books; ancient books were generally in the form of scrolls. Some of these codices were quite substantial: one comprises some eighty-six leaves containing ten of Paul's letters (Metzger 1992: 37–8). These documents provide important information on the earliest forms of New Testament texts in circulation, and some date as early as the second century. There are numerous papyri also of non-canonical scriptures, of which the most important are the thirteen codices preserving Coptic translations of Greek apocrypha found at Nag Hammadi in upper Egypt in 1945 (see chapter 5's case study). In addition to scriptures, the papyri preserve important documentary evidence for the study of early Christianity. Private letters show the development of Christian sayings such as 'God knows', 'if God wills it', and so forth. There are also official documents relating to periods when Christians fell under the scrutiny of the imperial government, such as certificates from the reign of Decius (249–51) proving that sacrifice had been made to the pagan gods, and an inventory of church property made during the persecution under Diocletian (see chapter 6).

However slight the material evidence for pre-Constantinian Christianity may be, it is still instructive. From the Dura Europos building and the catacombs we gain glimpses of places for meetings and burial; from inscriptions and papyri, the development of popular (as opposed to literary) modes of expressing Christian identity. Concentrations of data from specific geographical areas (such as the inscriptions of the Tembris valley or caches of papyri from certain parts of Egypt) permit insights into the development of Christianity in particular regions. Yet the material evidence needs to be interpreted with care. There are often problems of chronology: some inscriptions and papyri contain precise dates, but other artefacts have to be dated according to more subjective criteria, such as the style of letter-forms or painting. Above all, the archaeology should not be used merely to flesh out pictures derived from literary sources, or to push certain theological agendas. Less than a hundred years ago, it could be argued: 'The study of Christian archaeology, which is subsidiary to that of Church history and theology completes, with its monuments, what we can learn from documents about the events of the primitive Church, and *confirms what theology teaches* about the dogmas of Christianity' (Marucchi 1929: v, emphasis added). It is to be hoped that we have come a long way since then.

Using the sources

How are we to use this astonishing array of sources? Some suggestions have been made above, and the next three chapters will provide examples of interpretation, but it is perhaps appropriate here to state some basic principles.

It is clear that the study of early Christianity cannot be pursued by reading only a few normative texts, such as the New Testament writings and Eusebius' *Ecclesiastical History*. Any approach to the topic needs to account for the whole range of sources, all the while bearing in mind that different types of source will answer different sorts of question. It is important also to consider the broader context within which Christianity developed. Students and scholars trained in classical disciplines will naturally think first of the Graeco-Roman context, but other factors need to be considered too. Recent studies have emphasized the need to consider Christian origins very closely with contemporary Jewish traditions, since Judaism can shed light on Christianity, and vice versa (see chapter 4).

It is important to approach the ancient evidence (whether textual or material) in ways that are sensitive to the historical context within which that evidence came into existence. This is a particular problem for anyone who has come to regard the New Testament as part of their own living Christian tradition, where the biblical texts are primarily sources of divinely inspired teachings rather than historical documents. Such sensitivities are necessary also for the study on non-biblical sources, whether Christian, Jewish, or pagan. It is crucial to remember that non-Christian sources have a logic and purpose of their own: they are not simply there to provide interesting insights into the world of the early Christians. This might seem like stating the obvious, but it is easy to relegate Jewish and pagan writings to the level of mere background, from which specific details are plucked to add to the picture drawn from Christian sources. For example, source books that present extracts from non-Christian writings perhaps discourage students from reading more of those sources or working out the broader literary, political, and social contexts in which they were produced.

It is important also to be aware of our own limitations as interpreters of the ancient evidence. In chapter 2, we saw how early Christianity was often interpreted by earlier generations of scholars in ways that buttressed certain theological arguments they were advancing. The same is true of their modern heirs, even if today's scholars are wont to be less polemical than their forebears. Analyses of early Christianity can be shaped, more or less explicitly, by the doctrinal allegiances of the individual scholar. For example, when scouring my university library for source collections to recommend to readers of this book, I happened upon a volume that assembled extracts of early Christian writers on the nature of the church according to the chapters and paragraphs of the constitution of the Roman Catholic church known as *Lumen Gentium* ('light of the nations') issued by the Second Vatican Council in 1964 (Halton 1985). Non-Roman Catholics (and some Roman Catholics also) might view such an editorial rationale with bewilderment. Other personal agendas can also guide interpretations. A distinguished feminist theologian (and scholar of Christian origins) has complained recently that the academic quest for the historical Jesus is driven by what she terms a 'malestream' agenda – one that is directed by people who are white, male, middle class, and European or North American (Fiorenza 2000). Even scholars who write with no explicit religious agenda can find themselves appealing to particular trends in Christian thought: I was rather surprised that a reviewer of my previous book thought that some of my analyses could provide a basis for ecumenical dialogue.

The limitations of modern interpretation are apparent also where great claims are made for the insights that can be drawn by applying theoretical models drawn from the human sciences, particularly sociology and anthropology. Recent decades have seen the rise, for example, of social-scientific criticism of the New Testament and more broadly sociological approaches to early Christianity as a whole (Esler 1995; Stark 1996). Some have criticized these approaches for imposing modern interpretative frameworks on ancient data; defenders argue, however, that *any* modern analysis of the ancient world does this, and that model-driven approaches at least make the use of such frameworks explicit (Esler 1995: 4–8). Other criticisms have focused on how social-scientific or sociological analysis often claims for itself the modes of expression of modern quantifiable research and therefore gives the misleading impression that it can produce a 'true', 'accurate', or 'factual' account of early Christianity based 'transparently' on 'data' (Klutz 1998; Fiorenza 2000). Modern scholars generally protest that they can only produce subjective pictures of the past, meaning that their accuracy can be compromised by the assumptions that researchers bring with them to their topic. The nineteenth-century optimism that 'scientific' history could produce accounts of the past 'as it really was' has fallen so out of favour that words like 'positivism', which is used to describe this approach, seem to be deployed these days almost as terms of abuse. For my own part, I have never laboured under the illusion that we can produce a picture of the past that is accurate in every detail: after all, a new piece of evidence or a different methodology can throw accepted interpretations into doubt at any time. Nevertheless, events *did* happen in the past, and I think we can aspire to accounts of them that are plausible by being sensitive to all varieties of sources and the problems they present. The rest of the book aims to show ways in which this can be achieved.

Chapter 4

Messiahs and missions: contexts for the origins and spread of Christianity

Before you opened this book, you probably had some picture of Christian origins already in your head. Christians facing lions in the amphitheatre might have figured prominently, but I suspect that the most striking images will have been of events described in the New Testament. Such images have become central to the culture of the modern west, and of other parts of the world too. The most potent, if disturbing, of these images must be that of Jesus being executed on the cross. In many Christian countries, the image, propagated in paint, stone and other media, is almost ubiquitous. Even for individuals who might class themselves as post-Christian, in whom the crucified Christ no longer inspires reverent awe, it can be evoked from other contexts, such as the closing musical number of *Monty Python's Life of Brian* (1979).

My point here is that, regardless of whether or not we revere them, such images of Christian origins are so familiar and ingrained in our culture as to seem uncontroversial: in some sense, they are deemed to be 'true'. The origins of Christianity, especially as outlined in the books of the New Testament, might seem to some people to require little qualification. Part of the public debate engendered by Mel Gibson's film *The Passion of the Christ*

(2004) hinged on questions of the 'truth' and 'historical reliability' of the New Testament accounts upon which it was ostensibly based.[1] As we saw in the last chapter, however, the various texts that make up the New Testament present many difficulties of interpretation. For all that, most people, whether they are Christians or not, would seem to agree that the basic picture of Christian origins is reasonably uncontroversial. That picture might look something like this: Christianity developed as an off-shoot of Judaism, from which it inherited some things, but rejected others; and Christianity was fired by a missionary zeal that saw it expand successfully and rapidly into the Mediterranean world of the Roman empire, leading rather inevitably to the conversion of Constantine at the beginning of the fourth century.

In this chapter I want to examine this picture, suggesting that in some respects it may not be as uncontroversial as it might seem at first. Of course, this is a large subject, so I will rein in the discussion to a few strictly defined themes. I will concentrate on the context – perhaps it might be better to think in terms of multiple contexts – in which Christianity developed in the Roman empire. I will begin with aspects of the Jewish background to the world of the early Christians, in terms of both the Palestinian context of Jesus himself and the nature of the relationship between emerging Christianity and contemporary Judaism. Next I examine the spread of Christianity, suggesting ways in which an understanding of the society and culture of the Roman empire can help explain how Christian expansion occurred. The chapter will conclude with a case study of one instance of Christian expansion, the missionary journeys of the apostle Paul. My aim will be to explore how our understanding of Paul's activities as they are described in the New Testament can be enriched by what classical scholars have elucidated about the social, cultural, and religious life of the eastern Mediterranean world in the first century AD.

Christian origins and the problem of Judaism

These days it is customary to speak of the Jewish background of Christianity. Books on Christian origins, especially on the period described in the New Testament, often include several pages, or even a chapter or two, on what is usually called the 'Jewish background' or 'context'.[2] In many respects this topic is relatively uncontroversial. Jesus himself was a Jew and so were his disciples. The apostle Paul was a Jew as well as a Roman citizen, and he made statements proclaiming his Jewishness, such as that he was 'circumcised on the eighth day [after his birth], of the people of Israel, of the tribe of Benjamin, a Hebrew born of Hebrews' (*Philippians* 3.5). Both Jesus, as he is represented in the gospels, and Paul constantly harked back to the Jewish scriptures that Christians call the Old Testament. One of the central debates found in the New Testament concerns whether the Christian message should be preached only to Jews or could be taught also to non-Jews (see chapter 3). This closeness of emerging Christianity to Judaism probably accounts for the fact that, at first, the Roman authorities had difficulty in distinguishing Christians from Jews (see chapter 6). Hence it is a feature of some classic modern scholarship on Christian origins in the New Testament to stress this element, as in Geza Vermes' book *Jesus the Jew* (1981), or E. P. Sanders' *Paul and Palestinian Judaism* (1977).

And yet, however uncontroversial such assertions might seem in our own age, they would not have enjoyed universal assent from earlier generations of scholars writing about Christian origins. It is easy enough to imagine what would have happened if anyone had suggested to Eusebius of Caesarea that Jesus was a Jew. The founding father of ecclesiastical historiography – who asserted, after all, that the Hebrew patriarchs were effectively Christians in everything but name (see p. 38) – would probably have suffered an attack of apoplexy. For Eusebius, and even more recent generations of Christian scholars, Judaism has seemed to represent a version of God's relationship with humankind that was manifestly inferior to that enshrined in Christianity. A residual hostility to Jews and Judaism (anti-Semitism) has long exercised a dangerous influence over the history of scholarship on Christian origins (Fiorenza 2000: 115–44).

It would be rash, however, to assume that, just because we are not anti-Semites (or Eusebius) and can acknowledge that

Christianity had a Jewish background, we have a clear understanding of the relationship that emerging Christianity had to contemporary Judaism. In what follows, I want to look at a few aspects of this question, showing that the nature of the relationship is often quite murky. I will begin by looking at how some aspects of Jesus' career, at least in terms of how it is represented in the canonical gospels, might be seen to share characteristics with the Judaism of his time. Then I will consider how there is a danger of reading Christian assumptions into evidence for Judaism at the time of Jesus, and how this can give rise to problems in efforts to understand the relationship between Christianity and Judaism. In particular, we will see that there is a problem with seeing Judaism as some sort of fixed religious system from which Christianity departed.

Bandits and messiahs: seeking a context for the historical figure of Jesus

For early Christian writers like Eusebius, for whom Jesus' status as Messiah was self-evident, the fact that Jews rejected him seemed like an act of criminal madness. This begs an important question, however: to what extent might Jesus' activities have matched contemporary Jewish expectations of what the Messiah should be? In certain of the gospel narratives, there is a clear implication that Jesus was indeed rejected by some Jews at least. Such accounts of rejection reach a crescendo with the circumstances surrounding Jesus' trial and death. When the Roman governor Pontius Pilate offered the Jews in Jerusalem the opportunity to secure the release of a prisoner, they chose Barabbas, apparently in preference to Jesus (a least, that is how the story is often represented). In the exchanges between Pilate and the crowds in Jerusalem that follow, repeated demands were made that Jesus should be crucified.

The circumstances of Jesus' condemnation and death are instructive, particularly in terms of establishing a historical context for his career. From the gospel accounts it seems clear that he was executed for some political crime. When he was arraigned before Pilate, he was charged with claiming the title 'king of the Jews', and when he was nailed to the cross a placard carrying this charge was fixed over his head (Fredriksen 2000: 120–5). The very manner of his death confirms that his punishment was intended as a deterrent. A Roman account of the rationale for crucifixion underlines this point: 'Whenever we crucify criminals, the most frequented roads are chosen, where many people can see it and be moved by fear. For punishments are concerned not so much with exacting vengeance as with setting an example' (Pseudo-Quintilian, *Declamations* 274).

Furthermore, Jesus was not crucified alone, but in the company of two other men. The synoptic gospels as in agreement that these two were criminals: *Luke* 23.32 and 39 simply calls them 'evil-doers' (*kakourgoi*), but *Mark* 15.27 and *Matthew* 27.38 specify their crime through use of the Greek word *lēstai* – bandits. In popular retellings of the crucifixion story (and some modern translations of the New Testament) these bandits are sometimes referred to as 'robbers' or 'thieves'. Such a designation is misleading, giving the impression that they were rather insignificant criminals. Evidence from Palestine in the age of Jesus (roughly from the mid-first century BC to the mid-first century AD) suggests, however, that their activities were anything but petty. From contemporary sources, such as Josephus' *Jewish Antiquities* and *Jewish War*, it is clear that banditry represented a serious threat to the socio-political order in parts of Judaea, Galilee, and surrounding areas (Freyne 1988). This volatile political situation is hinted at also in the gospels in the figure of Barabbas. In the *Gospel of John* (at 18.40) he is called a *lēstēs* (the singular of *lēstai*), and from other gospels it is clear that he was not a minor criminal: he had been involved in insurrection (*stasis*) and murder in Jerusalem (*Mark* 15.7; *Luke* 23.19).

Is it possible that the historical figure of Jesus was some kind of social revolutionary, similar to the various bandits who periodically disrupted life in Roman Palestine? Of course, the violence associated with such revolutionary activities is singularly missing from the accounts of Jesus' career in the gospels. Nevertheless, there are hints that, in spite of his eschewing violence, Jesus' challenges to the priestly authorities in Jerusalem were sufficient to attract the suspicion that he was some kind of revolutionary. In one of the gospel narratives, Jesus asks the guards sent to arrest him in the garden of Gethsemane if they think he is a bandit (*lēstēs*: *Mark* 14.48). Another link is suggested in the *Acts of the Apostles*' account of the debate of the High Priest and the Sadducees at Jerusalem about what action to take against Jesus' followers. The Jewish elder Gamaliel is reported as urging caution, saying that if the movement that acknowledged Jesus as Messiah was not inspired by God, then it, like the movements led by earlier insurrectionists, would fail (*Acts* 5.34–9). As a result of such hints, the issue of banditry has become something of a leitmotiv in much modern research into the historical Jesus.[3]

Even if Jesus can be identified as the leader of a protest movement that, in spite of its non-violence, came to be perceived as a threat by the Romans and their Jewish elite allies, how could the leader of such a movement come to be regarded by some as the Messiah? According to prophecies in Jewish scriptures (many of them quoted or alluded to in the New Testament) the Messiah was someone who would come in the future to deliver Israel, God's people, from its enemies. Now some Jewish resistance leaders certainly seem to have perceived themselves as possessing some religious significance. Among the bandit movements mentioned by Gamaliel in his speech in *Acts* was one led by a certain Theudas, whose revolt is also discussed by Josephus. During the governorship of Cuspius Fadus, early in the reign of the emperor Claudius (41–54), this Theudas led some four hundred followers to the river Jordan. He claimed to be a prophet and announced that he would part the waters of the river to allow his followers to pass through. In the event, however, his career was cut short by Fadus' cavalry, who slew Theudas and many of his associates (Josephus, *Jewish Antiquities* 20.97–8; cf. *Acts* 5.36). Theudas' prophecy about the waters of the Jordan was clearly modelled on Moses' parting of the Red Sea during the flight of the Hebrews from Egypt (*Exodus* 14). Yet, however much at a general level Theudas might seem to resemble Jesus, he did not, so far as we can tell, claim to be the Messiah.

Nearly a century later, during the reign of the emperor Hadrian (117–38), a Jewish rebel *did* claim messianic status. From 132 until 135, the Jews made a last, ultimately futile, effort to throw off the yoke of Roman rule. Their leader in this is usually called Simon bar Kosiba in Jewish sources, but in Christian ones is called Simon bar Kochba. Bar Kochba means 'son of the star' and seems to indicate a connection with messianic prophecy in the Old Testament book of *Numbers* that 'a star shall rise out of Jacob and a sceptre shall rise out of Israel' to vanquish the enemies of the people of God (*Numbers* 24.17). Although this form of Simon's name is known only from Christian sources, it seems certain that he was proclaimed Messiah by a contemporary rabbi. Meanwhile, the rebels minted coins naming Simon as '*nasi* (prince) of Israel'. The extent to which Simon's titles provide a parallel for Jesus is open to debate, but they show how a messianic claim could be associated with an individual involved in rebellious activity (Schürer 1973–87: I, 543–5; Smallwood 1976: 439–41).

The question at issue, however, is more complex than identifying the extent to which Jesus' activities (as represented in the gospels) find echoes in those of contemporary Jews, or whether certain Jewish rebel leaders claimed to be messiahs. If we focus on the question of messianic expectation, it is clear that Jewish writings from the age of Jesus do not present one unambiguous image of what the Messiah should be, but several. The Dead Sea Scrolls from Qumran, for example, describe a number of messianic figures: there is a kingly messiah modelled on David, and a priestly one associated with Aaron (Knibb 1999). If we examine the whole of Jewish scripture, apocrypha, and pseudepigrapha from the period 300 BC–AD 200, then the range of figures who might be expected to intercede with God on Israel's behalf becomes bewilderingly wide, encompassing not only royal and priestly messiahs, but also prophets and mysterious figures sent from heaven (Nickelsburg 2003: 91–108). Indeed, even in the New Testament, the expressions used to articulate Jesus' messianic status were similarly varied. For example, the genealogy that opens the *Gospel of Matthew* (1.1–7) emphasizes the royal messiah linked to David, whereas in the *Letter to the Hebrews* Jesus is portrayed as an anointed priest. The image of Jesus as 'the son of man' (that is, some sort of heavenly figure in human form) derives from the description of 'one like a human being coming with the clouds of heaven' whose 'dominion is an everlasting dominion that shall not pass away' found in the Old Testament book of *Daniel* (7.13–14).

If Jesus' immediate followers expressed his messianic status in such a varied fashion, then that suggests his identification as the Messiah was something that needed to be established through argument, not something that was an easily recognizable and uncontroversial fact. The variety of messianic concepts found in contemporary Jewish writings similarly suggests that the concept of the Messiah was not clearly established as being one precise thing. Furthermore, the emphasis in much New Testament scholarship in elucidating messianic ideals in the Judaism of Jesus' time reflects a peculiarly Christian concern that risks distorting the nature of Jewish beliefs in the first century. It was possible for Jews to conceive of God intervening in human affairs on his own without the intercession of any messianic, prophetic, or heavenly agent (Nickelsburg 2003: 90–1, 123–35). Thus it is possible (perhaps even probable) that many Jews would not have agreed with, or even seen the necessity for, the Christian claim that Jesus was the unique agent of God's plan for humankind. To put it another way, the onus was on Jesus' followers to convince Jews that Jesus was the Messiah. If the Jews rejected that idea, it was not because of any hardness in their hearts (as the Christian version so often goes), but because those who advocated Jesus' messianic status were not sufficiently persuasive.

If we look at the question of Jesus' relationship with contemporary Judaism in this light, then we see that there are problems associated with the traditional notions of a Jewish 'background' or 'context'. That gives the impression that there was somehow a static, coherent, and even unitary Judaism out of which Jesus (and later Christianity) emerged. It is more helpful to think of the New Testament portrait of Jesus being produced in the context of a varied matrix of Jewish speculations on the role of God in the world and the extent to which divine intervention might (or might not) be mediated through a Messiah. Within Judaism itself, these ideas were expressed in diverse ways as Jews sought to make sense of their precarious position in the world, where God's chosen people were frequently subjected to political domination by heathen foreigners like the Romans. Another manifestation of the tensions within contemporary Judaism was its fragmentation into various groups. Within Palestine, there were sects such as the Pharisees and Sadducees mentioned in the New Testament, or the Essenes, whose thinking is probably reflected in the texts found at Qumran. In addition, there were divisions within Judaism over other matters. Also in Palestine, but more particularly in the Diaspora (the Jewish communities found in cities scattered throughout the Roman empire), differences of opinion arose about the extent to which there should be any accommodation with the social and cultural habits of the gentiles (pagan Greeks and Romans) (Barclay 1996). In recognition of this diversity, some (but not all) scholars speak in terms of plural 'Judaisms'. It is perhaps within this plurality of Jewish responses to the world and its problems that we can best attempt to understand the career of Jesus of Nazareth, and the emergence of the movement that gradually became Christianity.

The evolution of Judaism and Christianity

The problems of the relationship between Judaism and Christianity do not abate with either the death (and, for his followers, resurrection) of Jesus or the end of the period described in the New Testament. In recent scholarly debate, much effort has been invested in seeking to define the nature and chronology of what is usually called the 'parting of the ways', the process that gave rise to Judaism and Christianity as two distinct religions.[4] If it is now uncontroversial to assert that figures such as Jesus and Paul were Jews, then it has become equally common to acknowledge that this was also true for a sizeable number of early Christians. Debates about the relationship between nascent Christianity and Jewish traditions recur throughout the New Testament. Although it must be the case on purely demographic grounds that gentiles (that is, pagans) came to make up a greater proportion and ultimately a majority of converts (see pp. 116–17), the issue of Christianity's relationship with Judaism did not disappear.

Eusebius' account of the cleavage between Judaism and Christianity was by no means the first Christian literary treatment of the theme. Justin's *Dialogue with Trypho* and Tertullian's *Against the Jews* were specifically concerned with the issue, but it was also present in a wide range of early Christian literature, including accounts of martyrdom, such as the *Acts of Polycarp*, and liturgical works, like Melito of Sardis' *On the Pasch*. In many of these works, the portrait of the Jews is unflattering: in the *Acts of Polycarp*, for example, Jews are prominent in the crowd that bays for the martyr's blood. Yet there is a danger of mistaking the image in these literary texts of vigorous hostility between Jews and Christians as an accurate representation of how life was actually lived. As one scholar of the topic has put it: 'Literature, especially ideological and doctrinal, tends to stress differentiation, whereas social and religious experience tends to be more untidy' (Lieu 1996: 278).

Later in this chapter, when we consider why people converted to Christianity, we will see just how indistinct the boundaries between paganism, Judaism, and Christianity could be. At this juncture, I want to limit the question to Jewish and Christian identity. In some respects, Jews and Christians had much in common. Both Jews and Christians laid claim to the same scriptures and, with them, similar traditions; arising out of this, both assumed that their own group was the *verus Israel* (the true Israel), the true people of God. In the face of this shared heritage, Christian writers, especially bishops, asserted the superiority of Christianity's claims.

They did so, however, against a background of considerable overlap and interaction between Jewish and Christian communities and practices. At the beginning of the second century, bishop Ignatius of Antioch reproached the Christians of Magnesia and Philadelphia in Asia Minor for mixing their faith in Jesus Christ with Jewish practices. However much bishops might assert this incompatibility, the attraction of Judaism for some Christians remained strong. Some three centuries after Ignatius, another bishop of Antioch, John Chrysostom, reproached members of his flock for attending services in the synagogue (Wilken 1983). It would be erroneous to suppose that this closeness of Judaism and Christianity was simply an artefact left over from the days of Jesus and the apostles. At Edessa in Syria, for example, the close relationship between Judaism and Christianity seems to have been a late development, only beginning in the third century (Drijvers 1992).

Such factors have important implications for the relationship between early Christianity and Judaism. In the brief sketch of the conventional view of Christian origins offered at the beginning of this chapter, it was noted that Christianity inherited some things from Judaism. It has often been assumed that primary examples of this inheritance were Christianity's missionary impulse and the willingness of Christians to endure martyrdom for the faith. More recently, however, scholars have questioned such assumptions. Although it is true that many Jewish communities in the Diaspora attracted interested non-Jews (gentiles/pagans) who were known as 'God-fearers' (see p. 123), this is not quite the same thing as Judaism actively and systematically seeking out converts. In general, Jewish proselytism (the seeking out of converts) only developed much later, and even then seems to have been practised only to a limited degree (Goodman 1994). Similarly, the extent to which Christian martyrdom owed anything to the example set by Jews – such as those who died defending Jewish traditions against violation by the Syrian king Antiochus IV in 168/7 BC (*2 Maccabees* 6–7; cf. Frend 1965: 42–50) – has been questioned (Bowersock 1995: 9–21). It has been argued furthermore that the development of Jewish ideas of martyrdom occurred mainly in the first few centuries AD in a context where Jewish and Christian ideas influenced each other (Boyarin 1999).

Christianity's debt to Judaism needs to be rethought. There is a growing consensus that Jewish and Christian ideas about proselytism and martyrdom did not develop sequentially, with Christianity inheriting them from Judaism; rather, they developed in parallel, perhaps even through some process of mutual influence. It is important to bear in mind that Judaism was not some fixed system of practices and beliefs, but was itself subject to evolution as much as Christianity was. The early Christian centuries coincided with a period of profound trauma for the Jews, which forced upon them significant developments in terms of their religious life. This is particularly true of the place occupied by Jerusalem in Judaism. The first Jewish revolt against Rome in 66–70 ended with the destruction of the great temple in Jerusalem that had been the centre of Jewish cult. After the second Jewish revolt led by Simon bar Kochba in 132–5, Jerusalem itself effectively ceased to exist: in its place stood the Roman city of Aelia Capitolina, named after the emperor Hadrian, whose family name was Aelius, and Jupiter Capitolinus, the patron deity of Rome. Such destruction and desecration wrought tremendous changes in Judaism, as the primary cultic focus on Jerusalem and its temple was eclipsed, and a new religious leadership, the rabbis, gradually emerged. Thus, just as the first three centuries AD saw the development of Christianity, so too they saw the evolution of a new form of Judaism. There were contacts between them, as we have seen, but these were not instances of Christianity slipping back into its Jewish background. Instead, they were features of a more dynamic process that saw the emergence of not one, but two religions.

Mission and conversion: the expansion of early Christianity

Whoever Jesus was, and whatever the nature of his followers' relationship with contemporary Judaism (or Judaisms), it is indisputable that the movement that regarded him as the Messiah turned out to be very successful. By the third century Christians were constructing churches like that found at Dura Europos and digging their own catacombs at Rome; they were also increasingly attracting the hostile attention of the Roman imperial authorities (see chapter 6). How did Christianity develop from a few beleagured disciples in Judaea to a worldwide movement in such a relatively short space of time?

This is a difficult question to answer because of the shortcomings of the sources. We have already seen that the many medieval accounts of early missionaries founding churches in different parts of Europe are too tendentious to be taken seriously (p. 46). Our most important ancient narrative, Eusebius' *Ecclesiastical History*, is rather less helpful on this topic than might be expected from a work that was devoted to recounting the triumph of Christianity in the Roman world. His own statements on the dissemination of Christianity are limited to accounts of apostles taking the gospel with them to different parts of the world, and his sources for this are either the New Testament itself (particularly the *Acts of the Apostles*) or a rather nebulous 'tradition' (*paradosis*: *Ecclesiastical History* 3.1.1). He tells the story, now universally regarded as pure invention, of the early conversion of king Abgar of Edessa in northern Mesopotamia, and his exchange of letters with Jesus himself (*Ecclesiastical History* 1.13). That Eusebius tells us so little is hardly surprising. For him, paganism was a disease, and Christianity was its cure: Christian success was inevitable and was guaranteed 'by the power and help of heaven' (*Ecclesiastical History* 2.3.1). No further explanation was necessary.

For modern historians, who are prone to ask why a small religious sect could come to be the religion of the Roman empire, further explanation *is* necessary. Even so, answers are scarce. Like Eusebius, other early Christian writers were convinced that the success of their religion was guided by God. Moreover, they often made statements about the progress of Christianity, but the historical reliability of such remarks is doubtful given that they appeared in polemical or apologetical works. Thus Irenaeus of

Lyons spoke around 180 of Christians in Germany, Spain, Gaul, the East, Libya, and Egypt (*Against Heresies* 1.10.2) – but he did so in order to make a point about the worldwide unity of the church against heretics who were trying to divide it. Not much later, the north African writer Tertullian provided a comprehensive list of peoples and regions in the (then) known world and remarked: 'The name of Christ is disseminated everywhere, believed everywhere, revered by all the peoples listed above, it reigns everywhere, and is everywhere adored' (*Against the Jews* 7.9). Tertullian's testimony is no more reliable than that of Irenaeus. It comes in a polemic in which Tertullian argued for the superiority of Christianity over Judaism and claimed for the Christians and not the Jews biblical proclamations such as that in *Psalm* 19 (18 in the Septuagint) that God's glory would be heard to the ends of the earth.

Such claims will not do for today's more critical historians. Any attempt to get beyond them, however, and to come up with a historically plausible, demonstrable, and quantifiable understanding of Christian expansion remains difficult. This is because Christian communities simply appear, without warning as it were, in our sources. The surviving correspondence of bishop Cyprian of Carthage, for instance, contains a letter from a church council of *c.* 256 to 'the presbyter Felix and the laity living at Legio and at Asturica, and to the deacon Aelius and the laity living at Emerita' (Cyprian, *Letters* 67). This is the first clear evidence for Christianity in Spain (the cities mentioned are, respectively, modern León, Astorga, and Mérida). The presence of a presbyter and a deacon suggests some form of hierarchical organization in these Spanish communities, but how much is not clear (why are no bishops mentioned?). The existence of the letter itself implies contact between Spanish Christians and their north African brethren. Beyond that, however, we can ask questions, but only grope for answers. When, how, and by whom were these Spanish congregations founded? Were they even founded, or did they come into existence by some other, perhaps accidental, process? We do not know. Nor can we even guess how many

Christians the word 'laity' might mean (Clarke 1984–9: IV, 141–5). The same is true for many Christian groups throughout the Roman world which appear in the sources, particularly in lists of bishops at councils in the third and fourth centuries, with no prior warning of their existence (Humphries 1999: 46–53).

Numbers and variables

None of this is to say, of course, that historians are not interested in seeking to explain what is usually called 'the rise of Christianity' (Frend 1984; Stark 1996). There has been considerable interest recently in trying to plot the growth of Christians by various means. A major impetus for such research recently was the publication in 1996 of *The Rise of Christianity* by Rodney Stark. He freely admitted that he is no specialist in early Christianity, or even in the history of the ancient world. He is, rather, a sociologist who has worked on various modern religious movements, particularly those that might be termed cults or sects. Stark used methods developed in his previous researches and proposed a number of models that could be tested against ancient evidence in an effort to explain the growth of Christianity. He applied his scrutiny to topics such as the mission to the Jews, the reasons why Christians might volunteer to become martyrs, and the probable numbers of Christians in the Roman empire. Scholars working in the field broadly welcomed his approach, albeit with some reservations. Indeed, an issue of the *Journal of Early Christian Studies* was largely devoted to assessing the value of his work (Castelli 1998; K. Hopkins 1998; Klutz 1998).

One of Stark's most important contributions was to speculate on the number of converts to Christianity in the Roman empire (Stark 1996: 4–13, 129–45). A similar approach was being undertaken around the same time by the Cambridge ancient historian (and trained sociologist) Keith Hopkins in an article that was published in the *Journal of Early Christian Studies* debate on Stark (K. Hopkins 1998). Both Stark and Hopkins noted that such an approach was disadvantaged by the absence of quantifiable data – indeed, Hopkins called his study 'an experiment' and his methods 'frankly speculative and exploratory' (1998: 155). Both hypothesized that on the basis of a Christian population of 1000 in AD 40, and with a growth rate of between 3.35% per year (Hopkins) and 40% per decade (Stark), then the total number of Christians could have reached 10,000 by the early second century, 200,000 by the early third, 6 million by the early fourth, and over 30 million by the mid-fourth.

Such calculations – like the guesses about Christian numbers (either in total or as a proportion of the empire's population) made by earlier scholars such as Edward Gibbon, Adolf von Harnack, and Ramsay MacMullen (cf. Stark 1996: 6; K. Hopkins 1998: 191–2) – are necessarily speculative. Even for periods for which we have better data, quantitative surveys can yield only ambiguous results: two recent studies of conversion to Christianity among the Roman empire's senatorial aristocracy in the fourth and fifth centuries, for example, have argued for very different rates at which religious change took place (Barnes 1995; Salzman 2002; cf. Humphries forthcoming a). Nevertheless, the figures suggested by Stark and Hopkins have about them a certain plausibility. Both suggest that the third century saw a massive leap in Christian numbers. Other evidence suggests that this was indeed a period of considerable growth: there was a greatly increased output of Christian literature; a hierarchy of bishops emerges much more clearly now than at any earlier time (see chapter 5); and persecutions by the Roman state became more frequent and more aggressive (see chapter 6). Certainly, many more Christian communities can be identified in the sources for the third century than for the period before it.

The hypothetical increase in Christian numbers suggested by Stark and Hopkins is, in its own way, as crude an attempt to explain the expansion of Christianity as the portrait of self-explanatory success found in ancient Christian writings. There must have been many variables in the process. Perhaps there were decreases in Christian numbers at times of persecution. There were very likely regional differences too. I noted above the evidence from Cyprian for the existence of only three Spanish Christian communities in the mid-third century. For the same period, and from the same body of evidence, we know that there were dozens of Christian communities in north Africa. Other disparities are suggested by the sources. Pliny the Younger's famous letter to the emperor Trajan about Christians in Bithynia in north-western Asia Minor at the beginning of the second century mentions that Christianity had attracted 'many people of every age, every social rank, both men and women', that it had spread not only to the towns but also to 'the villages and countryside', and that consequently pagan temples had been 'almost entirely deserted' (*Letters* 10.96.9–10). What are we to make of this picture of the backwoods of Asia Minor apparently teeming with Christians? Perhaps Pliny (or the staff who reported details to him) was exaggerating. At any rate, we cannot take his account at face value (see chapter 6's case study). No other contemporary source written by a pagan gives anything like a comparable picture of Christian success: in their accounts of Nero's anti-Christian pogrom in 64, Suetonius simply mentions the movement in passing, without pronouncing on numbers, while Tacitus only implies (by virtue of the numerous punishments inflicted upon them) that there was a large group of Christians in Rome in Nero's time. Certainly, neither Suetonius nor Tacitus makes any mention of Christians as a serious threat in their own day.

How are we to account for the description of Christianity as being strong in some parts of the empire, but weaker in others? It is likely that this discrepancy simply reflects a reality where Christianity expanded at different rates and from different starting points in different provinces. Some indication of variable growth can be surmised from plotting on a map the places where Christian communities are known from sources such as Eusebius, Cyprian, and the lists of bishops attending church councils. (Examples of such maps can be found in Lane Fox 1986: 274–5, which is based on Meer and Mohrmann 1959: 10–11.) The results of such an exercise are striking for two reasons that Robin Lane Fox has characterized as the scatter and density of Christian communities (1986: 271–3). It is clear that by the beginning of the fourth century, Christianity was more evenly distributed across the eastern provinces in Asia Minor, the Middle East, and Egypt than it was in Europe. There were areas of particular density too, a factor that is most easily appreciated in the west, where we find concentrations of Christian communities in north Africa, central Italy, and the province of Baetica in southern Spain. Elsewhere, in Gaul and the Balkans for example, the presence of Christianity was spread more thinly.

What conclusions can such a spread suggest? It is obvious that Christianity enjoyed greater success in some areas than in others. The regions where it was strongest include, in Asia Minor and the Middle East, areas where we can observe in the New Testament some of the earliest missionary endeavours by apostles like Paul. The concentration of Christian communities in Egypt, north Africa, and southern Spain might suggest similar early missionary efforts there. In north Africa, this might well have been the case: accounts of martyrdoms and casual references in Tertullian suggest that Christianity had reached not only the major cities, but also smaller settlements and the countryside. The evidence taken as a whole, however, is ambiguous. Eusebius' information on Christianity in Egypt is sketchy before the time of bishop Demetrius of Alexandria around the year 200, although the existence of New Testament biblical papyri shows that Christians were present in Egypt before this. In Italy, we know of Christians at Rome from the time of Nero, but information about the rest of the peninsula is vague until the third century. Spanish Christians, as we have seen, only appear in the mid-third century, and then in paltry numbers. If we were to judge the sparseness of Christianity in Gaul as evidence for the religion's late arrival there, however, then we would have to reconcile that with the account of the persecution at Lyons in 177. Eusebius (*Ecclesiastical History* 5.1) quotes a document written shortly after the purge that implies a flourishing Christian community: among the martyrs of 177, nine are mentioned by name, and there are references to members of a hierarchy of clergy, both in Lyons and in neighbouring Vienne. Such details suggest two organized Christian communities in southern Gaul – but how long they had been there is impossible to know. In sum, the data for actual communities yields only a limited picture, but that is one of a patchy and uneven pattern of Christian expansion.

Missionaries, social networks, and diffusion

How did Christianity come to these various regions? From its earliest existence, the religion seems to have possessed a strong missionary impulse. At the beginning of *Acts*, the risen Jesus, just before his ascension to heaven, tells the assembled disciples that the holy spirit would come upon them and that they would bear witness to his gospel until the ends of the earth (*Acts* 1.8). We have already seen that similarly vague geographical expressions characterize early accounts of Christian success, and that precise references to missionaries are, with the exception of the apostles, absent. There presumably were missionaries, but our information on them is vague. The pagan Celsus, as reported by Origen, wrote in unflattering terms of anonymous preachers roaming the world; Origen's response does not provide any more detail (Origen, *Against Celsus* 3.9). Tertullian wrote, equally vaguely, that Christians could be found everywhere, on country estates, in camps of the imperial army, and in tenements in the cities (*To the Nations* 1.14). Christians produced apologetical literature that aimed to explain the tenets of their faith to pagans (and Jews), and some such works, such as Clement of Alexandria's *Exhortation to the Greeks*, sought to persuade them to convert. From the whole of Christian antiquity before Constantine, however, there is only one Christian missionary whose strategies are explained and described: Paul. His letters, and the account of his journeys in the *Acts of the Apostles*, give a detailed, but incomplete, account of how one individual, together with a small group of associates, endeavoured to spread the gospel (Clarke 1996: 851–66).

In terms of missionary goals, Paul seems to have had in mind a rather ambitious global programme, but in what is probably his last letter he admitted that in certain regions of the west 'the very name of Christ has not been heard' (*Romans* 15.20). The communities of the Jewish Diaspora seem to have played a significant role in Paul's strategy (Levinskaya 1996). *Acts* in particular depicts him as going first to the Jewish gathering place (termed either *synagōgē* or *proseuchē*) in each of the cities he visited throughout the eastern Mediterranean. In such places he could expect to find not only Jews, but also gentile/pagan god-fearers (on whom see p. 123). Not all such cities and their Jewish communities afforded identical opportunities. Philippi in Macedonia, for example, had been a Roman colony settled by military veterans since the late first century BC. Here the Jews seem to have been a rather marginal group: *Acts* tells us that their meeting place was outside the city gates (16.13; cf. Oakes 2001: 58–9).

Even in its emphasis on these Jewish networks, *Acts* is far from a satisfactory history. A major theme of its narrative is the hostility of the Jews to Paul's preaching in contrast to the more receptive audience he found among (some) gentiles/pagans. At Ephesus, for example, Paul taught in the synagogue for three months before Jewish hostility drove him to seek other accommodation among the gentiles (*Acts* 19.8–10). Some of Paul's letters attest to hostility towards the Jews: he warned the Christians of Philippi to 'beware of the dogs, beware of evil workers, beware of those who mutilate the flesh' (*Philippians* 3.2), a reference to the Jews and their practice of circumcision. Elsewhere, it looks as if his intended audience was wholly of gentile/pagan converts, such as when he asked the Corinthians to recall their worship of 'idols' (*1 Corinthians* 12.2). Certainly, by the time the deutero-Pauline letters were written, the target of missionary activity was deemed to be predominantly pagan/gentile. This does not mean that a Jewish phase in Christian missionary activity came to an end some time in the first century: we saw earlier in this chapter that the close relationship between Christianity and Judaism lasted well into late antiquity, meaning that some form of Jewish mission must have outlasted Paul.[5] Nevertheless, it is clear that the central place of Jewish communities in Christian missionary strategies must have declined. The reasons for this are simply numerical: the Jews accounted for only a small proportion of the empire's whole population, and many Jews refused to convert. If Christianity was to grow, then it would need to take its missionary effort to the gentiles/pagans (K. Hopkins 1998: 216). Indeed, it is clear that the presence of Jewish communities cannot be invoked everywhere to explain the arrival some time later of Christianity: for example, there seems to have been no Jewish community in Carthage before Christianity arrived there, already by the second century (Rives 1995: 226).

What other missionary strategies can be deduced from the New Testament accounts of Paul? One, clearly, is that his mission was primarily urban: it is not for nothing that Wayne Meeks summed him up in the phrase 'Paul was a city person' (Meeks 1983: 9). The reason for this urban focus was, presumably, that cities provided opportunities for the communication of the gospel to the widest possible audience since it was there that large gatherings of people could be found. Hence it is no surprise to find Paul preaching in the agora (market place) in Athens (*Acts* 17.17). Not all cities could offer equal opportunities, since the profile of their populations would have differed (as we noted in connection with the marginality of the Jewish population at Philippi). The cities that would have offered the best scope for spreading the Christian message were those that boasted not only a large local population, but also a multitude of transients who might then take the message elsewhere. That such considerations might have influenced Paul can be glimpsed in his use of Ephesus as a base for operations for over two years, 'so that all the residents of Asia, both Greeks and Jews, heard the world of the Lord' (*Acts* 19.8–10). This last remark might look like exaggeration on the part of the author of *Acts*, but it receives confirmation from Paul's own hand when he explained to the Corinthians that he would stay in Ephesus because 'a wide door for effective work has opened to [him]' (*1 Corinthians* 16.8). The reasons for the suitability of Ephesus are not hard to divine. It was a major centre of trade, industry, and Rome's administration in the province of Asia, and for these various reasons it was home to a large and diverse population. Such diversity was reflected in the city's religious profile: there were native Asian cults (including that of Artemis of the Ephesians), Graeco-Roman gods, and religious groups from other parts of the Roman empire, such as Jews and worshippers of the Egyptian goddess Isis (Koester 1995). For these various reasons, it was an ideal centre from which to disseminate Christian teachings to as wide an audience as possible.

It is also clear from the New Testament that Paul's journeys do not give a complete picture of Christian missionary activity for this early period. Paul's arrival in Ephesus had been preempted by reports of a rival mission by the Alexandrian Jew Apollos (*Acts* 18.24–8). When Paul was sent to Rome for trial he found Christians already in Puteoli on the bay of Naples as well as in the imperial capital (*Acts* 28.14–15; cf. *Romans* 16.3–16). Clearly there were Christians other than Paul who were seeking to spread the gospel. This is hinted at in information about Paul's associates the Jew Aquila and his wife Priscilla. Aquila himself was from Pontus in Asia Minor, but had travelled to Rome, whence he and Priscilla had come to Corinth, where they met Paul (*Acts* 18.1–2). At Ephesus they confronted Apollos (*Acts* 18.19, 26) and later assisted Paul there (*1 Corinthians* 16.19) before returning to Rome (*Romans* 16.3).

Such glimpses of itinerant bearers of the gospel are suggestive of the ways in which Christianity might have spread around the Roman world. The presence of Christians in some numbers at Rome already before Paul's arrival there is hardly surprising: the city was filled with foreigners and their cults (Noy 2000). Likewise Puteoli was a major trading centre linking Rome and the wider Mediterranean world. It too had a considerable population of migrants who brought their religious practices with them. It has been suggested that some early Christians might have been traders who spread the gospel (Frend 1964), but it is difficult to identify specific traders among known early Christians. We are told, for example, that the second-century Christian teacher (later condemned for heresy) Marcion had been a ship-owner on the Black Sea coast of Asia Minor (Tertullian, *Against Heresies* 30.1); but it cannot be shown *for certain* if it was maritime trade that brought him to Rome (cf. Lampe 2003: 241–4). Perhaps a better way of viewing the link between trade and Christian expansion is to think in terms of trade networks and the ways in which they facilitate the movement of people and ideas (Humphries 1998). This might explain the presence of numerous Christians in Baetica in southern Spain by the early fourth century, since this region was important in Mediterranean-wide trade in olive oil. North Africa too was an important region in the imperial economy. Yet traders and trade networks may not explain the presence of Christians everywhere. In southern Gaul, for example, Christians seem to have been present at Lyons, inland on the Rhône, before Massilia (Marseilles), the region's greatest port. In the case of Lyons, the early presence of Christianity there can be attributed to its importance in a variety of social networks, since the city was the administrative and cultural hub of life in the region.

Surviving literature from the earliest period implies that Christianity in the west was linked to immigrant populations. Until the early third century, the language of western Christianity was Greek, not Latin. Similarly, texts such as the *First Epistle of Clement* from the Roman Christians to their brethren in Corinth and the letter (quoted by Eusebius) on the martyrs of Lyons that was sent from 'the servants of Christ living in Vienne and Lyons in Gaul to the brethren in Asia and Phrygia' (*Ecclesiastical History* 5.1.3) show that early western Christians saw themselves as having natural contacts with the eastern provinces.

In some (perhaps many) cases, the spread of Christianity may have been quite accidental. It has been noted that Paul's journey to Rome piggybacked on major trade routes linking the city with the eastern Mediterranean. While he resumed preaching when he got to Rome, this was in no sense a formal missionary journey: he was travelling, after all, as a Roman prisoner. Similar accidental circumstances led to the first appearance of Christianity among the barbarian Goths living north of the empire's Danube frontier. If information about the fourth-century Gothic bishop Ulfilas can be trusted, then Christianity came to the Goths from Christian prisoners captured in raids by Gothic pirates on the northern coast of Asia Minor in the mid-third century (Heather and Matthews 1991: 143–4). For many places in the Roman world, however, the presence of Christianity cannot be explained with full clarity: Christian churches simply appear. In the absence of direct and unambiguous evidence, therefore, we should be cautious of accepting notions that Christianity spread primarily through an organized missionary strategy emanating from the faith's eastern point of origin. 'Secondary' missions are possible too, such as that postulated for the churches of southern Gaul, which suggests that they were evangelized from Rome, not from the eastern provinces (Lane Fox 1986: 273). But the idea that Christianity spread only through organized missions is probably much too neat; the reality was very likely more haphazard.

Conversion

Why did people convert to Christianity in apparently increasing numbers? Again, this is a difficult question to answer in terms that are satisfactory for modern historians. In the gospels Jesus displays his power through miracles; in turn, Paul performs miracles that persuade people to convert (Klauck 2000a). The miraculous element is not limited to the New Testament, but is found in later authors too. Eusebius famously describes in his *Martyrs of Palestine* how, during the persecution under the emperor Maximinus Daia (305–13), a Christian from Caesarea in Palestine was executed by drowning (4.14–15). As soon as he was thrown into the sea, however, there was an earthquake and the sea threw up his body in front of the city's gates, prompting the whole of the astonished population (so Eusebius tells us) to convert on the spot. Such miraculous stories have been taken seriously by some historians (MacMullen 1984: 25–9). The world into which Christianity expanded, after all, was one where there was no sharp division between the supernatural world of cosmic powers and the natural world of humankind.

Such stories occur in accounts penned by authors convinced of the heavenly intervention they set out to describe in their accounts of miracles: the authors of the gospels *believed* that Jesus could work miracles; the author of *Acts* was equally convinced that Paul could do likewise; and Eusebius, as we have seen, assumed that Christianity's success had been guaranteed by heaven. Modern researchers tend to be sceptical of the miraculous and prefer more sociologically plausible accounts. Thus they seek explanations in anxieties about the world (Dodds 1965) or in response to moments of crisis, such as the outbreak of plague or famine (Stark 1996: 73–94; Reff 2005). Perhaps it was the case that as Christian numbers apparently mushroomed in the third century conversion became easier because it brought membership of a substantial and supportive social network. Yet the third century also saw bloody persecutions of the Christians, and conversion at such times seems to defy reason (MacMullen 1984: 29–30; K. Hopkins 1998: 226). Even so, it may be the case that the steadfastness of Christians in the face of death impressed onlookers in a world where fatal illness could strike suddenly and without warning (thus Justin Martyr, *Apology* 2.12).

For the most part, however, we are often left groping for answers that our sources do not provide. Mass conversions – like that at Caesarea following the sea's regurgitation of the martyr's body – are described by onlookers, often with polemical of apologetical agendas. Indeed, even the famous story of Paul's conversion on the road to Damascus is told in full only by the author of *Acts* (9.1–19; 22.3–16; 26.9–21); Paul's own references to it in his letters are rather more oblique (e.g. *1 Corinthians* 15.8–9; *Galatians* 1.12–17; *Philippians* 3.4–7; cf. Marshall 1980: 166–72). First-hand accounts are rare and apply only to a handful of individuals. The second-century apologist Justin Martyr described his experiences in his *Dialogue with Trypho*, a work of apologetic directed against Jewish doubters of Jesus' status as Messiah. By his own account, Justin was on a quest for God through philosophy, which brought him to follow (in succession) the Stoics, the Peripatetics, the Pythagoreans, and the Platonists, before he found truth in Christianity (*Dialogue with Trypho* 2–3). A similar story was told by Augustine of his conversion in the late fourth century: his quest brought him at various times to Platonism and the doctrines of the Persian mystic Mani (see p. 163). The similarity between Justin's and Augustine's accounts suggests, perhaps, some literary artifice (cf. Nock 1933: 256). Their experiences, however, must have been very different: in Justin's day, Christians were few in number, while Augustine lived in a culture where Christianity was becoming increasingly the norm. Another reason for conversion is found in the writings of the late third-century north African Arnobius of Sicca, who claimed that he turned to Christianity because he had become disgusted at pagan sacrificial ritual (1.29) – but his revulsion is expressed in terms of stock Christian denunciations of paganism, and so might reflect Arnobius' later reinterpretation of his conversion experience. This suggests that converts could construct pictures of their conversion that fitted with their perceptions of their altered religious status: for Justin and Augustine, Christianity was superior to other forms of enlightenment; for Arnobius, it was more satisfying than pagan sacrifice. We can see a similar picture emerge for the conversion experience of the first Christian emperor, Constantine. There has been much debate about the extent to which he might have been influenced by Christians in his family. However that may be, Constantine's first overtly Christian action was to fight the battle of the Milvian Bridge on 28 October 312 with the Christian God as his champion. In the letters that he wrote in later years, he never forgot his debt to the God who had granted him victory.

The variety presented by such examples suggests that conversion could occur for diverse reasons, which defy attempts at generalization. We should also bear in mind that the religious experience of individuals in the ancient world was diverse and more fluid than categories such as 'pagan', 'Jewish', and 'Christian' suggest. We have already seen in this chapter how the boundaries between Judaism and Christianity were extremely porous well into late antiquity. This hints at how religious curiosity could lead to conversion. The *Acts of the Apostles* mentions repeatedly how Paul made converts of Greeks – that is, pagans/gentiles – when preaching at Jewish gatherings. Such Greeks are called *sebomenoi* (or *phoboumenoi*) *ton theon*, meaning 'God-fearers' (Levinskaya 1996: 120–6). They apparently attended the synagogue out of interest in learning about the Jewish religion. Inscriptions, especially from Asia Minor, suggest that these gentile/pagan 'god-fearers' were not (as was once supposed) the convenient invention of the author of *Acts*. They describe individuals, most of them apparently non-Jews, as *theosebeis*, which means 'god-worshippers' and the designation is perhaps analogous to the 'god-fearers' mentioned in *Acts*. Moreover, the inscriptions show that many of these 'god-worshippers' occupied prominent positions as patrons of their local Jewish communities (Levinskaya 1996: 51–126). Perhaps, as people with a speculative interest in other forms of religion, they were predisposed to listen sympathetically to Paul's preaching.

Recent study of sources (mainly inscriptions, again) relating to the cult of Theos Hypsistos ('the most high god') has underlined the blurring of religious boundaries in antiquity (Mitchell 1999; cf. Levinskaya 1996: 83–103). This cult was widespread throughout the eastern Mediterranean and Near East between the Hellenistic period and late antiquity. The focus of devotion was a remote, abstract deity who was often associated with messengers called 'angels' (in Greek, *angelos* means a messenger). In some places, the cult had strong pagan characteristics, through association of Theos Hypsistos with Zeus and other gods. This was not, however, its only manifestation. The term *theos hypsistos* was used by Diaspora Jews to describe their own God in Greek. It is often impossible to tell whether inscriptions recording dedications to Theos Hypsistos refer to a pagan god or the Jewish one. Indeed, many such dedications come from cities that had Jewish Diaspora communities. Furthermore, the worshippers of Theos Hypsistos – in both pagan and Jewish contexts – described themselves as *theosebeis*, precisely the term used to designate the pagan/gentile 'god-worshippers' who attached themselves to Jewish synagogues. Christians too were associated with the cult of Theos Hypsistos. Various early Christian writers condemned worshippers of Theos Hypsistos, whom they termed Hypsistarii or Hypsistiani, and whom they regarded as dangerous heretics. Inscriptions from Asia Minor suggest that some Christians, like Jews, could describe their God as *theos hypsistos* (Mitchell 1999: 122–3). The various manifestations of the worship of Theos Hypsistos suggest that religious boundaries were blurred 'and the beliefs and doctrinal positions of Christians, Jews, and [pagan] god-fearers continued to overlap throughout antiquity' (Mitchell 1999: 127).

A striking example of how religious traditions could intersect is attested by the fifth-century ecclesiastical historian Sozomen. He recounts how the emperor Constantine came to build a basilica by the oak at Mamre. This had been the site of the Hebrew patriarch Abraham's vision of three angels (*Genesis* 18.1–8). Christians later interpreted this as a vision of God, and therefore of Jesus Christ, in the form of the Trinity (Siker 1991: 178–82). Sozomen tells us of a remarkable festival celebrated at the site:

> Here the inhabitants of the local country and those from further afield – Palestinians, Phoenicians, and Arabians – gather every year in summer to observe a brilliant festival . . . This festival is attended by all peoples: by Jews, because they claim descent from the patriarch Abraham; by Hellenes [i.e. pagans], because angels appeared to men there; and by Christians, because he who appeared to that pious man was later born to a virgin for the salvation of humankind.
>
> (Sozomen, *Ecclesiastical History* 2.4.2–3)

Although Sozomen states that Constantine endeavoured to stamp out this mixed religious festival, the whole tenor of his account suggests that it was still being celebrated in his own day.

Any account of the success of Christianity in securing converts in the Roman world must take account of this fluidity of religious boundaries. Conversion to Christianity was an option – but not the only one for those who were interested in religious speculation. It was possible to convert from Christianity to something else, as did the emperor Julian (361–3) when he forsook Christianity and embraced a philosophical form of paganism. While it is true that the number of converts to Christianity increased during the first few centuries AD, it would be wrong to assume that this was the only possible route for the religious history of the empire to take (S. G. Wilson 2004). If we were to think that, then our analysis would be no better than that of Eusebius.

Case study: inscriptions and the missionary journeys of Paul

The purpose of this chapter's case study is to examine how external (i.e. non-Christian) evidence can be exploited to illuminate events described in early Christian texts. My focus will be on the missionary journeys of the apostle Paul. Although we possess a number of Paul's letters, it is above all on the *Acts of the Apostles* that we must rely for an outline narrative of his activities. The letters themselves provide no coherent narrative, even if they reveal much about Paul's ambitions and his concerns for the Christian communities founded by him and under his care. The book of *Acts* is an appealing specimen of ancient narrative, full of incident and adventure. But how reliable is it as history? We saw earlier (pp. 65–6) that some modern historians of the Roman world have been impressed by its verisimilitude, but that is not quite the same thing as strict accuracy. The first two parts of this case study will examine how the evidence of contemporary inscriptions can be exploited to provide a historical framework within which the narrative of *Acts* might be interpreted. In the third part, I will look at how inscriptions might allow us to guess at how Paul's missionary message was heard.

Inscriptions and chronology

However much *Acts* might seem, at first reading, to be a 'straight' history, it lacks one of the crucial elements upon which historians depend: dates. This is not to say that there are no chronological indicators in the text at all. For example, the account of Paul's last trial in Jerusalem before he was sent to Rome opens with the statement 'three days after Festus had arrived in the province [of Judaea], he went up from Caesarea to Jerusalem' (*Acts* 25.1). Similarly, there are indications of the length of time Paul spent in various places in the course of his travels, such as the 'three months' and 'two years' he resided at Ephesus (*Acts* 19.8, 10), or the three months spent wintering on Malta during the journey to Rome (*Acts* 28.11). The chronological markers in *Acts* are therefore all relative; absolute dates are entirely lacking. There are no references to Roman consular years, the regnal years of Roman emperors, or even to local calendars – all of which were used in various parts of the Roman world. In their absence, scholars have tried to fix certain dates, notably those of the terms of office held by Roman governors of Judaea. Such endeavours are deemed important, since upon them will depend any attempt to reconstruct a precise picture of Paul's career in terms of how long his missionary journeys lasted, and the length of time he spent in one city or another. For example, while *Acts* leaves off its account of Paul's journeys with his arrival in Rome, one recent reconstruction of his journeys dates his arrival there early enough to allow him time to undertake extra journeys to Spain and Greece (Murphy-O'Connor 1996: 359–64).

Among the cities visited by Paul was Corinth. This was an important centre for both trade and Roman provincial administration: in short, it boasted precisely the sort of profile that we have seen made certain places ideal for Paul's missionary activities (pp. 117–18). The fledgling Christian community of Corinth was important enough to be the recipient of two of Paul's genuine letters. Moreover, while sojourning in the city Paul wrote his *Letter to the Romans* and possibly also his *First Letter to the*

Thessalonians. The account of his stay at Corinth in *Acts* 18.1–17 implies that he spent some considerable time in the city. It also offers one of the most precious chronological indicators for his career, for it was in Corinth that there occurred a Jewish attack on Paul 'when Gallio was proconsul [i.e. governor] of Achaia [as the Roman province of central and southern Greece was called]' (*Acts* 18.12).

Gallio is one of the Roman officials mentioned in *Acts* about whom we have external evidence, with the result that he has been called 'the lynch-pin of Pauline chronology' (Murphy-O'Connor 1992: 149). The crucial evidence comes from an inscription in Greek found at Delphi in central Greece. It records privileges granted to Delphi by the emperor Claudius (41–54) and mentions that the basis for the emperor's actions was a report sent to him by his 'friend and proconsul Lucius Iunius Gallio'. In terms of chronology, the important part of the inscription is the first two lines. Unfortunately these lines are fragmentary (as indeed is the inscription as a whole), and in the translation that follows here I indicate reconstructed portions of the text by printing them in square brackets (i.e. []); parts of the text that remain uncertain are indicated by an ellipsis (. . .). Even so, enough survives to allow an attempt at reconstruction. The lines read:

> Tiber[ius Claudius Caes]ar A[ugustus] G[ermanicus, holding the tribunician power for the . . .-th time, acclaimed *imperator*] twenty-six times, f[ather of the f]ather[land, sends his greetings to . . .]
>
> (Oliver 1971; cf. Smallwood 1967: no. 376)

Although the text is fragmentary, these lines can be reconstructed with some confidence because the language of imperial titles in inscriptions is very formulaic. The crucial detail as regards dating is the mention of Claudius' acclamation with the title *imperator* twenty-six times: the Greek numeral ΚΣ (twenty-six) is clear in the surviving text. However, acclamations as *imperator* were made on occasions of military victories, and thus they could happen at any time, and at irregular intervals, during an emperor's reign: for example, an emperor might receive several such acclamations in any given year, but none at all in another year. In the case of Claudius, for example, it seems that his conquest of Britain raised the number of his acclamations as *imperator* from three in 43 (before the invasion) to at least five, and perhaps as many as nine, in 44 (after the invasion) (Levick 1990: 143–4). Precise dates corresponding to years can be calculated from the emperor's holding of the tribunician power. In the Gallio inscription that detail is missing, but we can attempt to determine it by establishing when Claudius received his twenty-sixth such acclamation.

The easiest approach is to begin by determining the upper limit for the date. A perfectly preserved inscription in Greek from Cys in Caria in south-western Asia Minor gives Claudius' titles as follows:

> Tiberius Claudius Caesar Germanicus Imperator Divine Augustus, Pontifex Maximus, holding the tribunician power for the twelfth time, consul five times, acclaimed *imperator* twenty-six times, father of the fatherland.
>
> (Smallwood 1967: no. 135)

It is the emperor's holding of the tribunician power that enables us to date this inscription more precisely. An emperor received this power on his accession to the throne and it was renewed on the anniversary of that event every year thereafter for the rest of the reign. Claudius became emperor on 25 January 41; therefore he held the tribunician power for the twelfth time from 25 January 52 until 24 January 53. Since the Gallio inscription also mentions Claudius as having been acclaimed *imperator* for the twenty-sixth time it is possible that it, like the Cys inscription, dates to that year.

That the Gallio inscription is *no later* than the year from 25 January 52 to 24 January 53 is demonstrated by another inscription, this time in Latin, from the Porta Praenestina (now the Porta Maggiore) in Rome. This text commemorates Claudius' completion of the Claudian aqueduct. It gives the emperor's titles as follows:

> Tiberius Claudius, son of Drusus, Caesar Augustus Germanicus, Pontifex Maximus, holding the tribunician power for the twelfth time, consul five times, acclaimed *imperator* twenty-seven times, father of the fatherland.
>
> (Smallwood 1967: no. 309)

From this text we can surmise that Claudius' twenty-seventh acclamation as *imperator* also happened some time in the year when he held the tribunician power for the twelfth time, that is between 25 January 52 and 24 January 53. Moreover, we can date this even more precisely. In his work *On the Aqueducts of the City of Rome*, written in the late first century, Frontinus records the completion of the Claudian aqueduct. His text has become slightly corrupt in its transmission, but it can be confidently reconstructed (Rodgers 2004: 73, 183–4). It gives the following information about the date:

> These works Claudius completed on the most magnificent scale and dedicated in the consulship of [Faustus] Sulla and [Salvius] Otho, in the eight hundred and third year since the foundation of the city [i.e. Rome], on the Kalends of August.
>
> (Frontinus, *On the Aqueducts of the City of Rome* 13.2)

It has been noted that there is something awry with Frontinus' dates: the eight hundred and third year since the foundation of Rome ought to be 50 (Murphy-O'Connor 1992: 150–1). Frontinus, however, clearly used a different calculation for the foundation of Rome than that used by many other authors (a system derived from the antiquarian writer Varro) and his dates 'since the foundation of the city' are routinely a year or two out (Rodgers 2004: 139–40). More significant is his notice of the consuls for the year: Faustus Sulla and Salvius Otho are known from many other sources to have been consuls in 52 (Rodgers

2004: 184; cf. Bickerman 1968: 184). Thus Frontinus and the inscription from the Porta Praenestina agree on the year 52. Moreover, Frontinus specifies that the date of the dedication of the aqueduct was the Kalends, that is the first day, of August. This makes it likely that (a) the Porta Praenestina inscription records Claudius' titles as they were on 1 August 52; and (b) he had already received his twenty-seventh acclamation as *imperator* by that date. If that is correct, then the twenty-sixth acclamation must have occurred earlier than this, and therefore the Gallio inscription must date to some time before 1 August 52, perhaps in the first half of that year.

If the upper limit for the date of the Gallio inscription is the first half of 52, can we set a lower limit? Unfortunately, not a single inscription correlates Claudius' twenty-fifth acclamation as *imperator* with a year in which he held the tribunician power. There is, however, an inscription that lists his twenty fourth acclamation, and gives the emperor's titles as follows:

> [To Tiberius] Claudius, son of Drusus, Caesar Augustus Germanicus, Pontifex Maximus, holding the tribunician [power] for the eleventh time, acclaimed *imperator* twenty-four times, consul five times, censor.
>
> (*Corpus Inscriptionum Latinarum* III, no. 1977).

Thus Claudius had been acclaimed *imperator* twenty-four times in the year from 25 January 51 to 24 January 52. His twenty-fifth acclamation must therefore have occurred either later in that year or in the one following. We could try to fix the date further if we knew more about the sequence of Claudius' acclamations. Unfortunately, the surviving data are fragmentary. Two further inscriptions correlate a twenty-second acclamation also with the year 25 January 51 to 24 January 52 (*Corpus Inscriptionum Latinarum* III, nos. 476 and 7206). This means that he must also have received a twenty-third acclamation in that year, even if no inscription attests it. This has prompted scholars to correlate Claudius' acclamations as *imperator* with the following years:

(a) In the year 25 January 51 to 24 January 52, he received his twenty-second, twenty-third, and twenty-fourth acclamations as *imperator*.
(b) In the year 25 January 52 to 24 January 53, but *before* 1 August 53 (as we can surmise from the Porta Praenestina inscription and Frontinus), he received his twenty-sixth and twenty-seventh acclamations as *imperator*.

This means his twenty-fifth acclamation happened either late in 51 or early in 52. Even with this uncertainty, it looks most probable that the twenty-sixth acclamation belongs to the first half of 52 and, with it, the inscription mentioning Gallio.

As a result, we can date Gallio's term as proconsul quite precisely. Such governorships were allocated to senators by lot on an annual basis, with governors serving a single year in office from the spring of one year until the spring of the following one (Talbert 1984: 348–53, 497–8). Therefore, if the letter of Claudius preserved in the Delphi inscription is dated to the first half of 52, then Gallio must have sent his report to Claudius some time before that. The usual conclusion is that Gallio's term of office stretched from the spring of 51 to the spring of 52.

In addition, we can speculate further about Gallio's proconsulship. His brother was none other than the philosopher Seneca, who records in one of his writings that Gallio did not complete his tour of duty in Greece. He states: 'When he began to feel ill in Achaia, he boarded a ship immediately, stating that the illness was not one of his body, but of the place' (Seneca, *Epistula Morales* 104.1). As a result, it has been postulated that Gallio left Achaia very soon after taking up office there, perhaps before the end of November 51, after which date sea travel would have become hazardous owing to inclement weather (Murphy-O'Connor 1992: 154–8). Unfortunately, however, we cannot know for sure exactly when Gallio gave up on his proconsulship and returned to Rome, although Seneca certainly gives the impression that his stay in Achaia was not a long one. When the various pieces of evidence are weighed, it looks most likely that Paul encountered Gallio some time in the second half of 51, or very early in 52 at the very latest. This is a considerable advance on the vague chronology offered by *Acts*.

Paul's Roman patron?

It is well known that Paul was once called Saul. This Aramaic name is associated with his career before his conversion, when, as an official of the high priest of the Jerusalem temple, he was charged with persecuting Jesus' followers. His Roman name Paul is associated with his post-conversion career as an apostle. The familiar story of Paul's conversion on the road to Damascus is most fully elaborated by the author of *Acts*, rather than by Paul himself (see p. 121). What is interesting, however, is that *Acts* does not notice Paul's change of name at this point of the narrative, but continues to call him Saul. Only later, when the apostle was at Paphos on the island of Cyprus, does *Acts* introduce us to 'Saul, who is also called Paul' (*Acts* 13.9). Why the delay in noting Paul's change of name? Intriguingly, Paul's most important convert on Cyprus was the island's Roman governor, Sergius Paullus. The fact that Saul now adopted a name identical to that of the governor (both are spelled 'Paulos', with a single 'l', in the Greek text of *Acts*) has prompted questions about some sort of link between Saul's change of name and his connection with Sergius Paullus. Here, however, there has been some considerable difference of opinion between ancient historians and New Testament scholars.

Let us consider first the most common opinion of New Testament commentators, which can be boiled down to a simple formula: the change of name from Saul to Paul is associated with Sergius Paullus merely as a literary flourish. Thus, in the view of Hans Conzelmann's authoritative commentary in the *Hermeneia* series, the author of *Acts* 'uses the opportunity provided by the name of "Paul's" first convert (Sergius *Paulus*) to introduce Paul into the mission under his generally known name. The connection with Sergius Paulus is therefore purely literary, not historical' (Conzelmann 1987: 100, spelling and emphasis in the original). Other commentators have surmised that as Paul was a Roman citizen, he would have possessed the *tria nomina* (three names) commonly possessed by Romans (e.g. Gaius Julius Caesar), and that Paulus (or Paullus) was probably one of these. Similarly, he probably also had an additional name (a *supernomen* or *signum*) by which he was commonly called; hence his Aramaic name Saul. Therefore, it has been argued that while *Acts* 'observes the coincidence that the governor of Cyprus was also called Paul . . . there cannot have been any connection between this fact and Paul's own name which he had received at birth' (Marshall 1980: 220; cf. Klauck 2000a: 52). Such assertions are, however, very speculative. If Paul did indeed possess the *tria nomina*, then we have no idea what those names were, or even if Paul(l)us was one of them. Given this uncertainty, it is perhaps unsurprising that other scholars, mainly ancient historians, have sought a much closer link between the apostle and the governor.

The most recent advocate of such a connection is Stephen Mitchell (1993: II, 6–7). For him, the telling fact in the narrative of *Acts* is the itinerary it ascribes to Paul after leaving Sergius Paullus and Cyprus:

> Then Paul and his companions set sail from Paphos and came to Perge in Pamphylia [the central coastal region of southern Asia Minor]. John, however, left them and returned to Jerusalem; but they went on from Perge and came to Antioch in Pisidia.
>
> (*Acts* 13.13–14)

The Roman colony of Antioch in Pisidia, located on a mountain plateau, seems an unusual next step in Paul's journey. Why did he bypass the populous coastal cities of Pamphylia, such as Perge itself, in favour of a town some 300 kilometres inland and in the mountains? One suggestion is that Paul was ill, perhaps with malaria, and sought out a healthier climate at upland Antioch.

Certainly, Paul's *Letter to the Galatians*, which may have been addressed in part to the Christians of Antioch in Pisidia, notes that he had been ill the first time he came among them (*Galatians* 4.13–14; cf. Mitchell 1993: II, 5–6). Even so, there were other highland towns that Paul might have visited rather than Antioch. In Mitchell's view, the key to solving this riddle lies in Paul's connection with Sergius Paullus, for his family, the Sergii Paulli, were among the leading citizens of Antioch in Pisidia. The basis for Mitchell's view is a series of inscriptions from the city itself or its surrounding territories:

(1) A Latin inscription giving a dedication 'To Lucius Sergius, son of Lucius, Paullus, the younger, a member of the board of four men for the upkeep of the roads, military tribune of the sixth legion *Ferrata*, quaestor' (Jacquier 1916: 246). This man was clearly of senatorial rank, since he was a quaestor. His name was also identical with that of his father, which is why he is described as Lucius Sergius Paullus the younger (*filius* in Latin).

(2) Another member of the family – probably a daughter of the elder Lucius Sergius Paullus and hence the sister of the younger Lucius Sergius Paullus discussed in (1) above – is known from a Greek inscription that mentions a 'Sergia Paulla, daughter of Lucius', who was married to another leading citizen of Antioch in Pisidia, Gaius Caristanius Fronto. The name of the emperor Domitian (81–96) has been partially erased from this inscription, helping us to date Sergia Paulla to the end of the first century. Further information of her husband is provided by another inscription from the city. It lists his distinguished career and confirms the chronology: he served in various military and administrative posts under Vespasian (69–79), Titus (79–81), and Domitian (81–96). In addition, he had been promoted to the senate (for both inscriptions, see Cheesman 1913: 260–6).

(3) A further member of the family, Sergia Paullina, daughter of Lucius, is attested as a major landowner in central Asia Minor in the early second century (Mitchell 1993: I, 151–2, and II, 7).

If the younger Lucius Sergius Paullus mentioned in (1) was indeed the brother of the Sergia Paulla mentioned in (2), then we can assume that the career of this younger Sergius Paullus must have been contemporary with that of Caristanius Fronto: that is, the second half of the first century. This means that his father, also called Lucius Sergius Paullus, must have been active a generation earlier, in the middle of the first century. If so, he was perhaps the same man as the governor of Cyprus encountered by Paul. An elder Lucius Sergius Paullus of the correct date is listed as a senator who was one of the curators of the Tiber banks on an inscription from Rome under Claudius (*Corpus Inscriptionum Latinarum* VI, no. 31545). He was perhaps also the Lucius Sergius Paullus who was a suffect consul in *c.* 70.

This is the man Mitchell identifies as the Sergius Paullus whom Paul converted. If this deduction is correct, then the reason for Paul's journey from Cyprus to Antioch in Pisidia, bypassing the coastal cities, becomes apparent. Sergius Paullus, impressed by Paul, suggested to him that he should take his preaching of the gospel to Anticoh in Pisidia, where the governor's family had strong connections (Mitchell 1993: II, 7). Mitchell's case is mainly circumstantial, but it has an air of plausibility about it. That said, it is difficult to predict if it will ever command the assent of New Testament commentators. The link between the Sergius Paullus of *Acts* and the Lucius Sergius Paullus who had been a curator of the Tiber banks under Claudius had been drawn before Mitchell, but New Testament scholars were reluctant to accept it. In the view of one commentator on *Acts* writing before Mitchell, the identification was 'weakly based' (Marshall 1980: 219). More recently Hans-Josef Klauck has similarly regarded the link with scepticism (Klauck 2000a: 50–1). It is not impossible that the governor of Cyprus and the curator of the Tiber banks were different individuals. However, given the prominence of the Sergii Paulli at Antioch in Pisidia displayed in the inscriptions, the case for Sergius Paullus suggesting the city to Paul as a target for his mission surely must remain a possibility.

Hearing the gospel

The account in *Acts* of Paul's encounter with Sergius Paullus makes it clear why the governor converted to Christianity – if indeed he did so: it is possible that the author of *Acts* exaggerated Paul's success with him (Klauck 2000a: 50–4). Sergius Paullus is depicted as a man with broad religious interests. At the time Paul met him, the governor was in the company of 'a certain magician, a Jewish false prophet, named Bar-Jesus' (*Acts* 13.6). It was Paul's refutation and miraculous striking blind of Bar-Jesus that persuaded Sergius Paullus to believe in Christ (*Acts* 13.7–12). Such miracles loom large in early Christian accounts of conversion (see pp. 120–1). We know little, however, apart from anecdotal evidence relating to individuals, about how people reacted to missionaries preaching the gospel. One way in which we might guess at the response to Christian teaching is to examine the language and rhetorical strategies used by Christian authors. This avenue of research has been pursued vigorously, both for New Testament texts and for the writings of later centuries.

Here I want to survey briefly some suggestions that the language used by Paul in his letters – and by the authors of the New Testament more generally – might have resonated in very particular ways with their audience. I will focus on two Greek words in particular: *sōter*, meaning saviour, and *euangelion*, meaning gospel. I will not list every instance of each word: such details may be found in reference works such as Hawthorne and Martin 1993 under the respective entries for the English words; more detailed accounts will be found under the Greek words in the multi-volume *Theological Dictionary of the New Testament* (see p. 229). Such words might seem these days to have inescapably Christian connotations. A comparison with inscriptions and other texts, however, suggests other possibilities.

Although the description of Jesus Christ as saviour is central to modern expressions of Christianity, use of the word *sōter* in early texts is rather sparse. In the undisputed letters of Paul, the term appears only twice. His instructions to the Ephesians about the Christian household include the statement: 'the husband is the head of the wife just as Christ is the head of the church, the body of which he is the saviour (*sōter*)' (*Ephesians* 5.23). Addressing the Philippians, he told them: 'our citizenship is in heaven, and it is from there that we are expecting a saviour (*sōter*), the Lord Jesus Christ' (*Philippians* 3.20). After Paul, the term *sōter* becomes more common. There are ten instances of the word in the Pastoral Letters, which, as we saw in chapter 3, are probably not by Paul (Hawthorne and Martin 1993: 868–9). The term also appears in other New Testament epistles (e.g. *2 Peter* 1.1; *Jude* 25). From there, it became a common descriptor for Jesus Christ in early Christian literature.

The term *euangelion* (gospel) is central to the vocabulary of the New Testament (Stanton 2004: 20–5). The Greek word is usually translated as 'gospel', an Old English word meaning 'good news' (hence the *Good News Bible*) or 'glad tidings'. The biblical accounts of Jesus' ministry ascribed to Matthew, Mark, Luke, and John are each called *to euangelion* (the gospel). Paul used the term in a variety of ways too. Often he spoke simply of *to euangelion* on its own, a phrase that implies '*the* gospel'. At other times, he wrote of 'the gospel of God' (e.g. *Romans* 1.1), 'the gospel of Jesus' (e.g. *1 Thessalonians* 3.2), and even, at two points, 'my gospel' (*euangelion mou*: *Romans* 2.16, 16.25). Also common in his writings is the verb *euangelizesthai* derived from *euangelion*: literally it means 'to gospel' or, less idiosyncratically, 'to spread the good news'; it is the root of the English verb 'evangelize'.

For the inhabitants of the eastern provinces of the Roman empire in the first century, such words would have had a very particular resonance that might have influenced how they 'heard' the preaching of Christian missionaries. They were used routinely in decrees (and inscriptions recording them) connected with the worship of Roman emperors as gods. Emperor worship, one of the most significant developments in the history of paganism in the Roman period, seems to have originated as a spontaneous reaction among eastern provincials to the success of imperial government. Its roots lay in the Hellenistic period, when kings of the eastern Mediterranean had been routinely accorded honours as if they were gods. With the advent of Roman power, such honours were transferred to successful Roman generals, such as Sulla, Pompey, and Caesar in the first century BC. After the conclusion of the late Republican civil wars, many of which had been fought out in the Greek east, these honours were offered to the emperor Augustus and his successors by provincials keen to express their gratitude for the restoration of peace.

Both *sōter* and *euangelia* (the plural of *euangelion*) are found in inscriptions (and other texts, such as papyri) relating to emperor worship. In 9 BC, for example, the federal council of the cities of the province of Asia adopted a new calendar that calibrated the beginning of each new year with the birthday of Augustus (23 September). A few extracts from their decree (found in fragments of varying completeness at five different locations) will illustrate the nature of the language employed:

> since Providence, which has divinely disposed our lives, having employed zeal and ardour, has arranged for the most perfect culmination for life by producing Augustus, whom for the benefit of humankind she has filled with excellence, as if [she had sent him as a saviour (*sōter*)] for us and our descendants, [a saviour (*sōter*)] who brought war to an end and set all things in order . . . And since the beginning of good news (*euangelia*) on his account for the world was the birthday of the god [i.e. Augustus] . . . for this reason, with good luck and for our salvation (*sōteria*), it has been decreed by the Greeks in Asia that the New Year's first month shall begin for all cities on the ninth day before the Kalends of October [i.e. 23 September], which is the birthday of Augustus.
>
> (Text in Sherk 1969: no. 65 D; translation adapted from Sherk 1984: 125–6)

Although the lines describing Augustus as a saviour (*sōter*) have been restored by the editors of the inscription, their presence in the text seems likely. Not only are many other emperors (and before them Hellenistic kings and generals of the Roman Republic) called *sōter*, but the inscription also expresses the Asians' hopes for their 'salvation' (*sōteria*). There is no such ambiguity about the use of the term *euangelia*, which appears not only here but also elsewhere in the inscription.

The extent to which this inscription echoes with ideas similar to those found in early Christianity is brought home to me every year when I present it to my students (by sheer serendipity, the lecture in question takes place only weeks before Christmas). They are struck by how the description of the emperor correlates closely with statements about Jesus from the New Testament. The parallels go further. Augustus proclaimed himself, and was recorded in countless inscriptions, as 'the son of a god', meaning the deified Julius Caesar. For his followers of course, Jesus was *the* son of *the* one true God. And just as Roman emperors claimed authority over the whole of the earth, so too New Testament texts proclaimed that Jesus' message will be heard to the ends of the earth.

To what extent could Paul and other early Christian authors have been aware that their use of such language mimicked terms that were central to emperor worship? An indication that they might have done is suggested by their use by Paul's older contemporary, the Jewish writer Philo of Alexandria (*c.* 15 BC–*c.* AD 50). In his *Embassy to Gaius* he twice used the verb *euangelizesthai* to describe the arrival of news at Alexandria of Gaius' accession to the throne in 37 (*Embassy to Gaius* 99, 231); he also described Gaius as 'a saviour (*sōter*) and benefactor' who would bring blessings to Asia and Europe (*Embassy to Gaius* 22), that is effectively to the whole world. If the Jew Philo could use language associated with emperor worship in ways that look self-conscious, why not also Paul and the early Christians?

This possibility has been explored by a number of scholars working on the New Testament. The harbinger of this approach was Adolf Deissmann in his *Licht vom Osten*, published in 1908 and translated into English as *Light from the Ancient East* (Deissmann 1910). The question has been revived recently by Peter Oakes in a study of Paul's *Letter to the Philippians* and Graham Stanton in an analysis of the meaning of the word 'gospel' (Oakes 2001; Stanton 2004). They all agree that the echoes of terms from emperor worship in New Testament writings are perhaps most significant in terms of how preaching might have struck the ears of contemporary audiences in the Greek-speaking eastern provinces of the Roman empire (Deissmann 1910: 342; Oakes 2001: 174; Stanton 2004: 48). This was, after all, a society filled with temples, decrees, and inscriptions associated with the worship of the emperor as a god. For Stanton the relationship is closer: the Christian proclamation of the 'good news' of Jesus Christ was in direct competition with proclamations of 'good news' concerning the emperors; furthermore, the Christians' good news was articulated by the singular noun *euangelion*, and was therefore *the* good news *above all*, superior to the plural good news proclaimed about emperors (Stanton 2004: 33–5).

While appeal to inscriptions relating to emperor worship might explain some elements in the early Christian message, it would be unwise to push the argument too far (and patently absurd to assume it might explain everything). For example, one of the commonest terms used to designate Christ in the New Testament is 'Lord' (*kurios* in Greek). While this term is sometimes applied to emperors, it is rare in public inscriptions before the middle of the first century AD (Oakes 2001: 171–2). We also need to bear in mind that so many of the early Christians were, as we have seen, Jews, for whom these words would have had specifically Jewish connotations. For example, terms like *kurios* and *sōter*, and even the verb *euangelizesthai*, were found in the Septuagint, the Greek translation of the Hebrew scriptures, and words expressing similar ideas are found in the Hebrew originals and in texts from Qumran. Comparison with the vocabulary of emperor worship is instructive, but it provides only one echo of the original reverberations of New Testament texts.

Inscriptions, Paul, Acts, and history

The survey given above hints at ways in which our comprehension of the career of the apostle Paul can be enriched and enlarged by study of the society and culture of Rome's eastern provinces at the time of his missionary journeys. The study of pertinent inscriptions has provided a chronological anchor for his travels; it has provided a suggestive solution to the reasons underlying his otherwise unexplained visit to Antioch in Pisidia; and it has hinted at ways in which the gospel message might have been heard by some of its target audience. There are, however, limits as to what such an analysis can tell us. Paul, after all, was a Jew, and no amount of elucidating his Roman context will compensate if that pertinent fact is ignored. In addition, we should not be misled by the verisimilitude of *Acts* into mistaking it for dispassionate history. Its positive portrayal of the Roman authorities is in contrast to a depiction of Jews and Jewish authorities that is often alarmingly hostile. As much as the letters of Paul, or indeed the tracts of apologists in the second and third centuries, *Acts* is a text with a particular argument to communicate. Any reading of it needs to bear this in mind.

Chapter 5

Doctrine and power: orthodoxy and organization in early Christianity

At various points in this book I have noted that Christians of later ages have looked back to early Christianity to validate their own beliefs and practices (see especially chapter 2). One of the major concerns of such backward glances in our own times has been to find some form of primeval Christianity that is somehow pure and free from corruption. The ultimately fruitless quest of Elaine Pagels for 'a "golden age" of purer and simpler early Christianity' has been mentioned already (p. 21). Seventeen centuries ago, Eusebius of Caesarea also sought to show for very different reasons how a pure form of Christianity endured from the time of Christ and the apostles down to his own day, in spite of threats from persecution and heresy (pp. 36–8). Behind Pagels' and Eusebius' quests lies an assumption that there exists a point to which we can return when there was a single form of Christianity undivided by ecclesiastical and theological disputes. Such aspirations to Christian unity are as old, it seems, as Christianity itself. The *Letter to the Ephesians* ascribed (almost certainly falsely) to the apostle Paul, for instance, asserted against those who would divide the church that 'there is one body and one Spirit, just as you were called to the one hope that belongs to your call, one Lord, one faith, one baptism, one God and Father of us all, who is above all and through all and in all' (*Ephesians* 4. 4–6).

In this chapter I want to explore this theme of unity in early Christianity, looking in particular at issues of doctrine and organization. This will involve discussion of the institution of the church, the debate between rival views of orthodoxy (and heresy), and the role played by bishops in emerging Christianity. I will begin with a specific example that might suggest a metaphor for the question more broadly. We will see that the development of a hierarchy of bishops in the church was closely related to efforts to preserve those beliefs that came to be regarded as true and therefore defined as orthodox, in opposition to other beliefs that were seen as false and therefore labelled heresy. The chapter will conclude with a case study that will investigate how a collection of texts discovered in Egypt in 1945 has compelled scholars to reassess questions of orthodoxy, heresy, and authority in early Christianity.

How many bishops attended the council of Nicaea?

In the early summer (perhaps June) of 325, by order of the emperor Constantine, an assembly of bishops met at the city of Nicaea in north-western Asia Minor. This assembly, or council as such a gathering is usually called, has assumed immense importance in the history not just of early Christianity, but of Christianity and the church more generally. The council of Nicaea is regarded as the very first ecumenical council, when bishops from throughout the inhabited world (*oikumenē* in Greek, hence 'ecumenical') assembled to debate matters of faith. Its deliberations chiefly focused on a dispute about the nature of Jesus Christ's divinity, and his relationship to God the Father and the Holy Spirit – in other words, about the nature of the Trinity. A priest from Alexandria in Egypt called Arius had argued recently that Christ was not of the same divine substance as God the Father. The council condemned these opinions and affirmed the unity of the Trinity. A statement of faith known as a creed (from the Latin verb *credo*, meaning 'I believe') was issued by the council, after which it was called the Nicene creed. This statement is still regarded by most Christian groups as the basic definition of orthodoxy.

But how many bishops attended the council of Nicaea and subscribed to its creed? This question might seem to be of relatively minor importance, but in seeking to answer it we discover much about how the history of the council of Nicaea was written and interpreted to suit later theological agendas. We get some inkling of the complexities of this issue if we return to the issue of the creed formulated by the council. For the Nicene creed recited by modern Christians the world over is not, in fact, the statement of faith issued by the bishops at Nicaea in 325; it is, rather, a revision of that creed formulated by another council of bishops that met at Constantinople in 381 (J. N. D. Kelly 1972: 296–301).

This is plainly a confusing set of affairs; but how did it arise? If we return to the question of how many bishops were at Nicaea we can begin to formulate an answer. The simple fact is that we do not really know. None of our roughly contemporary sources tells us the exact number. They give instead rather vague formulae such as 'more than 250' or 'about 300'. Modern scholars can do no better and place the number of bishops at the council somewhere between 250 and 300 (Hanson 1988: 155–6). Yet churchmen in the later fourth century claimed to know the exact number, not strictly of all bishops who attended the council, but of those who subscribed to the Nicene creed. That number was 318 precisely.

What are we to make of this? It could be argued, perhaps, that fourth-century churchmen simply knew better than we do, or that they had better sources (such as copies in their archives of the Nicene creed followed by a list of signatures, which they diligently counted). Given the vagueness of other (and earlier) fourth-century sources, however, this seems unlikely. Another possibility presents itself, and suggests a rewriting – or at least a reinterpretation – of the history of the council of Nicaea to suit later theological agendas. This is connected to the fact that what modern Christians call the Nicene creed is actually the formula drawn up at Constantinople nearly sixty years later. For while Constantine supported the creed drawn up at Nicaea in 325, in the remaining twelve years of his reign he changed his mind about it quite drastically. By the time of his death, many bishops who had been condemned at Nicaea for not agreeing to the creed were back in favour, while supporters of the Nicene creed now risked being sent into exile.

This is not the place to get bogged down in the complexities of the theological disputes over the nature of the Trinity that raged throughout the fourth century. It is enough to point out that for much of the period those bishops who were in the ascendant (in political terms, with the backing of an emperor) either ignored the creed of Nicaea or regarded it as heresy, and supported instead other creeds close to (but not identical with) the theology of the priest Arius. In the end, and again with imperial support, the adherents of the creed of Nicaea won the day at the council of Constantinople in 381. There they reaffirmed the Nicene creed, but reformulated it to take account of more than half a century of theological wrangling. Reformulated or not, however, the creed of Constantinople was regarded as being true to the orthodoxy of the creed of Nicaea.

This act of theological gymnastics did not appear out of the blue in 381. It reflected a tradition of theological debate that had developed among supporters of Nicaea during the fourth century. They had argued consistently that Nicaea's status as a council – and so, therefore, of its creed – was special. Nicaea was the first ecumenical council, they maintained, and therefore its decisions should enjoy priority. They asserted also that it had been called under the inspiration of God. Proof of this could be seen in the number of bishops who supported its creed. The precise number of 318 was not random, but resonated with symbolic meaning. It was the number of servants who had assisted the Old Testament patriarch Abraham against his enemies (*Genesis* 14.14). In Greek numerals, moreover, the number was written as TIH: the T symbolized Jesus' cross, while IH was the first two letters of

Jesus' name in Greek (*Iēsous*). Hence it was argued that the number of bishops at Nicaea was a fulfilment of biblical prophecy. This reveals how the champions of the Nicene creed accorded the council a special status that was used to affirm the orthodoxy of its statement of faith. In short, the council of Nicaea was not simply a historical event in the way that we would define one; rather, it was a symbol of orthodoxy and unity that had been pre-ordained by God.

Yet this unity reflected as much an aspiration as a reality. The debates at Nicaea revealed not only what united Christians in 325, but also what divided them. For example, the council issued a letter proclaiming that Easter should be celebrated at the same date everywhere – a sure sign that it had not been. In addition, the assembled bishops made decisions known as 'canons' (i.e. rules) that sought to clarify right practice on a wide range of issues of ecclesiastical administration and Christian conduct. Again, their very existence implies a diversity that the council endeavoured to harmonize. It was noted at the outset of this chapter that the aspiration towards unity in terms of Christian faith and organization is one that is as old as Christianity itself. As the debates at Nicaea demonstrated, however, this aspiration was held in tension by the fact that in different parts of the empire Christians organized their churches in different ways, and professed beliefs about doctrine that were subtly (or sometimes drastically) different. One of the challenges of studying early Christianity is to allow room not only for the unity upon which church tradition has laid such great emphasis, but also for the diversity against which the advocates of that unity struggled so vigorously.

The ideal of unity in early Christianity

The Roman world into which Christianity expanded was characterized by considerable diversity (Garnsey and Saller 1987). One reflection of this can be seen in the empire's languages. The

Romans themselves spoke and wrote Latin, and they imposed their tongue as the language of public business in the western empire; but in the provinces of the eastern Mediterranean the language of civic politics and administration was Greek. There were also various local languages, such as Egyptian, Aramaic, and Palmyrene in the east, Punic in north Africa, and Celtic in Gaul and Britain. These linguistic variations matched broader cultural divergences, which were reflected, for example, by different religious traditions (in terms of gods, rituals, temple design, and so forth). Economic life too operated differently in different provinces – and different systems could exist side by side within single provinces. Social structures were also diverse. A proportion of the empire's population lived in cities, but many others lived in villages or in isolated farmsteads. In some parts of the Roman world, such as in the mountains of Rough Cilicia in southern Asia Minor or along the desert fringes of north Africa, tribal societies endured throughout the empire's existence. Some regions also boasted curious social customs, such as brother–sister marriage in Egypt. Social divisions between rich and poor, elites and peasants, will have fostered differences in education, lifestyles, and life-expectancy within individual communities.

To what extent did this mosaic of cultural, social, and economic diversity have an impact on early Christianity? One influence was already traced in the last chapter, where we saw that Christian communities developed at different rates of growth and at different times in different places. Yet it was a characteristic of early church writers to stress the essential unity of the Christian movement. Some time around AD 250, bishop Cyprian of Carthage wrote a work tellingly entitled *De Catholicae Ecclesiae Unitate* – this is usually rendered in modern versions as something like *On the Unity of the Catholic Church*, in which the term 'catholic' means that the church was universal. In this work, Cyprian stressed how the church throughout the world was a community united in faith, practice, and organization under the leadership of its bishops:

> We ought to hold firmly and defend this unity, especially we bishops who preside over the church, so that we may prove also that episcopal authority is itself one and undivided. Let no-one mislead brotherhood through lying; let no-one corrupt the faith by perfidious perversion of the truth. The episcopal power is something of which each part holds the whole together.
>
> (Cyprian, *On the Unity of the Catholic Church* 5)

Some seventy years earlier, another bishop, Irenaeus of Lyons, had similarly written that the essential unity of the Christian faith had been maintained in spite of its dissemination far and wide across the face of the world:

> The church, having received this preaching and this faith . . . though dispersed in the whole world, diligently guards them as living in one house, believes them as having one soul and one heart, and consistently preaches, teaches, and hands them down as having one mouth. For if the languages of the world are dissimilar, the power of tradition is one and the same. The churches founded in Germany believe and hand down no differently, nor do those among the Iberians, among the Celts, in the Orient, in Egypt, or in Libya, or in those established in the middle of the world.
>
> (Irenaeus, *Against Heresies* 1.10.2, trans. Grant 1997)

Together, Irenaeus and Cyprian bear witness to the notion that Christianity, in terms of both faith and organization, was united to a single purpose.

Yet neither Irenaeus not Cyprian was offering a disinterested description of Christian unity. Both of them were asserting it in polemical works against enemies whom they accused of trying to tear Christianity apart. Irenaeus' work was directed against a group usually called the Gnostics who were spreading teachings about Jesus Christ that challenged the idea that there was a single faith to which all Christians subscribed. Cyprian similarly wrote against a background of competition. Just before he composed *On the Unity of the Catholic Church*, Christians (along with the rest of the empire's population) had been ordered to perform sacrifice to the pagan gods (see pp. 194–5). Many had refused and were imprisoned; some of these were executed and came to be regarded as 'martyrs', witnesses for the faith. Others, however, either succumbed to the demand to offer sacrifice or fled into hiding in fear of their lives. When the crisis abated, there was a vigorous debate about whether those Christians who had lapsed, either by sacrificing or by running away, should be readmitted into the church. This was a question that concerned Cyprian very directly, for he himself had hidden from the imperial authorities. It was a move that disappointed many Christians, not just at Carthage, but also in Rome. The result was a schism that divided the church of Carthage into rival factions and threatened a split with the church of Rome. As the recriminations piled up, Cyprian felt bound to defend his actions. Against his opponents he asserted that the church should be united and that this unity was the responsibility of its bishops.

Thus the emphasis on Christian unity in the writings of Irenaeus and Cyprian was a response to patent manifestations of disunity that they themselves faced on matters of faith and the integrity of the church as an institution. What is more, that unity was held in tension by a demonstrable tendency towards fragmentation and diversity in terms of organization, ritual practice, and belief. Thus the disagreements and differences that had confronted the bishops assembled for the council of Nicaea were nothing new: they were typical of early Christianity.

Organization and personnel

Members of most Christian churches today – and outside observers of them – are familiar with some form of hierarchy of persons established in positions of authority. These may be called, at the lower end of the scale, deacons, ministers, priests, and vicars; at the upper end there may be bishops and archbishops.

Some churches also have a figure in overall authority, such as the pope for Roman Catholics, or the ecumenical patriarch for the Greek Orthodox. Many of the terms used for these offices are derived from ancient languages and the continuity of terminology is an important element in the traditions of various churches. By its very nature, tradition emphasizes the unchanging nature of things, and there is a danger that terms used by early Christians (such as 'bishop' and even 'church') will be assumed to mean similar things both in antiquity and in the modern world. The reality, of course, is more complex, at least if we regard the church as a sociological phenomenon and not as something ordained by God. As we will see later in this chapter, the whole notion of ecclesiastical hierarchies was regarded as inseparable from Christian ideas about the role of God in human history and the function of the church as representing God on earth. It is essential to keep this point in mind in the investigation that follows, even when discussing the church as a human institution, since our sources were written by Christians who were convinced both of the reality of God and of the important role that he entrusted to the church.

Let me begin with the basic terminology. I noted above that modern terms for ecclesiastical institutions are often derived from ancient words. In English, this phenomenon is complicated slightly by the use of words derived from Germanic languages in the early middle ages. Such is the case with the English word 'church' (compare *Kirke* in modern German), which is used to translate the Greek word *ekklēsia*. The ancient word is more apparent in modern French *l'église*. The modern English terms bishop, presbyter/priest, and deacon, however, are close enough to their Greek counterparts *episkopos*, *prebuteros*, and *diakonos*. Of course, when these Greek words were first used by Christians in antiquity, they did not carry with them the connotations that their modern English equivalents have of an organized ecclesiastical system. Instead, they carried a range of different meanings, which can be highlighted by translating them literally. Thus *ekklēsia* could mean an 'assembly'; an *episkopos* was an 'overseer' or 'supervisor'; a *presbuteros* was an 'elder'; and a *diakonos* was a 'server' (from the Greek verb *diakein*, 'to serve').

All of these terms were used in antiquity in a variety of contexts apart from the Christian one. In classical Athens, for instance, the *ekklēsia* was the political gathering of the adult male citizens for deliberative purposes, while an *episkopos* could denote, among other things, an overseer of a city in the Athenian empire. That such terms came to be used by Christians to describe their own organizational structures could have been influenced by their continued use throughout antiquity as terms for civic institutions in the cities of the Greek east (Georgi 1995). It is equally (or more) likely, however, that Jewish tradition exercised an influence. Both *episkopos* (meaning God as a judge and men in positions of authority) and *ekklēsia* (meaning God's people) were used in the Hellenistic Greek translation of the Hebrew scriptures known as the Septuagint (Meeks 1983: 75–84). Whatever the origins of their use by Christians, it is clear already by the time of the Pauline letters that such words were being deployed in specifically Christian contexts: thus *ekklēsia* designated not only individual congregations of the faithful, but also their entire community throughout the world (Meeks 1983: 108).

Another feature that is suggestive of how emerging Christianity was influenced by its surrounding culture was the swift rise to prominence of a male-dominated leadership. Women do appear in certain prominent positions in the New Testament. Apart from Christ's companion Mary Magdalene, we also hear of women performing some kind of official (or semi-official) function in the churches of the age of Paul. *Acts*, for instance, recounts the story of Paul raising from the dead a certain Tabitha at Joppa. She is described as being responsible for 'good works and acts of charity', particularly towards widows (9.36–42). Paul himself refers to Phoebe, who was a 'deacon' (*diakonos*) of the Corinthian church and, like Tabitha, a benefactor (*Romans* 16.1). Later authors also refer to deaconesses and other influential women, particularly widows and virgins (Witherington 1988: 113–17, 149–51, 199–205). In general, however, authority lay with men.

Two of the deutero-Pauline pastoral epistles (*1 Timothy* and *Titus*), moreover, describe that authority in terms of the ancient household norms of patriarchal supremacy, and similar male-dominated stereotypes came to be the rule in early Christian writings. For some modern interpreters, this rise of masculine authority represents a triumph of the patriarchal environment over the more egalitarian teachings of Jesus himself (Fiorenza 1983: 288–94).

The rise of bishops to positions of prominence within the church occurred for various reasons. If we concentrate on the church as a human institution, then we can easily see how an administrative 'overseer' will have become more necessary as individual churches became larger and began to control greater resources. Such circumstances are implied by Eusebius of Caesarea's description of the church at Rome in the middle of the third century as comprising a bishop, forty-six presbyters, seven deacons, seven sub-deacons, forty-two acolytes, and fifty-two exorcists, readers, and doorkeepers, as well as supporting more than 1500 widows and paupers (*Ecclesiastical History* 6.43.11). Of course, what happened in the imperial capital may not be typical of what happened elsewhere. But it is clear from, for example, the church building remains at Dura Europos and descriptions of churches in sources describing the persecution under Diocletian that Christian groups were in possession of considerable properties by the end of the third century. Such properties, and the communities that they imply, needed someone to run them.

Modern historians of the ancient world have devoted much attention to such worldly functions of bishops, particularly for the period after Constantine when bishops began to acquire legal and administrative duties that effectively turned the church into an arm of the Christian Roman empire (Bowersock 1986). It is important not to forget, however, that the role of the bishop (and indeed of the clergy more generally) was primarily spiritual. Such is the reason given for the authority of leaders in some of the New Testament writings, such as the deutero-Pauline letters and the epistles ascribed to John. What bishops oversaw above all was the teaching of Christian doctrine. These concerns are echoed precisely in the first documents we possess from the pens of Christian bishops, such as the letters of Ignatius of Antioch (Kee 1995).

It is likely that the emergence of a church hierarchy was a gradual, even haphazard process. At first, leadership in Christian communities devolved on Jesus' surviving disciples (such as Peter and James) and the apostles associated with them (such as Paul). As this living link with the ministry of Jesus began to die out, however, there was an apparent need to appoint certain individuals to positions of authority. We can see this in some of the later New Testament writings, such as the deutero-Pauline *First Letter to Timothy* and *Letter to Titus*, where persons in leadership positions are described as *episkopoi* and *presbuteroi*. By the early second century we find a quite highly developed sense of hierarchical leadership, especially of the *episkopos*, in Ignatius of Antioch's letters. Again, this authority is conceived of in sacred terms: 'Be subject to the *episkopos* and to one another, as Jesus Christ was subject to the Father and the apostles were to Christ and the Father, so that there may be unity of both flesh and spirit' (*Letter to the Magnesians* 14.1). In Ignatius' view, such structures were inseparable from the very notion of a Christian *ekklēsia* (*Letter to the Trallians* 3.1). It is, perhaps, with Ignatius that we can begin to talk of 'bishops' and 'the church'.

How early and how firmly ecclesiastical authority was established is difficult to ascertain. It is possible that the situation was fluid for some considerable time. The *First Epistle of Clement* implies considerable dissension within the Christian community at Corinth over issues of leadership some time around the year 100. About a decade later, Ignatius of Antioch's letters repeatedly insisted that the Christians of Asia Minor should obey their clergy, especially their bishops – but this might be special pleading on Ignatius' part for a hierarchical structure that was not yet firmly established (Campbell 1994: 216–22). Recent studies of doctrinal disputes at Rome suggest that there was no bishop in overall control of the city's Christians even by the middle of the second century, and that Rome's Christians were caught between, on the one hand, centralizing tendencies enshrined in notions that the church ought to be united, and, on the other hand, the practical reality that the various leaders of individual congregations often disagreed with each other. According to this interpretation, it was only in the late second century, or even the early third, that a bishop with authority over all Rome's Christians finally emerged (Brent 1995; Lampe 2003; Thomassen 2004).

The institution of a clerical hierarchy was important not only within individual cities. Paul's letters to various Christian groups testify to their propensity to divide over issues of faith and practice. As an itinerant missionary, Paul could not supervise in person the communities that he established and so was compelled to write letters to them. Bishops, presbyters, and deacons helped safeguard against divisions by providing clearly identifiable leadership figures who could, moreover, endeavour to maintain unity not only within their own communities, but in the church throughout the Roman world. As with Paul, correspondence was a key element to this task, as is shown by some of the earliest post-New Testament Christian documents, such as the *First Epistle of Clement* to the church at Corinth and Ignatius of Antioch's letters to various congregations in Asia Minor and at Rome. Christian leaders also met for discussion. The *Acts of the Apostles* describes the apostles and elders (*presbuteroi*) meeting at Jerusalem to debate the question of gentile conversion (15.1–3). By the middle of the second century we begin to glimpse meetings of Christian bishops that could be called church councils. Eusebius of Caesarea describes such meetings of bishops to discuss the theological implications of the teachings of Montanus (see p. 163) and to debate the correct date for Easter observance (*Ecclesiastical History* 5.19.3–4; 5.23–4). By the third century, the procedures for church councils were becoming increasingly formalized, as is clear from the correspondence of Cyprian of Carthage (Amidon 1983). Such episcopal cooperation extended in some places to bishops officiating at the consecration of their colleagues, a practice attested from the mid-third century at Rome (albeit in the context of a schism) and Carthage (Eusebius, *Ecclesiastical History* 6.43.8; Cyprian, *Letters* 67.5).

The developments outlined above point to similar experiences in different churches across the Roman empire. It is clear, however, that there was also much variation. For example, the practice of a bishop being consecrated by his peers seems only to have begun at Alexandria with the election of Athanasius in AD 328 (Gryson 1973: 395–9). Equally, fourth-century church councils disagreed about the precise number of bishops who ought to participate in the consecrations of their colleagues (Hess 2002: 146–61). The fourth century also saw the formalization of episcopal hierarchies, where certain bishops held a higher authority over others in the same region. In the third century, such a phenomenon may be observed in the case of the city of Rome and in north Africa under the episcopate of Cyprian – in the latter case, however, this may have had as much to do with Cyprian's forceful personality as with the formalities of ecclesiastical administration (Rives 1995: 303).

From the reign of Constantine onwards, leadership functions seem to have devolved on certain metropolitan sees, which were, for the most part, located in cities that were also the headquarters of Roman administration in the provinces. In some cases, this merging of the structures of ecclesiastical and imperial administration provoked problems: in Palestine, the bishop of Jerusalem claimed special status by virtue of his city's historical importance for Christians, but he faced challenges from the bishop of Caesarea, whose city had long been the provincial capital. A further problem that emerged in the fourth century was defining what sort of centre should boast a bishop. At a council held in Serdica (modern Sofia) in 342 or 343, it was argued that bishops should not be appointed to villages or small towns where a single priest would suffice, lest the episcopal title and authority risk suffering humiliation (Hess 2002: 154–7). This resolution flew in the face of the reality in many parts of the empire, especially in regions where Christianity had made early gains. In north Africa bishops were found even in small towns (Lepelley 1981: 371–6), while in Asia Minor a distinction developed between *episkopoi*, who were the bishops of cities, and *chōrepiskopoi* ('country-bishops') in rural districts (Mitchell 1993: II, 70–1). In the latter case, this apparently organic development from the pre-Constantinian period led to conflict as attempts were made in the fourth century to impose a uniform ecclesiastical hierarchy throughout the empire. The correspondence of bishop Basil of Caesarea in Cappadocia (*c.* 330–79) includes an angry denunciation of country-bishops who were flouting his authority (*Letter* 54).

Ritual

Tensions between unity and diversity are found also in the practice of early Christian worship. There seems to have been broad agreement that there were certain normative rituals, such as initiation into Christianity through baptism, the celebration of the Eucharist, and prayer (both individual and communal). Similarly, certain days required some form of liturgical celebration, both at regular intervals throughout the year (Sunday worship) and on major feast days, of which Easter was the most important. For all that, there is evidence of some variation in how these rituals were observed in different parts of the Mediterranean world. This is suggested by the voluminous evidence for the liturgy in the fourth century, by which stage many local traditions had become firmly entrenched. We saw at the beginning of this chapter that the council of Nicaea debated the correct date for Easter observance in the face of diverse regional practices. This question continued to be debated by churchmen throughout the fourth century and beyond. Another manifestation of local variation can be seen in the surviving remains of churches. In north Africa, for example, the altar was located in the centre of the nave while church buildings as a whole were oriented towards the west; elsewhere in the Roman world, altars were usually located in or near the apse, while the churches themselves were oriented towards the east. (J. B. Ward-Perkins and Goodchild 1953: 56–66). In general, and despite the aspirations of bishops at councils, liturgical traditions were characterized by considerable regional variation (Bradshaw 1992: 111–30, 158–60).

The reasons for this variety are perhaps to be sought in the diverse traditions about Jesus that circulated in the early Christian centuries, thus prompting different liturgical forms of celebrating him. For example, Eusebius reports a controversy that arose in the second century because certain churches in Asia, who claimed this was their ancient tradition, celebrated Easter on the same day as the Jewish Passover, which could fall on any day of the week, and not on Easter Sunday. Against this Asian peculiarity, bishops elsewhere in the Roman world protested that by 'apostolic tradition' Easter ought to be celebrated on a Sunday. The bishops of Asia remained obstinate, however, citing their own precedents and traditions from the disciples Philip and John (*Ecclesiastical History* 5.23–4). Recent study of the work *Peri Pascha* (*On the Pasch*) by the early second-century bishop Melito of Sardis has suggested that this Asian practice could originate in a Christian celebration coinciding with the Jewish feast of Passover that commemorated not only the deliverance of the Israelites from Egypt as described in *Exodus*, but also the deliverance of God's new chosen people, the Christians, through the Messiah Jesus, whose coming the Old Testament *Exodus* narrative prefigured (Stewart-Sykes 1998). Moreover, this Asian practice might reflect a regional divergence as old as the gospel traditions themselves. Whereas the synoptic gospels attributed to Matthew, Mark, and Luke describe the Last Supper of Jesus and his disciples occurring on the day of the Jewish Passover, the gospel ascribed to John places it a few days earlier (see p. 72). Also, the eucharistic sayings of Jesus (promising eternal life to those who eat his body and drink his blood) are central to the Last Supper narratives in the synoptics. In the *Gospel of John*, however, they appear not in his account of the Last Supper, but much earlier in the story of Jesus' miraculous feeding of the five thousand (*John* 6.53–8), when explicit reference is made to the bread (*manna*) sent from heaven to the Israelites following the exodus from Egypt (*John* 6.31–2). Such divergences in the gospels point not only to the possibility of different understandings of Easter, but also divergent meanings of the Eucharist, at least in terms of how it was viewed in relation to the narrative of Jesus' ministry.

Orthodoxy and heresy

The most serious threat to Christian unity came not from divergent forms of organization or ritual, but from serious differences over doctrine – that is, over the teachings that constituted the very foundations of Christian belief. This is the debate usually characterized as being between orthodoxy (literally, correct belief) and heresy (from the Greek word *hairesis*, originally meaning simply 'choice', but eventually coming to denote religious speculations that deviated from correct belief). Although conflicts over doctrine often involved debates about the authority of the church's hierarchy, it would be naïve to imagine that worldly power was the only issue at stake. At heart, the dispute was about something altogether more serious and otherworldly: the salvation of Christian souls, something that could only be achieved through the true message of Jesus Christ.

The central place of the struggle between orthodoxy and heresy in the history of Christianity was neatly summarized by the Jesuit scholar Karl Rahner (1904–84), one of the most influential Roman Catholic theologians of the twentieth century:

> The history of Christianity is also a history of heresies and consequently of the attitudes adopted by Christianity and the Church towards heresy, and so involves a history of the concept of heresy itself. In all religions that possess any kind of definite doctrine . . . there are differences of opinion about that doctrine and as a consequence quarrels and conflict about it and about the socially organised forms in which the different religious views find expression.
>
> (Rahner 1964: 7)

It could be said that the debate is visible already in the origins of Christianity as a form of Judaism, when those who would come to call themselves Christians redefined their relationship with Jewish law and the traditions of ancient Israel, and advocated new truths based on Jesus' teachings. Just as Christianity splintered away from other forms of Judaism, so too, perhaps, there was a risk that Christianity itself might fragment, as different groups or individuals came to regard different versions or aspects of Jesus' message as more significant. Such divergences of opinion may be glimpsed in Paul's *First Letter to the Corinthians*, where the apostle sought to remind his audience that the true message of Jesus was not simply that he taught wisdom, but that through his death and resurrection he showed himself to be humankind's redeemer.

At the centre of such disputes lay disagreements about what precisely constituted Jesus' message and how (and by whom) it should be interpreted. The existence of various apocryphal writings shows that there were speculations about Jesus' message other than those contained in the writings of the New Testament. In the three centuries between Christ and Constantine, as Christianity intersected with the various systems of thought found around the Graeco-Roman Mediterranean, it was perhaps inevitable that those who heard the Christian message would seek to make sense of it in terms of the intellectual traditions with which they themselves were familiar. Such is the frank admission of the third-century Alexandrian theologian Origen. More to the point, Origen hints how this could fracture the unity of Christian orthodoxy:

> Since Christianity appeared to men as something worthy of serious attention . . . sects inevitably came to exist, not at all on account of factions and a love of strife, but because several learned men made a serious attempt to understand the doctrines of Christianity. The result of this was that they interpreted differently the scriptures universally believed to be divine, and sects arose named after those who, although they admitted the origin of the word, were impelled by certain reasons which convinced them to disagree with one another.
>
> (Origen, *Against Celsus* 3.12, trans. H. Chadwick 1953)

Such speculations (and later ones too, of course: differences of opinion did not come to a halt with Constantine!) came to be regarded as heresy when they fell foul of what the emerging leadership of the church deemed to be true doctrine.

A catalogue of these heresies will show how they presented versions of doctrine that reflect debate on the nature of Jesus' significance. One caveat is important, however. Our knowledge of early Christian heresies depends almost wholly on the writings of their self-appointed orthodox enemies. Among the extant works of early Christian writers are those that modern scholars term heresiologists, 'writers on heresy'. (We also have heresiology, which is the study of heresy, and the adjective heresiological.) The most important of these in the period before Constantine were Irenaeus, bishop of Lyons in Gaul, who wrote around AD 180, and Hippolytus, a presbyter of the church of Rome in the early third century. Their works catalogued the errors of heretics and refuted the doctrines they purveyed. Both Irenaeus and Hippolytus regarded the wedding of Greek philosophical speculation to the Christian message as a primary source of heretical corruption. In this respect, they seem to have had in mind similar intellectual trends to those that Origen described. Further information on early heresies can be found in later authors, notably Eusebius' *Ecclesiastical History*, and the later fourth-century heresiological catalogue known as the *Panarion* (literally, the *Medicine Chest* – a cure for heresies!) by bishop Epiphanius of Salamis on Cyprus. From these various sources we can discern several trends in Christian thought that produced doctrines that were condemned as heresy.

(1) *Debates on knowledge and wisdom*. Among the earliest groups to attract the wrath of the heresiologists were those who claimed that they possessed special knowledge (*gnōsis* in Greek) about Jesus and God. Indeed, Irenaeus' heresiological treatise, which is usually called *Against Heresies* (from the titles *Adversus Haereses* and *Contra Haereses* found in manuscripts of

the Latin translation of the work), seems originally to have been called *On the Detection and Refutation of the Knowledge (gnōsis) Falsely So-Called* (Rousseau and Doutreleau 1979: I, 31–5). Hence it is common to talk in English of Gnosis as the search for this special knowledge; to call those engaged on this quest Gnostics; and to describe the whole religious phenomenon as Gnosticism (see, however, the case study at the end of this chapter). Both Irenaeus and Hippolytus make it clear that there were several groups of Gnostics. In particular, Irenaeus is concerned to refute a group that he calls the Valentinians after the teacher Valentinus whose doctrines they followed. However, both heresiologists were aware that there were other teachers of Gnosis, meaning that modern scholars have often failed to pin down a single, easily identifiable phenomenon that might be called Gnosticism. Problems directly related to this issue will be explored in more detail in the case study at the end of this chapter.

(2) *Debates on the nature of Jesus Christ.* It was not only the nature of Jesus' teachings but also the character of his very existence that provoked debate. It is a commonplace of modern Christianity to talk of Jesus as both human and God incarnate at the same time. This seems to have been a difficult concept for some early Christians to accept: in particular, the brutal, public death of Jesus on the cross seemed difficult to reconcile with his divinity. Some groups, therefore, suggested that God had not actually taken on real human flesh in Jesus, but had only given the appearance of doing so: in Greek, the word *dōkesis* is used for this appearance, from which this doctrine is called docetism. The early presence of docetic tendencies is apparent from the letters of Ignatius of Antioch. Ignatius argued that docetic doctrines undermined Christian hopes of salvation and eternal life through Jesus' suffering, death, and

resurrection. Other early Christians sought to resolve the debate about the relationship between Jesus Christ and God by asserting his humanity at the expense of his divinity. A proponent of this view was Sabellius, a Greek who served as a presbyter at Rome in the third century, and after whom the heresy Sabellianism was named. He was not the only Christian to speculate about the relationship of Jesus Christ as Son to God as Father. The Alexandrian priest Arius (see p. 143) believed that the Son did not share the same substance (*ousia*) as the Father, but was only 'like' him. His views were condemned at the council of Nicaea, which asserted in its creed that the Son and the Father were 'of the same substance' (*homoousios*).

(3) *Debates about the relationship of Christianity to Judaism*. We saw in the last chapter that there was considerable debate among early Christians about the relationship of their faith to Jewish tradition and custom. In the middle of the second century Marcion, a Christian teacher from Pontus in Asia Minor, advocated a radical break with Judaism. According to Irenaeus, whose opinion was quoted by Eusebius, Marcion argued that the Christian god was superior to the Jewish god of creation. Furthermore, he advocated that Christians should reject the Jewish scriptures (the Christian Old Testament) as well as Jewish laws, on the basis that Jesus' teachings had ushered in a new covenant that annulled much that was found in the Jewish Bible.

(4) *Debates about prophecy and the end of the world.* According to the canonical gospels, when Jesus ascended to heaven after his resurrection, he promised to return again. Some early Christians expected this second coming (known as the *parousia* in Greek) to be imminent. The New Testament contains *Revelation*, which gives details of Jesus' return and the last days of the world. *Revelation* is the only book of prophecy to

have been deemed canonical by the church (and only after long debate: p. 67), but many others existed in antiquity (see p. 75). These indicate that there was a strong prophetic tendency in some sections of early Christianity, as there was among contemporary Jews. An extreme version of Christian prophecy is associated with the name of Montanus, a native of Phrygia in Asia Minor in the late second century. The heresiologists called his movement Montanism after him, or Kataphrygian after its place of origin. Montanus' followers themselves, however, seem to have designated their movement the 'New Prophecy'. We are told that Montanus, together with two female associates, claimed to utter divinely inspired prophecies, often accompanied by an ecstatic frenzy (Eusebius, *Ecclesiastical History* 5.14–16).

Although this catalogue does not exhaust the possible ways in which Jesus and his message could be interpreted, it is instructive of some of the tendencies in early Christian thought that came to be regarded as dangerous by the emerging Christian hierarchy. Some can be explained by the fusing (and subsequent metamorphosis) of Christian teachings with other religious and philosophical traditions. This was how the heresiologists viewed the Gnostics, for example. The defenders of orthodoxy also noted that the ecstatic prophecy associated with Montanus was characteristic of pagan cults in his native Phrygia. Such adaptations of Christian doctrines were not unique to Christianity within the empire. Beyond the eastern frontier in Mesopotamia, for example, there emerged in the third century a religion named Manichaeism (after its founder Mani), which merged Christian ideas and narratives with Near Eastern traditions of a cosmic conflict between good and evil, and light and darkness.

Church fathers such as Irenaeus and Eusebius characterized such trends as a conflict between truth and error. In the sketch offered here I suggest that it was symptomatic of the engagement of Christianity with different intellectual and religious traditions. Indeed, the maintenance of orthodoxy involved discerning between the right and wrong answers to quite legitimate questions about the nature of Jesus Christ and his significance for humankind. That this entailed a delicate balancing act can be seen from the apparent ease with which certain Christian writers slipped, as it were, from orthodoxy into heresy, as their theological investigations led them to postulate theses that the institutional church came to regard as heresy. For example, the stern morality of the north African Christian Tertullian was much admired by his contemporaries; but it eventually brought him into conflict with church authorities at Carthage and Rome over his views on the redemption of sin. In the end, Tertullian's views seem to have driven him to a rigorist position quite close to Montanism. Similarly Origen, perhaps the greatest early Christian commentator on scripture, came to be regarded with suspicion. His exploitation of Platonist philosophy in his theological speculations provoked some concern in his own lifetime. After his death, however, his ideas came to be regarded as more and more dangerous, especially in the context of debates on the Trinity in the fourth century. Increasingly it seemed as if Origen's speculative patterns of thought were incompatible with later, more rigid definitions of orthodoxy.

Although certain heresies arose at specific times or in particular places, many enjoyed considerable popularity elsewhere. Valentinian *gnōsis* flourished in Rome, as did the extreme anti-Judaism of Marcion. Similarly, Montanism, although it originated in Phrygia, came to north Africa. The reputation of the second-century Syrian theologian Tatian reveals other ways in which the struggle between orthodoxy and heresy was a complicated process. He began as irreproachably orthodox, a student of Justin Martyr at Rome. After Justin's death in 165, however, his extreme views on the renunciation of the world led him to be condemned as a heretic. For all that, his *Diatessaron* (a harmonization of the four canonical gospels in a single narrative) continued to be regarded as scripture in the Syrian church until the fifth century.

The history of early Christianity, then, is as much a complex story of the spread of competing opinions on the nature of the truth as it is of a pristine orthodoxy conquering the world while swatting away the periodic challenges of heresy.

Truth, tradition, text

The success of certain Christian groups deemed to be heretical and the tendency of certain individual Christians to deviate into what was called heresy suggest that the definition of orthodoxy was a difficult task. How it came to be defined involved attitudes not only to doctrine, but also to Christian tradition and scripture. This is apparent in Irenaeus' refutation of the groups he associated with false *gnōsis*. In his writings, he sought to demonstrate that Gnostic beliefs constituted error; he was also concerned to demonstrate how the truth of orthodoxy could be established. The substance of Irenaeus' argument drew together ideas about doctrinal truth, ecclesiastical tradition, and the authority of canonical biblical texts. Irenaeus asserted that the doctrinal line of the orthodox church was the same as that preached by Jesus and his immediate followers. By contrast, he regarded the proponents of *gnōsis* as being guilty of introducing novelties into those original Christian teachings. That the teachings of the orthodox church were true to the primordial principles of Christianity could be proved by tracing its history. This link had already been drawn by the author of the *First Letter of Clement* to the Corinthians, who argued that the apostles had been appointed by God's will, and in turn bishops had been appointed by the apostles (*First Letter of Clement* 42). In Irenaeus, this connection to the earliest days of Christianity was emphasized by tracing the succession of bishops at Rome (*Against Heresies* 3.3.3).

This emphasis on what is called the apostolic tradition, through which the teachings of Jesus and the apostles were handed down intact through an unbroken line to subsequent generations, manifested itself in others areas of Christian life. Particular liturgical practices were justified by appealing to traditions stretching back to apostolic times (see p. 157). While Irenaeus used the list of bishops of Rome as a way of guaranteeing the doctrinal truth of orthodoxy, he also saw the error of heresy as possessing its own tradition and succession, albeit a corrupt one. Thus the false teachings of the Gnostics were argued to stem from the errors of the magician Simon Magus described in the New Testament (*Acts* 8.9–20). Deviation from the apostolic tradition became, for the fathers of the church, the hallmark of heresy.

The debates on orthodoxy and heresy had one further, and very basic, repercussion. While Irenaeus and others might stress the truth of their doctrinal position and their direct succession to the age of the apostles, there was only one criterion by which orthodoxy could be judged: according to which scriptures were authoritative and true. Although arguments about what should constitute the New Testament canon dragged on until the fourth century at least (see chapter 3), it was in the context of these early debates on orthodoxy and heresy that the first arguments were made for closing the canon of Christian scripture. Thus Irenaeus condemned the proliferation of gospels used by his opponents and asserted that only four gospels – those attributed to Matthew, Mark, Luke, and John – should be regarded as true. Although Irenaeus seems to have ignored or passed over certain texts that came to be included in the canon (namely *Philemon*, *2 Peter*, *3 John*, and *Jude*), he quoted from or alluded to all the others. In particular, the fourfold gospel was central to his argument. That there should only be four gospels could be proved from scripture (the four creatures mentioned at *Revelation* 4.9; and the four covenants between God and humanity made through Noah, Abraham, Moses, and Jesus) and from nature (the four points of the compass, and the four winds) (*Against Heresies* 3.11.8). However subjective we may regard such arguments, they became widely accepted by the majority of Christian groups in the course of the next century (Stanton 2004: 63–91). For all that, the battle for orthodoxy, ecclesiastical order, and the New Testament canon was not won quickly. In many parts of the Christian world, other gospels continued to be read, sometimes for centuries afterwards.

Their existence, and their implications for the unity of early Christianity, will be the focus of this chapter's case study.

Case study: the Nag Hammadi discoveries and early Christianity

The mid-1940s were good years for the accidental discovery of long-forgotten but important religious texts by peasant farmers in the Middle East. In late 1946 (or early 1947: the date is disputed) Palestinian shepherd Muhammad edh-Dhib climbed a cliff at Khirbet Qumran by the shores of the Dead Sea in search of a lost goat. Instead he stumbled into a cave where he found the first of the Dead Sea Scrolls. This find is justly famous. Rather less well known, at least until recently, is the unearthing of another cache of documents only a year or so earlier. In December 1945 an Egyptian peasant of the al-Samman tribe called Muhammad Ali went with his brother Khalifa to Nag Hammadi (located between Asyut and Luxor in the upper Nile valley) to dig for the nitrate rich soil that they used as fertilizer on their family farm. We can only imagine what state of mind Muhammad Ali was in that day. A few months earlier his father Ali, who worked as a night watchman, had killed a marauder and been murdered in his turn in an act of blood vengeance. Some time later, early in 1946, Muhammad Ali and his brothers managed to identify their father's murderer. They killed him, dismembered his body, and ate his heart, but the blood feud was to continue for years afterwards. Perhaps, then, Muhammad Ali was slightly agitated on that December day. He possibly did not feel any more comfortable when his mattock snagged on something hard on the ground that further investigation revealed to be a jar, its lid sealed with bitumen. At first Muhammad Ali was frightened that it might contain an evil spirit. Then the thought occurred to him that it might contain treasure instead. He smashed the jar open but found nothing more than a number of papyrus codices bound in leather covers. Thus was the collection of early Christian texts known as the Nag Hammadi library brought to light.

The codices came to public and scholarly attention through a complex series of transactions. Muhammad Ali's mother seems to have burned some of them as kindling; how many is not known for sure, but twelve more or less complete codices and some sheets from another survive. By the end of 1946 one codex had come into the possession of the Coptic Museum in Cairo. Another made its way onto the antiquities black market and was offered for sale in New York and Paris before it was purchased by the Jung Foundation in Zurich in 1952 and given to the institution's founder, the psychologist Carl Gustav Jung, as a present. It too was later installed in Cairo's Coptic Museum, albeit after much legal wrangling. By 1975 the Museum was in possession of all thirteen of the extant Nag Hammadi codices. Publication of the library's contents was a protracted business too for various reasons, including the jealous rivalries to which academics are sometimes given and the upheavals in Egypt following Nasser's nationalist revolution in 1953. It took the intervention of UNESCO to guarantee a full photographic edition of the codices, a task only completed in 1996 (King 2003: 150–1).

It is probably safe to say that the contents of the Nag Hammadi library have revolutionized the study of early Christianity. The codices contained dozens of texts written in Coptic – the ancient Egyptian language written in an adapted Greek alphabet that is still used by Egypt's native Christian community. But they were no ordinary texts. The first codex that came to light in Cairo in 1946, and which is numbered as Codex III in the standard reference system for the Nag Hammadi library, contained a text called the *Apocryphon [Secret Book] of John*. Scholars had known of this work earlier, from another Coptic manuscript held in Berlin that had been published at the end of the nineteenth century (King 2003: 80). Codex III from Nag Hammadi, however, contained a slightly different version of the text. Moreover, it also contained similar works: a *Gospel of the Egyptians*, two works on the existence of a supercelestial realm beyond the visible world, and *The Dialogue of the Saviour*, a collection of sayings attributed to Jesus. The codex bought by the Jung Foundation, now numbered Codex I, was filled with similar texts, including an *Apocryphon of James* and a *Gospel of Truth*.

When the whole of the Nag Hammadi library was reassembled, the range of texts was astonishing: there were gospels (including the famous *Gospel of Thomas*), apocalypses, prayers, and books of secret wisdom. The scholarly world reeled (and postgraduates were directed to learn Coptic). It was generally agreed that the texts belonged to a library belonging to Christian heretics called Gnostics, hitherto known largely through the writings of early church writers who had condemned them. The texts revealed very different traditions about Jesus and his followers. Where once the story of orthodoxy and heresy had been studied largely from the perspective of those orthodox authors whose writings had survived, now it was possible to view the debate from the other side. Nevertheless, there has been little agreement about how the Nag Hammadi texts should be used. The purpose of this case study is to present some of the potential vistas that they offer. I will not devote much space to their theological content, however; that is a topic best explored by reading the tracts themselves together with the many fine discussions of them (see the works listed in chapter 7).

Conspiracy theories

Awareness of the Nag Hammadi texts has been filtering into mainstream popular culture since their first publication in English translation in 1977 (Robinson 1988). Some perceptions of them tend towards the idiosyncratic. The details of their discovery implied that someone in antiquity had gathered them together and hidden them. Their contents suggested that they were hidden because what they contained was heretical and threatening. The fact that their publication history was controversial and protracted prompted suspicions that something sensational was being kept secret. If we add these various factors together and stir in a dollop of imagination, then we might reach the conclusion that some sort of sinister conspiracy was at work that sought to keep the Nag Hammadi library hidden from view.

This view has found its way into a recent best-selling novel. In Dan Brown's *The Da Vinci Code*, an eccentric English historian presents the writings from Nag Hammadi as a true history of Christian origins that was suppressed by the early church but which was preserved through the centuries by a secret society. He shows the chief protagonists of the novel (a Harvard professor and a French policewoman) a leather-bound volume of 'Gnostic Gospels' and explains that they contain truths about the divine feminine that the church would rather forget. For what it is worth, *The Da Vinci Code* reflects how perceptions of the Nag Hammadi library and the Dead Sea Scrolls have become confused in some recesses of the popular imagination: at one point the eccentric English historian even refers to the Nag Hammadi codices as 'scrolls'.

Perhaps it will seem gratuitous of me to mention interpretations of the Nag Hammadi texts contained in a novel – the stuff of tabloid history, it might be said. However, *The Da Vinci Code* has sold extremely well and has been responsible for raising public awareness of the Nag Hammadi library. Other books have been published explaining (and sometimes denouncing) its contents.[1] It might be objected that *The Da Vinci Code* is only fiction, that its conspiracy theories hardly merit serious attention, and that anyone who *does* take them seriously is simply misguided. Even so, some aspects of the response to the novel, particularly the angry denunciations of it, remind us that there are modern Christians who are uncomfortable with the sorts of information that are included in the Nag Hammadi texts, and that the history of early Christianity is a subject in which people continue to vest powerful emotions.

Nag Hammadi and the Gnostics

I have mentioned already that the Nag Hammadi library provoked much excitement because it preserved more or less complete versions of texts that had been mentioned in the polemical treatises composed by early Christian writers against the heresy that modern scholars have called Gnosticism. For example, Irenaeus of Lyons had recounted how the Gnostics 'introduce an infinite multitude of apocryphal and bastard scriptures that they themselves have composed to stupefy the simple and those who do not know the authentic writings' (*Against Heresies* 1.20.1, trans. Grant 1997). When he came to defend the status of the canonical gospels, Irenaeus mentioned how the Gnostics used a *Gospel of Truth* (*Against Heresies* 3.11.9). In Codex I from Nag Hammadi was found a text that began: 'The gospel of truth is a joy for those who have received from the Father of truth the gift of knowing him' (Nag Hammadi Codex I, 16.31–3, in Robinson 1988: 40). Fragments of a similar work were found in Codex XII. It is possible that this is the gospel that Irenaeus condemned. Moreover, since the publication of the Coptic *Apocryphon of John* found in the Berlin codex, it was clear that the Greek original of this text (also found in Coptic translation at Nag Hammadi) must have been the source of a Gnostic myth described by Irenaeus at *Against Heresies* 1.29. Irenaeus and the later heresiologists had described the Gnostic threat as taking many forms. For many scholars, the texts unearthed at Nag Hammadi seemed to fit neatly with this polemical characterization. As Kurt Rudolph has put it: 'The Church Fathers already were conscious of what was for them the frightening variety of the Gnostic teachings . . . This picture is in fact fully and completely confirmed by the Nag Hammadi texts' (Rudolph 1983: 53).

That is why the Nag Hammadi discoveries were considered such a revelation: texts that the heresiologists presented as objects of scorn could now be read for themselves and the judgements of the self-proclaimed champions of orthodoxy assessed. For example, Irenaeus began his description of the beliefs of the Gnostic sect known as the Valentinians as follows:

> In the invisible and unnameable heights there was a perfect Aeon [i.e. a supernatural being], prior to all. This Aeon is called Pre-beginning and Pre-Father and Abyss. Since he was incomprehensible and invisible, eternal and unbegotten, he was in silence and in rest for unlimited ages.
>
> (*Against Heresies* 1.1.1, trans. Grant 1997)

Such ideas of an incomprehensible and unperceivable pre-existing deity are found in various of the Nag Hammadi tracts. In the *Apocryphon of John*, for example, Jesus talks of the Monad, an undivided supreme deity, in the following terms:

> The Monad [is a] monarchy with nothing above it. It is [he who] exists as [God] and Father of everything, [the invisible one] who is above [everything, who is] imperishability, existing as a pure light which no [eye] can behold.
>
> (Nag Hammadi Codex II, 2.25–32, in Robinson 1988: 106)

Similar statements about the unknowability of the supreme pre-existing deity occur in other texts in the Nag Hammadi library, such as the *Tripartite Tractate* in Codex I, the *Gospel of Philip* in Codex II, and the epistle of *Eugnostos the Blessed* in Codex III.

Perhaps the most striking feature of the Nag Hammadi texts is that they present well-known biblical stories in disconcertingly unfamiliar ways. The character of Mary Magdalene appears in the canonical gospels as one of Jesus' closest associates. The *Gospel of Philip* from Nag Hammadi gives that association a new twist:

> And the companion of the [Saviour is] Mary Magdalene. [But Christ loved] her more than [all] the disciples [and used to] kiss her [often] on her [mouth]. The rest [of the disciples were offended] by it [and expressed disapproval]. They said to him, 'Why do you love her more than all of us?' The Saviour answered and said to them, 'Why do I not love you like her?'
>
> (Nag Hammadi Codex II, 63.34–64.5, in Robinson 1988: 148)

In addition to the unusual narrative, we see here also the importance attached in these texts to seeking out the divine through insight and knowledge.

Several of the Nag Hammadi writings also provide variations on the story of the world's creation found in the book of *Genesis*. In the biblical account, it is God who created the world. In the various Nag Hammadi versions it is not the supreme pre-existing deity but a lesser and imperfect creator god who does this. He is decribed, moreover, in singularly unflattering terms. The *Testimony of Truth*, for example, offers the following commentary on the biblical story of the expulsion of Adam from Eden found in *Genesis*:

> But what sort of God is this? First [he] envied Adam that he should eat of the tree of knowledge. And secondly he said, 'Adam, where are you?' And God does not have foreknowledge, that is, since he did not know this from the beginning. [And] afterwards he said, 'Let us cast him [out] of this place, lest he eat of the tree of life and live forever.' Surely he has shown himself to be a malicious envier.
>
> (Nag Hammadi Codex IX, 47.14–30. in Robinson 1988: 455)

In this version, the creator god obstructs the path to fulfilment through knowledge. The message is underlined in other texts. The *Hypostasis of the Archons* tells of how, when the creator god first saw his creation, 'he became arrogant, saying "It is I who am God, and there is none other apart from me"' (Nag Hammadi Codex II, 94.21–2, in Robinson 1988: 167). Identical views are found in two other texts from the same codex, the *Apocryphon of John* and a treatise *On the Origin of the World* (Pagels 1979: 55–6).

In addition to these variations on the Bible, the Nag Hammadi texts appeared to confirm suspicions about the conflict between orthodoxy and heresy in early Christianity that had been mooted before their discovery. In 1934 the German scholar Walter Bauer had published *Rechtgläubigkeit und Ketzerei im ältesten Christentum*, a book that finally appeared in English translation thirty-eight years later as *Orthodoxy and Heresy in Earliest Christianity* (Bauer 1972). Bauer subjected the writings of the heresiologists to penetrating criticism, arguing that investigations of heresy were 'usually done with implicit, or even explicit assent to the view that any such divergence really is a corruption of Christianity' (Bauer 1972: xxi). He went on to state:

> Perhaps – I repeat, *perhaps* – certain manifestations of Christian life that the authors of the Church renounce as 'heresies' originally had not been such at all, but, at least here and there, were the only form of the new religion – that is, for those regions they were simply 'Christianity.' The possibility also exists that their adherents constituted a majority, and that they looked down with hatred and scorn on the orthodox, who for them were the false believers.
>
> (Bauer 1972: xxii)

Bauer's book initially met with a frosty reception, but the discoveries at Nag Hammadi suggested that he had been unusually prescient. Among the texts were not only depictions of the conventional Christian God as imperfect and deceitful, but also denunciations of 'orthodox' Christianity and its hierarchy. The *Gospel of Philip*, for example, teaches that true knowledge and enlightenment are hindered by the conventional names of things. Its selection of examples is instructive:

> Names given to earthly things are very deceptive, for they divert our thoughts from what is correct to what is incorrect. Thus one who hears the word 'God' does not perceive what is correct, but perceives what is incorrect. So also with 'the Father' and 'the Son' and 'the Holy Spirit' and 'life' and 'light' and 'resurrection' and 'the Church' and all the rest.
>
> (Nag Hammadi Codex II, 53.24–32, in Robinson 1988: 142)

A more emphatic attack is found in the *Apocalypse of Peter*, where the Saviour predicts to Peter that many will subvert the truth of his message to humankind:

> And there shall be others of those who are outside our number who name themselves bishops and also deacons, as if they have received their authority from God. They bend themselves under the judgement of the leaders. Those people are dry canals.
>
> (Nag Hammadi Codex VII, 79.22–31, in Robinson 1988: 376)

It is not hard to see why heresiologists such as Irenaeus, who invested so much in the tradition and authority of the church, should have been outraged by such teachings.

The problem of Gnosticism

Thus far we have seen how various of the Nag Hammadi texts present rather different points of view on scripture, salvation, and the church from those found in the heresiologists, and that scholars felt that it was possible at last to write a comprehensive account of the Gnostics from their own perspective. It became customary to talk in positive terms about a unitary 'Gnosticism' and even a definable 'Gnostic religion'. More recently, however, the validity of these conjectures has been questioned. The titles of studies such as Michael Williams' *Rethinking 'Gnosticism'* (1996) and Karen King's *What is Gnosticism?* (2003) hint at the nature of the disquiet. The basic terminology used in scholarly literature in the area has been thrown open for debate.

One upshot of these new investigations has been to remind us that the term 'Gnosticism' is a coinage of the early modern period, originating in the debate between Protestants and Roman Catholics (King 2003: 7). Modern scholars have used the word rather indiscriminately to designate a wide range of religions and their adherents that claimed special insight or knowledge. Indeed, some modern descriptions of Gnosticism include religious traditions that would have been quite alien to Irenaeus. Thus Kurt Rudolph, who eschewed the term Gnosticism for the more neutral 'Gnosis', included the Manichaeans, followers of the third-century AD Mesopotamian mystic Mani, and even the Mandaeans, a sect still to be found in small numbers in Iran and Iraq. He also saw the influence of Gnostic thought in medieval religious groups such as the ninth-century Bogomils in the Balkans and the twelfth-century Cathars of southern France (Rudolph 1983: 326–76). The possible reverberations can be found elsewhere, in modern literature and psychological theory – it was not for nothing that one of the Nag Hammadi codices was offered as a gift to Carl Jung.[2] Scholars such as Williams and King argue that the meaning of the term Gnosticism has become so diluted as to be almost useless as a precise historical category.

This debate has important implications for the Nag Hammadi library. In the first place, it was noticed quite early on in the investigation of the manuscripts that they were hardly a cogent Gnostic collection.[3] Generally speaking, the contents of the Nag Hammadi codices present such an astonishing diversity that scholars have found it difficult to agree whether or not texts were Gnostic, and even if they were, it was debated as to what sort of Gnostic teachings they reflected. Michael Williams comments that 'the failure in reaching a consensus on classification of writings as "gnostic" or "non-gnostic" . . . suggests that the problem may lie not in natural scholarly contentiousness so much as in a category that is unacceptably vague and probably fundamentally flawed' (Williams 1996: 49). His concerns have been echoed by Karen King, who argues 'that a rhetorical term has been confused with a historical entity. There was and is no such thing as Gnosticism, if by that we mean some kind of ancient religious entity with a single origin and a distinct set of characteristics' (King 2003: 1–2).

This is perhaps a natural conclusion when dealing with a modern term like Gnosticism; but what about words that are attested in antiquity, such as Gnosis and Gnostic? Again, they seem to have a broad range of meaning and are perhaps useless for defining a precise historical phenomenon. When Irenaeus used the Greek noun *gnōsis* ('knowledge') to identify the target of his polemic, he qualified it with the adjective *pseudōnumos* ('falsely so-called'). The issue for Irenaeus was that the form of knowledge against which he was arguing was a false one. Furthermore, Irenaeus' use of this term was inseparable from his argument that the church preserved a pristine orthodoxy that stretched back to the time of Jesus and the apostles: he lifted the phrase *pseudōnumos gnōsis* from the deutero-Pauline *First Epistle to Timothy* (6.20). Indeed, the formula would be used later more arbitrarily to designate heresy more generally. When Eusebius of Caesarea stated that the challenge of heresy would be one of the cardinal themes of his *Ecclesiastical History*, the exact form of words he used to describe it was *pseudōnumos gnōsis* (*Ecclesiastical History* 1.1.1).

The word 'gnostic' (*gnōstikos* in Greek, *gnosticus* in Latin), which can be either a noun or an adjective, is hardly used with any greater precision. Whereas Irenaeus used the term in the specific context of the heretics against which he was writing, we also know that the third-century pagan Neoplatonic philosopher Plotinus wrote a tract to which his student and biographer Porphyry gave the title *Against the Gnostics* (Porphyry, *Life of Plotinus* 16).[4] Porphyry states that Plotinus' enemies were Christians who developed their particular ideas from reading philosophy, a charge also found in Irenaeus (*Against Heresies* 2.14.2). But while Irenaeus' problem with these people was that they were perverting scripture, Plotinus' gripe with them was that they were abusing philosophy. It is hard to know if Plotinus and Irenaeus were describing the same group (they were, after all, writing a hundred years apart) or whether both used the word 'Gnostic' as a general term of abuse. Furthermore, the term 'Gnostic' could be used in a positive sense by Christians themselves. Such is the case with Clement of Alexandria (*c.* 150–215). In his *Stromateis* (*Miscellanies*), he used not only *gnōstikos* but also *gnōsis* to mean an enlightened Christian and the knowledge to which that Christian could aspire (e.g. *Stromateis* 6.18). Clement did not qualify *gnōsis* with an adjective such as *pseudōnumos*, so the knowledge he is describing is not tainted with any negative connotations. He seems, moreover, to be unique in using the words *gnōstikos* and *gnōsis* in a positive rather than pejorative sense. But Clement's writings hint that there may well have been Christians who aimed at a form of enlightenment that led to a closer relationship with the divine – precisely the sort of thing that the texts from Nag Hammadi suggest repeatedly. Whether or not the authors, copyists, or readers of the Nag Hammadi texts would have called this enlightenment *gnōsis*, as Clement did, cannot be known for certain. With the exception of Clement, it seems to be a general rule that the terms *gnōstikos* and *gnōsis* were deployed polemically to castigate a theological enemy. As a term of abuse, *gnōstikos* might simply have meant a 'know it all'.

If Gnosticism is a mirage and the terms Gnosis and Gnostic of questionable validity, how are we supposed to talk of the systems of thought revealed in the Nag Hammadi texts? King suggests that 'the term "Gnosticism" will most likely be abandoned' (King 2003: 218). If it is not, she argues, then at the very least use of the term will have to be more thoughtful and rigorous, eschewing the distortions imported from the early Christian discourse on orthodoxy and heresy. Williams has offered a more radical solution, to dispense with the term forthwith! He prefers to speak of 'biblical demiurgical traditions' (Williams 1996: 51–3, 263–6) which is more descriptive of the contents of the Nag Hammadi library and related documents: the traditions are biblical in that they arise out of recastings of scripture; they are demiurgical in that they allude to the demiurge, the inferior creator divinity.

Manuscripts and heretics

Most discussions of the Nag Hammadi library have tended to analyse it in connection with heresiological polemic. In terms of their historical significance, the texts are usually examined in the context of conflict between orthodoxy and heresy in the second and third centuries AD. It is assumed, correctly I think, that the manuscripts preserve Coptic translations of earlier Greek writings.

When those Greek originals were composed has been a topic for vigorous debate. For example, Elaine Pagels has proposed that the *Gospel of Thomas* was written earlier than the canonical *Gospel of John* (Pagels 2003). She suggests that this is why the *Gospel of John* presents such a hostile portrait of the disciple Thomas as the most unenlightened of Jesus' followers (such as the 'doubting Thomas' of *John* 20.24–9). In Pagels' view, this polemical caricature of Thomas was intended to subvert the teachings contained in the gospel that went under his name and which promised secret insights into Jesus' message. Pagels' dating, however, is a hypothesis – plausible it might be, but it cannot be proved. The absence of Greek originals of the *Gospel of Thomas* and the other Nag Hammadi texts means that they cannot be dated precisely. As it is, estimates for the dates of the various writings in the collection range from the first century to the third.

Discussions of the Nag Hammadi tracts in a second- or third-century context obscure a significant detail about them. What we possess are Coptic copies, not the Greek originals, and the manuscripts can be dated quite precisely. Their leather bindings contain a material known to archaeologists as cartonnage. This is made from scraps of papyrus pasted together and it gives the book covers rigidity. Study of the cartonnage of the Nag Hammadi codices has revealed a number of dated papyrus documents, the latest of which is a receipt written in 348. This gives the earliest date for the construction of the bindings. Thus the manuscripts belong to a historical context that is 150 years later than the one in which the texts themselves are usually discussed. Any explanation of the Nag Hammadi library must take account of this.

A starting point is suggested by place names in the cartonnage scraps that suggest the library was bound (and perhaps written) in the same region of Egypt where it was discovered. In the fourth century, this was the location of a number of important monasteries led by an ascetic called Pachomius. Some scholars have suggested that the name Pachomius (in its Coptic form Pachom) can be read in the cartonnage papyri, but whether this

AD

was the famous Pachomius or some other man of that name cannot be ascertained (Goehring 2001: 236–9). These factors have prompted some scholars to postulate a fourth-century context for the Nag Hammadi library. In particular, it has been argued that the books originally belonged to a monastery library and that they were buried at a stage when the monks became worried that the contents might land them in trouble.

A possible context for the burial has been sought in a letter written in AD 367 by bishop Athanasius of Alexandria. This document is the thirty-ninth in a collection known as his *Festal Letters* – letters that he wrote each Easter to Egyptian Christians on matters of discipline. *Festal Letter* 39 is concerned with 'the teaching of the worship of God', which, Athanasius stated, could be found only in scripture. In this letter, for the first time, we have a list of the twenty-seven books that now constitute the New Testament canon. Athanasius also noted certain non-canonical works – such as the *Wisdom of Solomon*, the *Wisdom of Sirach*, *Judith*, *Tobit*, the *Shepherd* of Hermas, and the *Didache* – that could be used for Christian instruction. Then he noted:

> Nevertheless, the former books [i.e. scripture] are canonised; the latter are (only) read; and there is no mention of the apocryphal books. Rather (the category of the apocrypha) is an invention of the heretics, who write these books whenever they want and grant and bestow on them dates, so that, by publishing them as if they were ancient, they might have a pretext for deceiving simple folk.
>
> (Athanasius, *Festal Letter* 39, trans. Brakke 1995: 330)

Athanasius ordered such apocryphal books to be rejected. It is suggested, therefore, that a community of monks, having received the letter, diligently collected any codices of heretical works they might possess, sealed them in a jar, and buried them where they lay hidden until Muhammad Ali chanced upon them.

Attractive though this story is, it is mainly a whimsical conjecture built on circumstantial evidence. Many scholars have rejected it outright (Rousseau 1999: xvii–xxxiii, 19–28). A recent examination of the evidence remarks circumspectly: 'While it may be less satisfying not to argue for a specific provenance, it may be, in the end, all we know' (Goehring 2001: 241). In spite of this it is clear that somebody in Egypt in the middle of the fourth century thought it was worth assembling these texts into codices. But who were they, and why did they do so? One suggestion is that the Nag Hammadi codices were not the property of heretics but were part of a library compiled for heresiological purposes, a collection of reference material consulted by those who sought to refute their teachings. Another, based on the different styles of handwriting and binding techniques found in the codices, is that the Nag Hammadi collection, even if it was found together, was assembled from disparate libraries. All such suggestions are conjectural: the codices themselves yield little information about who used them.

Even if it is impossible to identify categorically the owners and readers of the Nag Hammadi libraries, the very existence of the manuscripts points to something significant. They imply that there was in fourth-century Egypt some group (perhaps groups) that was reproducing and reading texts that traditional church history associates with the second and third centuries. This traditional form of church history owes its origins to Eusebius of Caesarea: for him, ecclesiastical history was in large measure a narrative of the triumph of orthodox, united, and universal Christianity over heretical and schismatic enemies who fell by the wayside. In large measure, modern histories of the church, and of Christianity more generally, have adopted this narrative framework. But the reality seems to have been considerably messier. For example, during the reign of the emperor Decius (249–50), when Christians were being forced to offer sacrifice to the pagan gods (see chapter 6), there arose at Rome a schism between those who had given in to the imperial demands and a group of hardliners led by the priest Novatianus. His cause was taken up by a Carthaginian cleric called (confusingly) Novatus, and their followers were known as the Novatians. The Novatian schism from the rest of the church is usually considered in a third-century context, which is where Eusebius discusses it (*Ecclesiastical History* 6.43–6). Yet a distinct Novatian church persisted long afterwards, and not just in Rome and Carthage. The fifth-century ecclesiastical historians Socrates and Sozomen mention that in their own day there was a Novatian church with its own bishop at Constantinople, and that Novatian communities could be found in neighbouring parts of Asia Minor (Mitchell 1993: II, 96–100). Meanwhile, inscriptions from Phrygia in northern Asia Minor attest to the presence there of Novatian and Montanist Christian groups throughout the fourth century and beyond (Mitchell 1993: II, 100–8). Similarly, histories of the debate over the nature of the Trinity and the nature of the relationship between Christ and God the Father known as the Arian controversy normally locate it in the fourth century. This conflict is sometimes described as coming to an end within the fourth century, when the institutional church reaffirmed the creed of Nicaea at the council of Constantinople in 381. Even after this, however, Christians whose beliefs can be categorized as 'Arian' continued to exist – the early medieval Gothic kings of Spain only renounced their Arianism and sought to bring their realm into the Catholic fold in the late sixth century.[5]

In this context, we can postulate that the existence of the Nag Hammadi codices shows that there were Christians in fourth-century Egypt with an interest in doctrines that did not conform to the church's strict definitions of orthodoxy. Moreover, they were not the only Egyptians in late antiquity with such tastes. Athanasius' thirty-ninth *Festal Letter* presupposes that this was the case. It can be proved also from more positive evidence. In 1886–7, excavations at Akhmim, also in upper Egypt, revealed the tomb of a monk datable to any time between the eighth and twelfth centuries. In the tomb was found a seventh-century parchment codex containing an extract from a gospel written from the perspective of Jesus' disciple Peter. Other fragments of this *Gospel of Peter* have been found on papyrus elsewhere in Egypt (Ehrman 2003: 13–28). But this text too had been condemned, as

Eusebius tells us, in the early third century by bishop Serapion of Antioch in Syria (Eusebius, *Ecclesiastical History* 6.12). For all that, it was still being read in Egypt some four hundred years later. The discoveries at Akhmim and Nag Hammadi, together with other stray fragments and manuscripts, suggest that there was a broad spectrum of interests, and perhaps also of beliefs, among Egyptian Christians throughout antiquity and into the early middle ages. Such material – together with evidence for the tenacity of heterodox and schismatic groups elsewhere in the Mediterranean world – points to a diversity in early Christianity that is not always highlighted in traditional narratives of church history.

Ancient texts and modern readers

This survey of the implications raised by the Nag Hammadi discoveries has touched repeatedly on the problem of how they should be interpreted within a framework of Christian history that owes much to models derived from early church writers like Irenaeus and Eusebius. It is unlikely, I suspect, that a scholarly consensus will be reached any time soon on the Nag Hammadi library. The various reactions to it, however, remind us that the interpretation of early Christianity is often driven by the personal sympathies of modern readers. Consider, for example, the *Gospel of Thomas*. This text has provoked so much debate, to the extent that some would advocate reopening the canon and including this gospel in an expanded New Testament (cf. Baarda 2003: 46–7). That may never happen, and some would say it *should* never happen. The prospect of any such debate would certainly have outraged Irenaeus. Yet the very fact that such a debate is happening reveals that some modern Christians have found something attractive in what is usually categorized as an apocryphal, even heretical gospel. In North America, for instance, it has been adopted as a favoured text by Christian reading groups dissatisfied with the teachings of the established churches.[6] Indeed, the modern appeal of texts from the Nag Hammadi library is probably broader still: when one new translation of the texts (Layton 1987) was reissued in paperback in 1995, its cover bore an illustration rich with esoteric symbolism and the new subtitle 'ancient wisdom for the new age'. If you eat lentils, hug trees, and don't wash, then this could be the book for you. . . .

The debate on the Nag Hammadi library is instructive about the passions that are invested in the quest for early Christianity. One of the most ardent popularizers of the texts in recent decades has been the Princeton historian Elaine Pagels. Her books often begin with confessional passages about her own spiritual longings that have impelled her to read these extraordinary texts. Her studies of the Nag Hammadi writings have drawn criticism on grounds that show how the boundaries between scholarship and faith can become blurred. One such critique reads:

> For some researchers, Elaine Pagels, for example, this process [i.e. the disappearance of the 'Gnostic' tradition] has seemed a great betrayal, the suppression of free-thinking and feminism by totalitarian bishops. But such a judgment fails to grasp the insidious nature of the Gnostic alternative and the tenuous position of bishops in the days of the determinative struggle.
>
> (Young 1991: 18–19)

More recently, it has been written of the whole question:

> [The *Gospel of Thomas*] is now being referred to by some as 'the fifth gospel' in order to shore up claims that its earlier layers provide access to a Jesus more congenial today than the Jesus portrayed by New Testament writers . . . [T]he assumption in some circles that Q and Thomas are 'gospel' for humankind today is to be repudiated. The primary reason for that is theological, not historical . . . In essence, this was Irenaeus' answer at the end of the second century. I believe that it still has theological validity today.
>
> (Stanton 2004: 3–4)

Such comments illustrate the different levels at which the debate on the Nag Hammadi library in particular and early Christianity in general takes place. Modern interpretations reveal much not only about the ancient texts, but also about their modern readers.

Chapter 6

Confronting Babylon: early Christianity and the Roman empire

Consider the following episodes from the New Testament accounts of Jesus' life, all of them familiar to anyone who reads the gospels:

> In those days a decree went out from Caesar Augustus that the whole inhabited world should be registered. This, the first registration [i.e. census], happened when Quirinius was governor of Syria.
>
> (*Luke* 2.1–2)

> [The Pharisees said to Jesus:] 'Tell us, then, what you think. Is it lawful to pay taxes to Caesar, or not?' But Jesus, aware of their malice, said, 'Why put me to the test, you hypocrites? Show me the money for the tax.' And they brought him a *denarius* [coin]. And Jesus said to them, 'Whose image and inscription is this?' They said, 'Caesar's.' Then he said to them, 'Give therefore to Caesar what is Caesar's, and to God what is God's.'
>
> (*Matthew* 22.17–21; cf. *Mark* 12.14–17; *Luke* 20.22–5)

> Pilate also wrote a placard and put it on the cross; it read, 'Jesus of Nazareth, the King of the Jews.' Many of the Jews read this placard, for the place where Jesus was crucified was near the city; and it was written in Hebrew, in Latin, and in Greek.
>
> (*John* 19.19–20; cf. *Matthew* 27.37; *Mark* 15.26; *Luke* 23.38)

Such passages are a reminder that Christianity originated in a world dominated by the political power of Rome. In early Christian literature, the empire and its institutions are omnipresent, punctuating not only Jesus' life, but also that of the religious movement that recognized him as the Messiah. The common images of early Christianity that we surveyed at the beginning of chapter 4 testify to this ubiquitous Roman presence: the crucified Jesus and Christians facing lions in the arena were consequences, after all, of early Christianity's collision with the imperial authorities.

In this chapter I want to explore the interrelationship between early Christianity and the institutions of the Roman empire. We have already considered some aspects of this question when we looked at Paul's missionary journeys (chapter 4). Yet what perhaps characterized imperial Rome's dealings with emerging Christianity more than anything else were the sporadic persecutions to which Christians were subjected. Eusebius of Caesarea's positive view that God had permitted the establishment of the Roman empire to facilitate the spread of the gospel message (p. 39) would seem, on the face of it, to be one that persecuted Christians in the centuries before Constantine would have been unlikely to share. I will begin, therefore, with a survey of persecutions in the pre-Constantinian period, elucidating some of the problems of interpretation that they present. Then I will examine some reasons why Christians might have felt alienated from the society and institutions of the Roman empire. This does not tell the whole story, however, so my next section will explore how and why some early Christians, even before Constantine's conversion, could protest their loyalty to the Roman empire and even seek its protection. The reasons for this diversity of experience are to be sought in the precise contexts within which persecution (and toleration) occurred. To that end, the case study that concludes this chapter will examine one very early instance of confrontation between Christianity and the empire.

An age of persecutions?

The history of early Christianity before Constantine's conversion can sometimes seem to be dominated by conflict with the Roman empire and outbreaks of persecution, when Christians were tortured and killed for their beliefs. We have already seen that tales of persecution and martyrdom fascinated later generations of Christians from Eusebius in late antiquity, through the middle ages and beyond (chapter 2). Indeed, vivid images of persecution and martyrdom often dominate the modern perception of early Christianity, as if they were broadly representative of the early Christian experience. Among the more influential, perhaps, is the painting *The Last Prayer* by J.-L. Gérôme (1824–1904), which shows a scene from the circus in Rome: in the background, some Christians have been fixed to burning crosses, while others kneel in prayer as they await their fate; in the foreground, two lions and a tiger emerge from a tunnel. This image has been reproduced on the covers of books dealing with the early Christians.[1] Its iconography has been echoed also in more popular media, for example in the depiction of the fate of Christians under the emperor Nero (played by a splendidly demented Peter Ustinov) in the 1951 film *Quo Vadis*.

Some of the verdicts pronounced on Christianity by pagan Romans suggest implacable hostility (see p. 198). Yet the main source for our grim picture of an age of persecutions and martyrs before Constantine is to be found in the writings of Christians themselves. In the early fourth century, Eusebius of Caesarea not only made persecution and martyrdom one of the central themes of his *Ecclesiastical History*, but also dealt with the subject in his *Martyrs of Palestine*. Around the same time, Lactantius devoted his treatise *On the Deaths of the Persecutors* to recounting Roman hostility to the Christians and, equally to the point, the ignominious demises suffered by those emperors who oppressed the church. Both Eusebius and Lactantius saw oppression of Christianity culminating in their own day with the so-called 'great' persecution initiated in 303–4 by the tetrarchic emperor Diocletian (284–305), which was swiftly followed by the conversion of Constantine (306–37). These narratives are supplemented by other texts, such as the letters of Cyprian of Carthage and the acts (from *acta*, meaning the records of court proceedings) of various martyrs. The spectre of persecution almost seems to haunt the literary output of early Christianity. Taken together, such sources often paint a bleak picture of a time when it seemed that the empire was waging a war against the Christians. Indeed, the Greek word for war, *polemos*, is used by Eusebius of Caesarea to describe the persecutions (*Ecclesiastical History* 1.1.2; 8.13.10).

Although the information given in such accounts is useful, the overall picture it yields is problematic. Some descriptions of persecution appear in texts that were written as critiques of Christians who had given in too easily to demands from the imperial authorities to offer sacrifice to the pagan gods, or against heretics who denigrated the value of martyrdom. These polemical contexts of early Christian accounts of persecution need to be weighed carefully if the texts themselves are not to mislead. For example, Eusebius' descriptions of persecutions in his *Ecclesiastical History* were far from transparent, but were calibrated to support his thesis that the Roman empire had a positive role to play in God's plan for humankind. When Christians were allowed to live in peace, he argued, the empire flourished (*Ecclesiastical History* 8.13.9–13). Prudent emperors were opposed to indiscriminate persecution (Trajan at 3.33; Hadrian at 4.9; Antoninus Pius at 5.13; Gallienus at 7.13). By contrast, those emperors who persecuted were clearly tyrants. Thus Eusebius introduced his narrative of Nero's persecution by emphasizing the emperor's overall depravity (2.25.1–2), while the account of Domitian's anti-Christian measures was preceded by a description of his capricious cruelty (3.17). When Eusebius came to the purges of his own day, he stressed the immorality of persecutors such as Maxentius and Maximinus Daia (8.14) – a view echoed in the writings of Lactantius. Eusebius similarly associated persecution with emperors who came to the throne through bloodshed, overthrowing rulers who had been favourably disposed to Christians, for example when Maximinus Thrax replaced Alexander Severus (6.28), and when Decius seized the throne from Philip the Arab (6.34). In addition, Eusebius could attribute persecution also to the shortcomings of Christians themselves. The outbreak of Diocletian's persecution, for example, had been preceded by decades of peace for the Christians, during which, Eusebius maintained, they had grown proud, lazy, and neglectful of their duties towards God. The resumption of hostilities was explained by Eusebius as the fulfilment of biblical prophecy that God would wreak vengeance on his people for their crimes against him (8.1.7–9). Eusebius' account of the persecutions was shaped, therefore, by his apologetical agenda. Moreover, it is littered with inconsistencies, errors, and omissions that make much of it doubtful history (Barnes 1971: 155–6).

A further difficulty with the traditional account (whether it is found in ancient sources or regurgitated in sentimentally pious modern works) is that it tends to treat the experience of Christians in something like isolation from the broader context of Roman law and administration within which the persecutions were enacted. For example, by laying emphasis on the horrors experienced by the Christians, it ignores the fact that brutal punishments were a common enough reality in the Roman empire. Moreover, killing people (criminals in the main) in gruesomely inventive ways in venues for public entertainment, such as the amphitheatre or circus, was a widespread phenomenon (Coleman 1990), not just a special form of sadism reserved for Christians. Thus the experiences of the early Christians at times of persecution were hardly unique.

Similarly, the portrait of the persecutions in Christian accounts (both ancient and modern) as a determined effort to expunge the religion entirely seems to be based on an overly optimistic impression of the efficacy of Roman government. All too often, it is assumed that the Roman empire was rather like a modern nation (albeit one of a decidedly totalitarian hue) that could impose its laws wherever and whenever it pleased with comparative ease. Such a view is implicit in Edward Gibbon's oft-quoted verdict on Roman government in the second century AD:

> If a man were called upon to fix the period in the history of the world, during which the condition of the human race was most happy and prosperous, he would, without hesitation, name that which elapsed from the death of Domitian to the accession of Commodus. The vast extent of the Roman Empire was governed by absolute power, under the guidance of virtue and wisdom. The armies were restrained by the firm but gentle hand of four successive emperors, whose characters and authority commanded universal respect.
>
> (Gibbon 1776–88 [1994]: I, 103)

These days historians of the Roman world are likely to contend that, in many respects, the efficacy of imperial administration was altogether more limited. There was little scope for any emperor (even one of Gibbon's 'good' ones) to have a direct influence on anything more than the small groups of individuals with whom he came into direct contact (either in person or through the process of law), much less the 'human race' as a whole. Until the reforms of the emperor Diocletian in the late third century, the bureaucratic apparatus of the imperial administration was too small to allow for a more intrusive style of government. Even the emperor's deputies in the provinces, his governors, could rely on only a small body of advisors and troops to help them with the business of administration. In the absence of large numbers of civil servants, therefore, the Romans had to rely on the cooperation of local elites the length and breadth of the empire to see that government ran smoothly (Veyne 1990). Such elites were based mainly in urban centres: for this reason the cities of the empire have been characterized as 'the secret of government without bureaucracy' (Garnsey and Saller 1987: 26).

If we view Roman government in this way, then the persecutions of the Christians begin to take on a very different complexion. Far from representing some kind of total war against the Christians by the Roman authorities, most persecutions were emphatically local events. Thus, while Eusebius might describe Nero as beginning 'to take up arms against the worship of the God of the universe' (*Ecclesiastical History* 2.25.1), this emperor's persecution was limited to the city of Rome. Eusebius also contended that Nero's campaign was renewed by Domitian (3.17), but again the evidence suggests a more limited impact. Some executions took place at Rome. There are signs in the New Testament *First Epistle of Peter* and *Revelation* that Christians in Asia Minor were being repressed also at this time (see p. 202), but this purge is more likely to have been provoked by a local famine than by any imperial directive (Frend 1965: 211–17). It looks likely that 'the tradition of Domitian the persecutor has been vastly exaggerated' (Jones 1992: 119).

Even when persecution was more widespread, its effect seems to have been sporadic. The reign of Marcus Aurelius (161–80) saw a number of purges, but they seem to have occurred mainly in the years 164–8 and 176–8 and to have been concentrated in Asia Minor, with an additional outburst also at Lyons in Gaul in 177. At no point are we told explicitly why these persecutions occurred, but it seems that local factors were the most obvious cause (Frend 1965: 5, 268–94). None of this is to say that the Roman imperial authorities were innocent of complicity in the persecutions. Martyrs were executed for their steadfast faith, but executions could only be ordered by imperial officers (governors in the provinces; prefects in Italy). That is why, until the end of the third century, persecution and martyrdom were exclusively urban phenomena: provincials may well have harboured anti-Christian feelings, but they needed the presence of a governor, holding his assize courts in the main cities, to condemn Christians to death (Bowersock 1995: 41–57).

Of course, there were times when the Roman government was able to envisage universal, rather than local, persecutions. Three are usually cited: under Decius (249–51), in the latter years of the reign of Valerian (257–9), and the 'great' persecution begun by Diocletian in 303–4, which lasted in some parts of the empire for ten years. More than any other, Diocletian's persecution seems to have been envisaged as applying to the whole of the Roman empire. There can be no denying that episodes in this anti-Christian purge were savage indeed. Consider, for example, the following haunting tale of the fate of an unnamed village in Asia Minor:

> At this time soldiers surrounded a small town in Phrygia, of which the inhabitants were all Christians, every man of them, and setting fire to it burnt them, along with the young children and women as they were calling on the God of all. The reason for this was that all the inhabitants of the town to a man, including its mayor (*logistēs*) and magistrates (*stratēgoi*) with all the officials and the whole people, confessed themselves Christians and refused to obey those who ordered them to commit idolatry.
>
> (Eusebius of Caesarea, *Ecclesiastical History* 8.11.1: adapted from Lawlor and Oulton 1927–8)

Yet when we consider the evidence for Diocletian's persecution as a whole, it is apparent that there was a considerable gap between imperial ambition and actual implementation. The efficacy of the imperial orders was dependent on the administration's resources for carrying them out. In some places, like the Phrygian village mentioned above, Diocletian and his fellow emperors were able to send troops to effect the purge. Some governors plainly enforced the imperial edicts with enthusiasm; others, however, seem to have done little. In some parts of the empire, such as Britain, Gaul, and Spain, the persecution seems to have had little if any impact (Humphries forthcoming c). Perhaps the most telling indication of the limits of persecution is the most obvious: it did not work (Frend 1959; Drake forthcoming).

A major difficulty in trying to see the persecutions as historical events arises from our almost total dependence on Christian sources (for an exception, see the case study at the end of this chapter). In some cases, such as Eusebius and Lactantius, they quote decrees of individual emperors. Interestingly, however, such quotations are mainly drawn from imperial proclamations bringing persecutions to an end, not from those that ushered them in (we have not a single word, for example, of any of Diocletian's four persecution edicts of 303–4). The result is that we rely on Christian sources not only for quotations from and summaries of imperial documents, but also for the historical framework within which to interpret them. Through their scrutiny of such texts, modern scholars generally agree that there was no universal edict against the Christians before the middle of the third century, even if local persecutions were quite common (Ste Croix 1963; Barnes 1968).

A major change in Roman policy occurred with the accession of the emperor Decius in 249. Christian sources give the impression that Decius compelled Christians throughout the empire to offer sacrifice (e.g. *Passion of Pionius* 3.1). Other contemporary Christian accounts, such as those preserved in the correspondence of Cyprian of Carthage or Dionysius of Alexandria (quoted by Eusebius, *Ecclesiastical History* 6.40–2), indicate that considerable disruption and hardship was unleashed upon the church. There also survive some forty-four papyrus certificates from Egypt that record sacrifices offered by individuals in accordance with Decius' orders. Some of these, however, suggest that sacrifices were demanded of the empire's population generally – one records the sacrifices offered by a pagan priestess – and not just the Christians. Although this Egyptian evidence is the most voluminous non-Christian record of religious affairs under Decius, there are hints from elsewhere in the empire of similar activities. For instance, an inscription from Aphrodisias in western Asia Minor records a letter from Decius thanking the city's population for their expressions of goodwill on his accession and noting how they 'made proper sacrifice and prayers' (Reynolds 1982: 141). Such evidence has prompted some scholars to doubt that Decius' policy amounted to a deliberate persecution. They see it, rather, as an effort to secure the goodwill of the gods, Rome's traditional defenders, for the emperor and his subjects at a time when the empire's fortunes were flagging because of barbarian invasions, civil war, and economic malaise. Since they could not sacrifice to pagan gods, the Christians simply fell foul of Decius' ostentatious display of traditional piety. Other scholars have objected, however, that by the mid-third century it would have been reasonably obvious to an emperor and his advisors that a command to universal sacrifice would have the effect of ensnaring Christians. Hence Decius' edict may well have been designed from the outset to punish Christians, whose 'atheism' towards the traditional gods could be regarded as putting the emperor and the empire in serious peril (Rives 1999).

This last factor is perhaps the most important explanation of why persecutions happened at all. Christian disregard for traditional religion – not just at Rome, but in communities throughout the empire – could be seen as subverting the *pax deorum* ('peace of the gods'), the compact between heaven and earth that was secured through acts of piety such as sacrifice and kept the gods favourable to humankind. The persecuting authorities repeatedly demanded sacrifice of those accused of being Christians: only through the performance of this ritual could prisoners demonstrate their devotion to the gods whose power held the universe in balance. Any disaster, natural or political, could prompt doubts about the gods' continued goodwill and provoke a frenzied quest for anyone likely to have offended the powers in heaven. Tertullian remarked pithily that if the Tiber flooded or the Nile did not, if there was drought, earthquake, famine or plague, then the popular cry went up: 'The Christians to the lion!' (*Apology* 40.1). Although Tertullian went on to joke about the absurdity of throwing the Christian multitude to a single beast, the connection between natural disasters and persecutions was real enough. A letter from Firmilian, bishop of Caesarea in Cappadocia, to Cyprian of Carthage records how, in the reign of Alexander Severus (222–35), a series of violent earthquakes in Cappadocia and Pontus provoked a local persecution (Cyprian, *Letters* 75.10.1). Aspirations towards piety for the sake of the prosperity of the empire are explicit in surviving statements made by the persecuting authorities themselves. The pagan emperor Galerius, as he lay dying painfully from a horrific disease in 311, issued an edict that halted the persecution, but which explained why he (and Diocletian) had embarked on the policy in the first place:

> Among the other measures which we are constantly drawing up in the interest and for the good of the state, we had previously wished to restore everything in accordance with the ancient laws and public order of the Romans, and to see to it that the Christians too, who had abandoned the doctrine [*secta*] of their own forefathers, should return to a sound mind.
>
> (Lactantius, *On the Deaths of the Persecutors* 34.1: a Greek translation of the same edict is given in Eusebius of Caesarea, *Ecclesiastical History* 8.17.6)

Other decrees of the tetrarchic emperors, such as an edict on incest from 295, the command to persecute the Manichaeans *c.* 300, and the famous edict on maximum prices of 301/2, similarly drew a connection between tradition, religion, and imperial prosperity (Humphries forthcoming c).

Christian alienation from Roman society

That the persecutions happened at all reflects not only what the Romans (whether emperors, governors, or provincials) thought of Christians, but also how the Christians had made themselves in some ways a distinctive group within the empire's population. This was not a question of simple distinctions: we have already seen how the division between Christianity and Judaism was one where the boundaries were often hard to identify precisely (chapter 4). In terms of the society of the Roman empire, the situation of Christians is neatly encapsulated in the second-century *Epistle to Diognetus* which states that Christians were no different from the empire's other inhabitants in terms of where they lived or how they spoke, but 'that they live as strangers in their own lands, share everything as citizens, and suffer everything as foreigners' (*Epistle to Diognetus* 5.5).

The writings of Tertullian provide a lively insight into such problems as they were faced by the Christians of Carthage in the late second and early third centuries. In a series of works, Tertullian warned his fellow Christians of the temptations to sin that surrounded them. His *On Spectacles* sought to show that attendance at shows in the circus, theatre, and arena was an offence to God because such entertainments were saturated in the trappings of pagan cult. The worship of the pagan gods was the focus of his *On Idolatry*: Tertullian instructed his audience to be alert for the dangers that lurked in all sorts of activities, from observance of the calendar, to the celebration of imperial victories, to the formulae used for swearing everyday contracts. For Tertullian, such temptations lay everywhere: he even wrote a work *On the Dress of Women* excoriating women for their fancy clothes, make up, and dyed hair; the same work also condemned men who liked to trim their beards into fashionable goatees or use cosmetics. In almost every way, it seemed, the Christian found himself (or herself) at odds with the mundane realities of Roman lifestyles.

We have already touched upon the most basic distinction that set Christians apart from the pagans: religion and religious observance. The Christians believed that there was only one God, whose plan for humanity had been mediated through his son Jesus, the Messiah. Such monotheism (as the worship of a single, exclusive deity is called, as distinct from polytheism, the worship of many gods) was not unique to the Christians. The Jews were monotheists too, after all. Like the Christians, the Jews had often been reviled by the pagan inhabitants of the Graeco-Roman world.

Sometimes they were the victims of violent pogroms. Yet they never experienced systematic persecution, as the Christians did (at least not until the empire itself became Christian). This is because the Jews possessed something that the Christians did not: an ancient heritage. The historian Tacitus, who wrote a hostile portrait of the Jews in the early second century, observed that Jewish practices, however repugnant they might be (for pagans), were 'sanctioned by their antiquity' (*Histories* 5.5). Like many good, old-fashioned Romans, Tacitus was devoted to the maintenance of the *mos maiorum* – long-standing traditions established by the ancestors. Hence the Jews, however despicable he might find them, deserved toleration because their social and religious traditions originated in the dim, distant past. This was not something the Christians could claim. As the biographer Suetonius put it, Christianity was 'a new and malevolent superstition' (*superstitio nova ac malefica*: *Life of Nero* 16.2).

In the view of traditionalist Romans, one of the damning features of Christianity was its origin in comparatively recent historical times. Equally unfortunate, here was a religion that regarded as divine a man who had been executed as a criminal by a Roman governor (Tacitus, *Annals* 15.44.3–4). Although most Christians claimed the Jewish scriptures for themselves as their Old Testament, the continued existence of Judaism after Jesus served to emphasize for many pagans that Christianity was a pernicious novelty. This had been the argument of the pagan philosopher Celsus in the later second century; it was also made, in the mid-fourth century, by the emperor Julian. The power of tradition and antiquity could make life difficult for any cult when it was confronted by Roman power. At some time around the year 300 (the precise date is the subject of disagreement), the emperor Diocletian wrote to the proconsul of Africa ordering him to hunt out the Manichaeans. This religion had been founded in the third century by the Mesopotamian mystic Mani. It did not help that the cult originated in the territory of Persia, one of Diocletian's bitterest enemies. But equally reprehensible was the novelty of the religion: in his letter to the proconsul, Diocletian stated that it was simply not right that a 'new', 'hitherto unknown', and 'depraved' sect should seek to overturn the benefits of Rome's ancestral religion (*Comparison of Roman and Mosaic Law* 15.3).

That Christian monotheists rejected the gods worshipped by pagans across the empire also had social ramifications that served to mark out Christianity as distinctive. Taking their lead from Old Testament prohibitions on idolatry, early Christian writers from Paul onwards argued that no Christian could participate in the public sacrificial rituals that were central to Graeco-Roman religious practice. Hence the test of sacrifice during periods of persecution. From the early second century, Roman and municipal officials were aware that devout Christians could not perform this ritual, so it could usefully be deployed as a way of ensnaring them (see the case study at the end of this chapter). But the insistence on sacrifice had a positive significance too: by making offerings to the gods, those accused of being Christians could advertise publicly that they really belonged to the pagan community. Rejection of sacrifice meant not only that Christians refused to take part in the central rituals of pagan cult, but also that they could neither eat the sacrificial meat nor participate in the public feasting that sometimes accompanied pagan rites (thus Paul, *1 Corinthians* 8). Rejection of pagan gods and rituals, therefore, went hand-in-hand with ostentatious exclusion from some central aspects of life in ancient communities.

Such behaviour could be construed as subverting the basic social order. It could be surmised also from other Christian practices. Since they lived, for much of the first three centuries, under the intermittent threat of persecution, Christians were prone to conduct their religious gatherings in seclusion. This could provoke the suspicion of imperial and local authorities. The Romans associated secretive behaviour with tendencies towards perversion and criminality. This link is apparent in the description offered by the historian Livy (writing under the emperor Augustus) of the orgies and conspiracies that accompanied the secret rites of Bacchus, which had been suppressed by the senate in 186 BC (Livy 39.8–14). The secrecy surrounding Christian rituals gave rise to similar suspicions. Snippets of information about Christian rituals, such as the symbolic consumption of the body and blood of Christ in the Eucharist, could prompt outlandish rumours that the Christians indulged in cannibalism at their clandestine meetings (Minucius Felix, *Octavius* 9.5). We will touch on this topic again in this chapter's case study.

Another aspect of Christian behaviour that marked the new religion as different derived from its emphasis on moral strictness and renunciation of the world and the temptations it offered to the body (Brown 1988). This is not to say that Romans were moral degenerates, as they are often portrayed in Christian confessional discourse (in Tertullian, for instance). That Livy's senators should have been so appalled by the dissipation of the worshippers of Bacchus is but one reflection of a Roman tradition of stern morality. For the Christians, however, the moral battle between good and evil was equated with a struggle within them between the spirit and the flesh. By focusing on the needs of the spirit, Christians hoped to triumph over the weaknesses of the flesh for gluttony and sexual immorality. This renunciation of the temptations offered to the flesh could lead to physical withdrawal from the world. By the end of the third century, the deserts of Egypt and the Middle East were coming to be occupied by individuals who sought to subject their physical bodies to the most rigorous deprivations of all the fleshly temptations that the world had to offer. The behaviour of such individuals was described as *askēsis*, the Greek term for the tough training regimen to which athletes adhered. Such 'athletes for God' were the first Christian ascetics, from whose endeavours the monastic movement developed (Harmless 2004). Of course, this was not a purely Christian phenomenon: Jewish groups, such as the Essenes, had also withdrawn to the desert to pursue their love of God free from the temptations of the flesh. Even so, the Christian enthusiasm for asceticism could be viewed as another manifestation of their broader rejection of the normal structures of society. This was certainly the case especially in the fourth and fifth centuries, when ascetic tendencies – particularly when they were espoused by members of the social elite, such as aristocratic women – could be regarded as undermining the traditional values that bound society together (Brown 1988; Salzman 2002: 167–9).

Christians might protest that such spiritual rigour made them morally superior to their pagan contemporaries. And yet, their very profession of Christianity could be deemed to threaten the total subversion of the moral norms of imperial society. At Carthage in 203, for example, a young woman of high status called Perpetua was arrested for her adherence to Christianity. There survives an account of her trial, some of it penned (it seems) by Perpetua herself and therefore, as the work of a female author, the subject of much study (e.g. Salisbury 1998). Although the text recounts Perpetua's story from a Christian perspective, it provides many insights into how pagans regarded Christianity as threatening. One episode describes how her father, visiting her in prison, appealed to her to take pity on his old age and 'give up [her] pride' (*Passion of Perpetua* 5.4). Perpetua refused, however, to her father's despair. Later, when she was brought before the governor Hilarianus for trial, her father came before the tribunal, this time with her infant son for whose sake he begged Perpetua to offer sacrifice to the gods. Hilarianus too asked Perpetua to have consideration for her father and son, but to no avail (*Passion of Perpetua* 6). Not even the bonds of family, the very basis of the Roman community, were enough to persuade Perpetua to recant. For her own part, she claimed to have experienced visions that confirmed to her that her spirit would be victorious: worldly ties and bodily punishments could not persuade her otherwise. In the end, together with the slave girl Felicitas, Perpetua was killed in bloody spectacles staged in the amphitheatre to commemorate the birthday of the reigning emperor's son.

Other accounts of martyrdom indicate the lengths to which Roman officials would go in an attempt to get Christians to abjure their faith: even when the prisoner was on the very brink of execution, sacrifice was demanded (*Passion of Pionius* 21). The determination of Christians to suffer death for the sake of Christ probably struck many pagans as sheer madness – the dying

Galerius, after all, sought to justify the 'great' persecution as aiming to bring Christians back to soundness of mind (see p. 196). In such circumstances we can express little surprise at the response of Arrius Antoninus, governor of the province of Asia in the mid-180s, when he was confronted by Christians who demanded that he martyr them. The governor shrugged them off, however, with the suggestion that if death was what they really wanted then they could hang themselves or throw themselves off cliffs (Tertullian, *To Scapula* 5.1).

Christian attitudes to the Roman empire

The incidence of persecution and Christian rejection of Graeco-Roman social and religious institutions might suggest that Christianity existed in a condition of continual confrontation with the culture within which it developed. The relationship, however, was rather more ambiguous, with early Christian attitudes to the Roman empire encompassing both outright hostility and efforts at accommodation. This is apparent already in the New Testament. *Revelation* gives a particularly bleak picture of the Christian view of the empire, refracted through the lens of Jewish apocalyptic ideology (Bauckham 1993). Rome appears in various coded guises. It is 'a beast' with 'seven heads and ten horns', each horn crowned with a diadem, and each head marked with 'blasphemous names' (*Revelation* 12.3, 13.1, 17.3). It is the whore, 'with whom the kings of the earth have committed fornication', who sits on the beast (17.1–6). It is allegorized as Israel's ancient foe Babylon, 'the dwelling place of demons', and so on (18.2–24; cf. 17.5). The attitude of the author towards Rome is implacably hostile, and the city's fall (and that of its empire too) is confidently foretold. Yet this was not the only Christian view of Rome possible. Around the same time as *Revelation* was being written, a more measured response was formulated by the author of the *First Epistle of Peter*. It too refers to Rome as Babylon (*1 Peter* 5.13), but equates Christian living with obedience to the empire: 'For the Lord's sake accept the authority of every human institution, whether of the emperor as supreme, or of governors, as sent by him to punish those who do wrong and to praise those who do right' (2.13–14). Through such good conduct on the part of Christians, it was hoped that pagans might be persuaded to come to know God in time to glorify him on Judgement Day. The letter's message in this regard was reduced to a simple formula: 'Fear God. Honour the emperor' (2.17).

Such tension between hostility and accommodation did not diminish for later generations of Christians. Even Tertullian, that purveyor of pungent criticisms of so many aspects of pagan society (see above), was keen to stress that Christians were not disloyal subjects of the emperor and that, however much they seemed to be at odds with traditional paganism, they should not be persecuted. In his *Apology*, his greatest appeal to the pagan elite on behalf of Christianity, he drove the point home:

> For we pray for the safety of our rulers to the eternal God, the true God, the living God . . . We are praying continually on behalf of all of our rulers, that their lives should be long, their power secure, their household safe, their armies strong, their senate loyal, their people honest, their world peaceful – everything for which man or Caesar could wish.
>
> (Tertullian, *Apology* 30.1, 4)

Indeed, Tertullian argued that Christians were likely to be the best of subjects: their special understanding of the apocalyptic horrors that would attend the end of time meant that they were likely to pray all the more earnestly that it should be postponed and that the empire should prosper (*Apology* 32.1). Against such a background, persecution could not be justified. Worse, it threatened to disrupt the peaceful order of things, an outcome that would benefit neither pagans nor Christians (*To Scapula* 5.2–4).

Tertullian's was not the only appeal. Other Christians before him, such as Athenagoras in his *Embassy on Behalf of the Christians* directed to the emperors Marcus Aurelius and Commodus in the late-170s, would also plead that the interests of Christians and the Roman empire were similar. Such positive attitudes to Rome reached a climax with the writings of Eusebius of Caesarea, for whom the conversion of Constantine to Christianity vindicated his view that the empire had an important role to play in God's plan for humankind. As we have seen, such a belief led Eusebius to associate outbreaks of persecution with tyrannical emperors only, a thesis that runs counter to many of the known facts about the Roman empire's dealings with Christianity. For example, it prompted Eusebius to assert that the emperor Philip the Arab (244–9) had actually been a Christian and that the persecution initiated by his successor Decius was in large measure a reaction against what Eusebius interpreted as Philip's outright support for Christianity (*Ecclesiastical History* 6.34 and 6.39.1). Modern scholars generally agree that Eusebius has overstated the nature of Philip's attachment to Christianity. At best, the emperor may have had a positive interest in Christianity that restrained him from initiating a persecution himself (Barnes 1968). Indeed, Eusebius also tells us that Philip and his wife Severa received letters from the theologian Origen (*Ecclesiastical History* 6.36.3).

What evidence there is suggests that the third century, at least during periods when persecution was in abeyance, saw Christianity gaining some degree of intellectual and social respectability – albeit one that falls short of actual approval. Philip the Arab was not the first emperor to express an interest in the religion. Eusebius recounts also that Julia Mammaea, mother of the emperor Alexander Severus (222–35), invited Origen to the imperial palace at Antioch to discuss matters religious (*Ecclesiastical History* 6.21.3–4). A later, but unreliable, source mentions that Alexander also had a statue of Jesus (along with images of Abraham and the deified emperors) in his shrine of household gods (*Historia Augusta, Life of Alexander Severus* 29.2). Later in the third century, Paul of Samosata called on the emperor Aurelian (270–5) to adjudicate in an ecclesiastical dispute arising from Paul's expulsion by his fellow bishops from the see of Antioch (Eusebius, *Ecclesiastical History* 7.30.18–19). Aurelian intervened (and found against Paul), but we should be wary of interpreting this as a signal of implied approval of Christianity: later in his reign Aurelian also resorted to persecution of the Christians, showing that imperial attitudes towards Christianity could be ambivalent. Indeed, detailed understanding of Christianity did not necessarily imply approval. In the years leading up to Diocletian's persecution, for instance, the philosopher Porphyry penned a detailed rebuttal of the Christian faith based on a thorough knowledge of both the Old Testament and the New.

Variations in the attitudes of the imperial authorities, and even of individual emperors, could be matched by the behaviour of Christian communities. In the mid-250s, when Gothic pirates sailed across the Black Sea and ravaged areas of Cappadocia and Pontus in Asia Minor, it seems that they received some assistance from local Christians. Such actions might well have been regarded as treachery by pagans. At the time, it also drew a stinging rebuke from the Christian bishop of the Cappadocian city of Neocaesarea, Gregory Thaumaturgus (the 'Wonder Worker'). In his *Canonical Letter*, which set down prescriptions for the behaviour of Christians on a number of matters, Gregory condemned those who had assisted the barbarians and called on them to repent (Heather and Matthews 1991: 1–12).

Such instances of imperial and ecclesiastical conduct remind us that the history of early Christianity in the Roman world is not one that can be reduced to a simplistic narrative of an 'age of persecutions'. The imperial authorities and pagans in general could be by turns tolerant or hostile, but there is no easy formula by which such activities can be explained. Two instances from the archaeological record are suggestive of the curious relationship between emerging Christianity and the culture that surrounded it. At some date in the early third century, the Christians of Dura Europos, a city on the empire's eastern frontier, adapted a building for use as a church. The renovations were quite substantial: two rooms were knocked together to form a meeting hall; another was provided with a baptismal font and decorated with frescos showing scenes from the New Testament. Moreover, the Christians were not the only inhabitants of Dura to be renovating buildings for religious use at this time: other structures were adapted for use as a Jewish synagogue, a temple of Mithras, and a temple of the Syrian gods of Palmyra. The building transformed into a church was in close proximity to the walls of the city, walls which were presumably patrolled now and again by the soldiers of the local garrison. Did none of them notice what the Christians were doing? It is hard to imagine, given the extent of the renovations, that they did not. But it seems that no one cared too much about it. The very presence of an elaborate church building suggests, perhaps, that the non-Christians of Dura regarded the Christians in their midst with something like benign neglect. If we turn our attention now to the west of the empire, we find that, around the same time (or perhaps slightly earlier), someone scratched an anti-Christian graffito in the plaster of a wall in a room on the Palatine hill in Rome (and so in the shadow of the palace of the emperors). It showed a figure offering a prayer to a crucified man who, rather disconcertingly, has an ass's head. Beside the picture is scratched a line in Greek that says: 'Alexamenos pray to god.' It seems to have been a common pagan jibe to present the focus of Christian worship as having the head of an ass: it is attested by Minucius Felix (*Octavius* 9.3, 28.7) and Tertullian (*Apology* 16.12). But what are we to conclude from this graffito? Answering this question highlights the problems of interpreting visual evidence. Maybe someone found Alexamenos' Christianity offensive, and sought to give offence in return. Or perhaps that someone simply found Alexamenos' religious eccentricity screamingly funny.

Towards Christendom: an uneven progress

The renovators of the Dura Europos church and Alexamenos in Rome lived at a time when Christianity was becoming increasingly prominent in the life of the empire. Between 200 and 300 there were numerous important developments. We have seen that Christian numbers increased considerably, reaching perhaps 6 million by *c.* 300 (chapter 4). This rise in numbers was accompanied by growing administrative sophistication, which saw the emergence of bishops as the key leadership figures within Christian communities. This process was important also for the definition of orthodoxy and its defence against the challenges of theological speculations that came to be regarded as heresy (chapter 5). Similarly, the third century saw the emergence of some of early Christianity's greatest intellects, notably Origen. Such growth brought Christianity greater attention from outsiders, sometimes manifested by hostility and persecution, at others by curiosity, perhaps even respect.

These developments might seem to conform to the old teleological view of Christian history, suggesting that full recognition and acceptance under Constantine was inevitable, albeit after a final test of Christian resolve in Diocletian's great persecution. This view of trauma eclipsed by triumph is too simplistic. Although the political fortunes of Christianity were indeed transformed by Constantine's conversion, the first Christian emperor turned out to be a peculiar champion for the church. Although ecclesiastical writers could regard him as the advocate of orthodoxy at the council of Nicaea in 325, his later rejection of the Nicene creed and its defenders made him a controversial figure. Moreover, while some Christians might have interpreted Constantine's adoption of Christianity as inaugurating an era of peace for the church (as indeed it is sometimes presented in modern accounts), for others the persecutions continued. Among the Christian communities of north Africa, for example, a schism arose over the conduct of Christians during the great persecution. One group, the Donatists – so-called because they followed the views of Donatus, a cleric elected by hardliners as bishop of Carthage in 311 – held that any Christians who had surrendered sacred scriptures to the persecutors should not be easily readmitted to the body of the church. Constantine, however, sided with the Donatists' more moderate opponents, the self-proclaimed 'catholics'. He tried to achieve unity in the African church through inquiry, debate, and persuasion at councils of bishops and through the efforts of imperial officials. When these tactics failed, however, the Donatists once again felt the force of imperial coercion, this time exerted by a Christian emperor in search of ecclesiastical harmony (Frend 1952; Tilley 1997).

If Constantine's conversion did not bring persecution to an end, neither did it cause the immediate cessation of pagan opposition to Christianity. Moreover, on two occasions in the fourth century it seemed as if emperors themselves were determined to bring the Christian triumph to an abrupt halt. When Julian, the last member of the dynasty of Constantine, succeeded to the throne in 361, he abandoned Christianity (if he had ever really subscribed to it) and sought to restore paganism. His death less than two years later, however, meant that his plans remained unfulfilled, tantalizing us with one of the great 'what ifs' of late Roman (and early Christian) history. Some thirty years later, Eugenius (393–4), who usurped the imperial throne in the west, similarly signalled his intention to reverse Christianity's fortunes. It is said that when he travelled through Milan on his way to do battle with his Christian rival Theodosius I (eastern emperor 379–95), Eugenius threatened the city's bishop Ambrose that he would soon turn Milan's cathedral into a stable (Paulinus of Milan, *Life of Ambrose* 31.2). In the end, however, Eugenius' plans too were confounded by defeat and death.

In spite of these threatened reversals, the story of Christianity in late antiquity is one of growing respectability and power. In the decades that followed Constantine's conversion, emperors (and later aristocrats as well) began to invest considerable amounts of their wealth in patronage of the church. Imperial law provided ecclesiastical personnel with important privileges, such as the right to validate wills and to preside over arbitration courts. But even these developments that seemed full of promise brought difficulties in their wake. The wealth of the church was a cause for concern that prompted caustic observations from pagans as much as from Christians. At the end of the fourth century, the pagan historian Ammianus Marcellinus complained that the extravagant wealth of the bishop of the city of Rome sat uncomfortably with Christian ideals of humility (27.3.13). Around the same time, the rich pagan senator Vettius Agorius Praetextatus is supposed to have quipped: 'Make me bishop of the city of Rome and I'll become a Christian immediately' (Jerome, *Against John of Jerusalem* 8). Power, as much as wealth, was a dangerous blessing. As bishops became increasingly important public figures, for example, so competition for bishoprics could be intense. At Rome in 366, an episcopal election degenerated into mob violence in which 137 people were killed (Ammianus Marcellinus 27.3.12). A few years earlier, some Christians at Alexandria expressed their disapproval of their unpopular bishop George by murdering him and parading his mutilated corpse through the city streets on the back of a camel (Ammianus Marcellinus 22.11.3; Socrates, *Ecclesiastical History* 3.2–3). Such developments are good examples of the complexity of the process sometimes still called 'the Christian triumph'. As Christianity became the dominant religion of the empire, so it assimilated to itself certain Roman cultural forms and social mores: the empire transformed Christianity as much as Christianity transformed the empire (Salzman 2002: 200–19). Perhaps many at the time would have nodded in sad agreement with the verdict of the monk Jerome who, looking back over some eighty years of imperial Christianity, observed of the church that 'when it came under Christian emperors, its power and wealth increased, but its virtues diminished' (*Life of Malchus* 1).

If the teleological view of Christian triumph looks less than positive when viewed from such perspectives, it is undermined also by other vistas on the history of Christianity. To assert that Christianity triumphed under Constantine is to adopt a view of history that, like that of Eusebius of Caesarea, places Rome and its empire at the heart of Christian history. Other narratives are possible, of course, that present a very different picture. Beyond the empire's frontiers, among the Goths and Persians for example, Christians continued to be persecuted long after Constantine converted. Similarly, while Eusebius was convinced that the rise of Christianity proved that God had forsaken the Jews, Judaism continued to flourish, and even make gains: in the ninth century, the tribal leaders of the Khazars in central Asia actually converted to Judaism. Finally, while Christianity certainly expanded in the territories of the Roman empire, not all those gains lasted. In Britain, the end of Roman rule and later the advent of the Anglo-Saxons seems to have weakened Christianity to such an extent that pope Gregory the Great (590–604) felt the need to send missionaries there. Even in the Middle East, where Christianity had been born, the faith experienced a decline in the aftermath of the Muslim Arab conquests in the seventh century. Such vignettes hint at the fragility of Eusebius' optimistic vision of the interlocked destinies of Christianity and the Roman empire. Even in late antiquity, some came to dissent from it. In the troubled years of the early fifth century, as Roman power faltered, the north African bishop Augustine of Hippo commenced his great meditation on the role of God in history, the *City of God*. For Augustine there could be no easy equation between Christian and Roman success: the mind of God was much too inscrutable to be read easily in the events of human history (e.g. *City of God* 14.11, 18.53; Markus 1988).

Case study: Pliny the Younger and the Christians

We noted earlier that our view of the history of Roman persecutions of Christianity is largely dependent on, and shaped by, Christian texts. There is only a pitifully small number of independent pagan sources that we might use as a control on the Christian accounts. There are, of course, the notices of Tacitus and Suetonius on the purge at Rome under Nero. For the 'great' persecution of the early fourth century, we possess a number of documents. Two fragmentary inscriptions from Asia Minor substantially confirm Eusebius' account (*Ecclesiastical History* 9.7.3–14) of a letter from the later tetrarchic emperor to cities eager to repress Christians (Mitchell 1988); while a papyrus from Egypt records the seizure of a church by local officials (White 1996–7: II, 166–70). Our most important pagan source for actual measures being taken against Christians is much earlier.

It consists of an exchange of letters from the early second century between Pliny the Younger and the emperor Trajan. In this case study we will look at some of the ways in which these letters can be interpreted.

The two letters in question come from the tenth book of Pliny's collection of letters, where they are numbers 96 and 97. The first nine books had been edited for publication by Pliny himself, but the tenth book was edited by some other person after his death. They are an important source not just for early Christianity, but for the government of the empire in this period: that is because the majority of them concern issues that arose when Pliny served as governor of Bithynia and Pontus in northern Asia Minor from *c.* 110 to 112. The letter concerning the Christians seems to have been written in the Pontic (i.e. eastern) part of the province, probably in the year 112 (Sherwin-White 1966: 691–4). In the text of the letters that follows, I have indicated the individual section numbers in bold numbers: this will make referring to them in the ensuing discussion much easier. I have also added certain Latin terms in parentheses and occasional explanations in square brackets.

The first letter is one from Pliny to Trajan, outlining a difficulty he has encountered in his government of the province:

> **1.** It is my custom, my lord, to refer to you all matters about which I am in doubt, for no one is better able to resolve my doubts and to inform my ignorance. I have never been present at examinations (*cognitiones*) of Christians: consequently, I do not know what is the nature of their crime or the extent to which they ought to be punished. **2.** Nor am I at all sure whether any distinction should be made between them on grounds of age, or if young people and adults should be treated alike; whether a pardon ought to be granted to anyone retracting his beliefs, or if he has once professed Christianity, he shall gain nothing by renouncing it; and whether it is the mere name (*nomen*) itself, even if innocent of crimes, which is to be punished, or rather the

crimes (*flagitia*) associated with the name. In the meantime, this is the line I have followed with those brought before me on the charge of being Christians. **3.** I have asked them in person if they are Christians. I have asked the question a second and third time of anyone who has confessed, threatening them with punishments: those who persist I order to be led away [i.e. to execution]. For, whatever the nature of their admission, I am convinced that their stubbornness and unshakeable obstinacy ought to be punished. **4.** There were others who were similarly insane who, because they were Roman citizens, I entered on the list of persons to be sent to the city [i.e. to Rome for trial].

Once I had begun to deal with this problem, as so often happens, the charges became ever more widespread and increasingly varied. **5.** An anonymous pamphlet (*libellus*) was circulated containing many names. I considered that I should dismiss any who denied that they were or ever had been Christians when they had repeated after me an invocation to the gods and had made offerings of incense and wine to your statue, which I had ordered to be brought in [i.e. to the courtroom] for this purpose along with the images of the gods, and furthermore had cursed Christ – none of which things, it is said, those who are genuine Christians can be induced to do.

6. Others, whose names were given to me by an informer, said that they were Christians and then denied it; they explained that they had been [Christians] but had ceased to be, some of them three years previously, others several years previously, and not a few even twenty years previously. All of these also worshipped your statue and images of the gods and cursed Christ. **7.** They declared, however, that the sum total of their guilt or error amounted to no more than this: that they had met regularly before dawn on a fixed day to chant verse amongst themselves to Christ as if to a god, and to bind themselves by oath, not for any crime, but to engage in neither theft, nor robbery, nor adultery, nor to commit a breach of trust and to deny a deposit when called upon to restore it. When these things were finished it had been their custom to disperse and reassemble later to eat food of an ordinary, harmless kind; but they had given this up after my edict (*edictum*) by which I had banned all political clubs (*hetaeriae*) in accordance with your orders (*mandata*). **8.** This made me decide it was all the more necessary to extract the truth by torture from two slave women, whom they call 'servers' (*ministrae*). I discovered nothing more than a depraved and immoderate superstition.

I have therefore adjourned the examination (*cognitio*) and hastened to consult you. **9.** The matter seems to me to be worthy of your consideration, especially in view of the number of persons at risk. For many people of every age, every social rank, both men and women, are being brought and will be brought into danger. It is not only the towns, but the villages and countryside too which are infected through contact with this superstition; yet it seems possible to check it and to set things right. **10.** At any rate, it is clear enough that the temples which had been almost entirely deserted hitherto are beginning to be frequented, and the sacred rites which had been allowed to lapse for a long time are being performed again, and flesh of sacrificial victims, for which until recently scarcely any buyer could be found, is on sale everywhere. It is easy to deduce from this that a great many people could be reformed if they were given an opportunity to repent.

(Pliny the Younger, *Letters* 10.96,
adapted from Radice 1969)

To this enquiry, Trajan replied as follows:

1. You have followed the right course of action, my dear Secundus [i.e. Pliny], in your examination of the cases of those who have been charged with being Christians. For it is impossible to lay down a general rule in something like

> a fixed formula. **2.** They [the Christians] must not be hunted out; if they are brought before you and convicted, they must be punished, excepting, however, anyone who denies that he is a Christian and makes this fact clear, by offering prayers to our gods, he is to be pardoned as a result of his repentance, however suspect his past conduct may be. But pamphlets (*libelli*) circulated anonymously ought to have no part in any accusation. For they are the worst sort of precedent (*exemplum*) and are not in keeping with the spirit of our age.
>
> (Pliny the Younger, *Letters* 10.97, adapted from Radice 1969)

It is impossible to overestimate the importance of these letters. They give the earliest account of Christianity, and a reasonably detailed one at that, as seen by pagan outsiders. But how are we to interpret them? There are various possibilities. Here I will begin by looking at what specific details can be gleaned from the letters themselves. Then I will look at the broader contexts in which they can be located.

Legal process and cultural bias

The overriding impression given by the letters is of some perplexity on the part of Pliny in particular. Even so, his description of the manner of his investigation is quite detailed. At two points in his letter (§§ 1 and 8) Pliny explicitly describes the legal procedure against the Christians as a *cognitio*. This term literally means an 'inquiry', and was not a trial by jury. Rather, the process took place in front of a magistrate – the emperor or his representative at Rome, the governor in the provinces – and the outcome largely depended on the whim of that magistrate (Millar 1992: 517–32). In Pliny's case, however, his ability to act on his own initiative was circumscribed because of his lack of experience of similar investigations into the activities of Christians; the very fact that he mentions that he had never attended such an investigation surely implies that he knew of such investigations, perhaps at Rome, in the recent past. He supplements this general statement about his lack of experience with three further questions that were vexing him especially (§ 2): about the distinctions (if any) to be made on grounds of age; whether renunciation of Christianity is adequate to secure a pardon; and, perhaps most significantly, about the precise nature of the charges against the Christians, specifically whether they were to be condemned simply for the 'name' (*nomen*) of being Christian, or for 'crimes' (*flagitia*) associated with the name. Given his inexperience, Pliny aims to explain to the emperor the nature of his conduct thus far in the investigation. Now that his inquiries have reached an impasse, he is keen to hear Trajan's guidance.

Pliny's confusion over the nature of the charge – *nomen* or *flagitia* – reflects a legal uncertainty about the treatment of Christians that was reflected in writings by Christians themselves. Apologists of the second and early third centuries – notably Justin (*Apology* 1.4), Athenagoras (*Embassy* 2), and Tertullian (*Apology* 3.20) – were keen to stress that there was no criminality whatsoever to be associated with the 'name' of being Christian. The very fact that they made such statements, however, suggests that the assumption of criminality was common. There is more positive evidence, too, from the period of Pliny's letter. Tacitus called Christianity a 'destructive superstition' (*exitiabilis superstitio*: *Annals* 15.44.4) while for Suetonius it was, as we have seen, 'depraved and malevolent' (*Life of Nero* 16.2; see p. 198). Presumably Pliny – who was a friend to both Tacitus and Suetonius (Sherwin-White 1966: 745, 759) – would have shared their view. Like them, he describes Christianity in § 8 of his letter in negative terms as 'a depraved and immoderate superstition' (*superstitio prava et immodica*). Furthermore, he assumes that Christianity poses a threat, as is clear from his assertions that men and women, adults and children, of all classes, and from town and country alike are involved in the cult, and his implication that traditional forms of pagan worship had been abandoned (§§ 9–10). These observations are almost certainly clouded by exaggeration on Pliny's part, but they fit the customary characterization of dangerous superstitions in the Roman mindset. Abandonment of traditional religion was a stock accusation made against Christians, as we saw earlier in this chapter. Similarly, Pliny's alarm about the widespread nature of Christianity is similar to Livy's damning portrait of the cult of Bacchus (see p. 199). Indeed, the sorts of orgiastic and violent activities that Livy associated with the rites of Bacchus were also suspected of Christian gatherings (Minucius Felix, *Octavius* 9). Pliny, of course, does not specify any such depravities in his letter, but that is hardly an objection: he says enough to make it clear that he views Christianity as a threat. We may be dealing with stereotypes here, but they were clearly potent ones.

Pliny explains also that he had some Christians brought before him (§ 3). He challenged them on the charge of being Christians, all the while reminding them of the punishment (namely execution) that lay in store for them if they were found guilty. Pliny's tactic of threatening the prisoners with punishment is one that is paralleled by the actions of Roman governors in accounts of martyrdom, such as the *Acts of Polycarp*. The formula of repeatedly asking about the charges is echoed also in the accounts of Jesus' trial before Pilate (*Mark* 15.2–5; *Matthew* 27.11–15). At this point of his investigation, Pliny notes that he had the prisoners led off to execution, except for those who were Roman citizens. They were to be sent to Rome for trial, a procedure that is reminiscent of Paul's appeal to Caesar (*Acts* 25.11–12)

Pliny notes, with a hint of weariness, that the number of accusations began to multiply in number and variety (§ 4). He refers to an anonymous pamphlet (*libellus*) that named numerous people as Christians. Clearly the situation was growing worse and Pliny, worried at this deterioration, began to pursue his investigations further. He was plainly aware that Christians could not offer sacrifices, so he ordered a number of prisoners to make offerings to statues of the emperor and the gods and to curse Christ (§§ 5–6). This seems to have satisfied him that these prisoners were innocent.

The flow of accusations did not abate, however, with new ones now supplied by an informer (*index*: § 6). The persons now accused admitted that they had once been Christians, but had since given up the cult. Some claimed to have done so as much as twenty years earlier – if that is accurate, then it would provide evidence for Christians in Pontus in the early 90s, thereby confirming the notice of Christians in that province in the *First Epistle of Peter* (1.1). Once more, offerings and curses were made, but by now Pliny's curiosity seems to have been encouraged. He must have asked the prisoners what Christianity entailed, because they went on to explain to him details of their prayer services and fellowship meals (§ 7). They emphasized that they swore to abjure criminal activity. The list provided by Pliny looks plausible, for very similar lists are found in the New Testament (esp. *1 Peter* 4.15).

Some of these prisoners further explained that they had given up Christianity after the emperor's ban, reinforced by Pliny as governor, on political clubs (*hetaeriae*). This detail apparently prompted Pliny's interest further, leading him to torture two slave women who had been 'servers' (*ministrae*, probably deacons) in the local church organization. This was not a form of punishment; rather, torture was routinely applied to slaves as a means of extracting confessions (Sherwin-White 1966: 708). The most Pliny was able to discover was that Christianity was a 'depraved and immoderate superstition'. At this stage in his investigations, Pliny decided to write to Trajan not only for advice, but also for confirmation that his conduct so far had been correct. He had already mentioned that his practice had been to allow those accused of being Christians an opportunity to repent (§§ 2, 5, 6). At the end of the letter he suggests that this is the best procedure (§ 10).

The most outstanding characteristic of Trajan's response to Pliny is its pragmatism. He confirms Pliny's assumption that it is for the 'name' alone that Christians should be punished; the issue of crimes (*flagitia*) is not addressed. He also stresses that legality must be observed: anonymous accusations, like those in the pamphlet, cannot be allowed to stand because they establish bad precedents that are entirely out of keeping with Trajan's ideals of government for his reign (*nostrum saeculum*: § 2). Perhaps the most interesting aspect of his response is his assertion that there should be no systematic persecution: Christians brought before Pliny and formally accused (*delati*: § 1) are to be subject to his court, but there is to be no hunt for Christians. Indeed, Trajan states that no fixed form of ruling can be given that could be applied generally. Here we have a good example of the essentially responsive nature of Roman provincial administration: governors should deal with problems when they arise, but they should not provoke further difficulties unnecessarily.

Placing Pliny and Trajan in context

It was perhaps inevitable, given that Trajan refused to lay down general rules for persecution, that this correspondence should attract the attentions of Christians themselves. The earliest Christian writer to note the letters was Tertullian in his *Apology*. One of his aims in this work was to highlight the inconsistency of Roman attitudes towards Christianity. He was writing against a background of bitter anti-Christian sentiment in Carthage and he sought to advise the city's magistrates of the futility of pursing a persecution. Pliny's letter and Trajan's response were marshalled in support of this agenda. From them, Tertullian argued, 'we find that inquisitions against us have been forbidden' (*Apology* 2.2.6). He gave a summary (not always accurate: Sherwin-White 1966: 692) of both letters, noting in particular the emperor's order not to hunt out Christians but only to punish those presented for trial. He argued that such a ruling was ambiguous: if Christians were not to be hunted, then surely they must be innocent; but if they were punished after a trial, then they must be guilty (*Apology* 2.2.8). Such inconsistencies, Tertullian asserted, were typical of the authorities' confused approach to the whole Christian question.

It was from Tertullian's *Apology*, not the original texts themselves, that the letters came to the attention of Eusebius of Caesarea, who chose to include a notice of them in his narrative of Rome's dealings with Christianity (*Ecclesiastical History* 3.33.3). What is most interesting about Eusebius' analysis of the episode is that he uses it to distance Trajan from the incidence of persecution. The last emperor to order a persecution, in Eusebius' view, had been Domitian (3.17), but this had come to an end with that emperor's assassination and replacement by Nerva. Eusebius draws an implicit link between the annulling of Domitian's acts by the senate and the end of this particular bout of persecution: one of the acts attributed to Domitian by Eusebius was the exile of the evangelist John to the island of Patmos (3.18); with the advent of Nerva, however, that exile came to an end and John returned to Ephesus (3.20.9). After a short reign Nerva was succeeded by Trajan. Eusebius notes that persecutions began to occur again, but emphasizes that they were the result of local, popular agitation rather than direction by the emperor (3.32.1). This argument is underscored by Eusebius' interpretation of Pliny's and Trajan's exchange. After citing Trajan's ruling that Christians should not be hunted out but could be punished if encountered, Eusebius observes that this *almost* removed the threat of persecution. That it did not was not the fault of the emperor; again the fault is said to lie with the populations and magistrates of individual cities (3.33.2). It seems as if Eusebius was endeavouring to distance Trajan from those tyrannical emperors who did persecute, yet was finding his thesis confounded by the patent reality that persecutions and martyrdoms had taken place in Trajan's reign (this was, after all, the period of Ignatius of Antioch's journey to Rome to meet his death). But why did Eusebius go to such lengths to distance the emperor from instances of persecution? The reason is twofold. First, and as we have already seen several times, Eusebius was at pains throughout the *Ecclesiastical History* to stress the essential harmony of Christianity's destiny with that of Rome. Secondly, Trajan also played an important role in one of the other central themes of Eusebius' narrative: by his extirpation of the Jewish revolt in various parts of the eastern Mediterranean in 115–17 (Smallwood 1976: 389–427), Trajan further compounded the calamities suffered by the Jews (4.2).

Both Tertullian and Eusebius sought to place the correspondence of Pliny and Trajan in the context of Roman attitudes to the Christians. That, perhaps, is the framework within which the letters are most frequently studied: they are a standard ingredient, after all, of sourcebooks on early Christianity (e.g. Stevenson 1987: 18–21; Novak 2001: 47–9). In part this context is suggested by the letters themselves: Pliny hints at the beginning of his letter at the occurrence of other trials of Christians, and Trajan notes the inadvisability of laying down a general ruling about them. Nevertheless, the context within which both governor and emperor were writing about the Christians was that of provincial administration. If we examine the letters bearing this in mind, further light may be shed upon them.

Pliny's status as governor of Bithynia and Pontus was unusual. In the first letter Trajan wrote to Pliny after the governor had arrived in Bithynia, the emperor impressed upon him the necessity of making it clear to the provincials that he had been sent there on a special mission (*Letters* 10.18.2). The nature of this mission is clarified by an inscription recording his career that was set up, after his death, at his birthplace Comum (modern Como) in northern Italy. (Most of the text is known only from a fifteenth-century transcription, but the reconstruction is for the most part uncontroversial; certainly, there is no doubt about the lines that are of interest here.) This states that Pliny had been 'legate with propraetorian authority of the province of Pontus and Bithynia, with full consular power, sent to that province in accordance with a decree of the senate by the emperor Caesar Nerva Trajan Augustus' (Smallwood 1966: no. 230; Sherwin-White 1966: 732). As a legate (*legatus*), Pliny was Trajan's direct appointee and representative in the province, albeit with the sanction of a senatorial decree. This is instructive, because ordinarily Bithynia and Pontus had been governed not by imperial legates, but by proconsuls selected by lot from the ranks of the senate. In other words, Pliny's appointment as governor was an extraordinary command; for some reason, Trajan sent him there instead of a proconsul. This sort of unusual arrangement was undertaken when an emperor wished to have closer supervision over the affairs of a particular province. What were the circumstances that prompted Pliny's appointment?

Various reasons have been suggested. One is that Pliny's appointment was somehow connected with administrative arrangements in the eastern provinces being put in place before Trajan's invasion of Parthia (Rome's enemy across its eastern frontier at this time) which began in 113, just a year after Pliny's death. This all seems unlikely, however: Pliny's career had been almost exclusively civilian, making him an improbable candidate to assist the emperor's strategic arrangements in the lead up to war. In fact, we need go no further than the letters in book X themselves to discover why Trajan felt it necessary to appoint Pliny as extraordinary legate to a province usually governed by proconsuls: the region was close to a state of chaos (Griffin 2000: 118–20).

There were several reasons for this. One was the intense rivalry between the cities of Bithynia and Pontus – a phenomenon eloquently attested in the period immediately prior to Pliny's appointment by one of the region's own sons, the noted orator Dio 'Chrysostom' ('Golden Mouthed', on account of his eloquence) of Prusa. This rivalry had manifested itself in a series of extravagant building projects, as the cities strove to outdo each other; but the financial management of many of these projects had been disastrous, and Pliny reported on several occasions that there were constructions of public amenities left unfinished because of a lack of funds (e.g. *Letters* 10.18, 37–40). There were problems too relating to public order. Persons condemned for crimes were still at large (10.31–2) and there were often bitter rivalries between factions within individual cities (10.59–60).

Perhaps more pertinent to the case of the Christians, there had been worrying incidents of subversive behaviour. In his account of the cross-examination of the individuals named as Christians by an informer, Pliny noted that they claimed to have ceased meeting with other Christians because of Pliny's edict (*edictum*) issued in accordance with the emperor's orders (*mandata*) that banned political clubs (*hetaeriae*). Pliny is referring here to the circumstances of his appointment and arrival in Bithynia and Pontus. *Mandata* were the specific instructions given to a governor on his appointment to a province (Millar 1992: 313–16). In Pliny's case, and bearing in mind the extraordinary nature of his appointment, these *mandata* were probably quite detailed: indeed, several other letters refer to Trajan's instructions concerning troop allocations (10.22.1), banishment from the cities (10.56.3), and financial donations (10.110–11). The *edictum* was issued by the new governor at the time he entered his province; it set out the terms of his administration. Questions about political clubs (*hetaeriae*) had obviously been of concern to Trajan: the ban on them was included in his *mandata* and had been confirmed in Pliny's *edictum*. The seriousness of the situation is hinted at by an exchange between governor and emperor concerning the establishment of a guild of firemen (*collegium fabrorum*) in the city of Nicomedia. Pliny asked if such an organization might be established there, since recent fires had caused substantial damage (10.33). In his response, however, Trajan was adamant that no such course of action should be taken, and cited the recent social disorders as reason for his decision:

> We must remember that this province, and particularly the cities, were troubled by political factions of this nature. Whatever their name, and for whatever reason we establish them, people who gather together for a common purpose soon form themselves into political clubs (*hetaeriae*).
>
> (10.34)

Another pair of letters throws further light on the issue. The city of Amisus was permitted to run its own affairs independently of the province, but when its citizens wished to establish burial clubs (*eranoi*), Pliny wrote to Trajan for guidance about whether this should be permitted or forbidden (10.92). It looks as if he had in mind the emperor's *mandata* about *hetaeriae*. Trajan replied that the club was permitted so long as it did not lead 'to riotous and illegal gatherings' (*ad turbas et ad inlicitos coetus*); but he was quite firm that 'in other cities, which are subject to our governance, institutions of this kind must be forbidden' (10.93). All of this is consonant with something Trajan wrote in another of his letters to Pliny: the governor had been appointed to guarantee that peace (*quies*) would be restored to the province (10.117).

It seems clear that Trajan and Pliny were nervous about secret societies disrupting the peaceful order of life in the cities. Could this explain something of their attitude to the Christians? Certainly, a link is often drawn between the mention of the *hetaeriae* in the letter concerning the Christians with that in the correspondence about the fire brigade at Nicomedia (e.g. Clark 2004: 19; cf. Downing 1995: 241, citing the Amisus letters also). A. N. Sherwin-White, who devoted much of his scholarly career to elucidating both Pliny and the Roman persecutions of the Christians, was wary of seeing the provisions against *hetaeriae* as the basis for Pliny's actions (1966: 708, 779). At best, we can say that those persons who ceased attending Christian gatherings after Pliny had issued his *edictum* were sensitive to the fact that they might be entrapped by such a measure, and liable to punishment as a result. Pliny's letter emphasizes above all that the impetus for the prosecution, and persecution, of Christians came predominantly from the local population. The reference to a pamphlet (*libellus*) and an informer (*index*) in bringing forward charges suggests that Christians were easy victims for anonymous accusations, especially at a time when emperor and governor were apprehensive about potential causes of sedition.

However instructive the correspondence of Pliny and Trajan might be about the dealings of one emperor and governor with a particular cluster of Christians at a specific date, the letters are a reminder also of how much we do not know. We can only guess at the motives that drove the accusations against the Christians; perhaps they too were a product of the rivalries that had caused much unrest in the cities of Bithynia and Pontus. Such gaps in our knowledge, however, are common enough. By the third century, there seems to have been a considerable body of imperial legislation concerning the Christians. The lawyer Ulpian (died

223) prepared a compendium of laws about provincial administration called *The Duty of the Proconsuls*. Its seventh book assembled responses (called rescripts, *rescripta*) of emperors to queries about the punishment of Christians. Not a word of this seventh book survives, however, and we are entirely reliant on the Christian Lactantius for the information (*Divine Institutes* 5.11.19). This brings into sharp focus the difficulties of studying early Christianity in the Roman world: as is so often the case, we depend in large measure on what the Christians themselves tell us.

Chapter 7

Discovering early Christianity

The previous chapters in this book have mapped out various ways in which early Christianity can be studied. Plainly a subject that boasts such a long and diverse intellectual lineage will have generated a great deal of published material. If we focus solely on the modern scholarship produced about the earliest Christian writings, those found in the New Testament, few people would be inclined to disagree with Stephen Mitchell's verdict that they 'have been overwhelmed by their interpreters' (Mitchell 1993: II, 3). So where are interested novices to the subject to begin their studies? How are they to gain access to this arcane and hotly debated world? This final chapter aims to provide such beginners with a map of the literature as it exists, suggesting possible entry points. Of course, like anything else in this book, what I give below is highly subjective: there is no single right way to approach early Christianity (but perhaps many wrong ways), so what follows is not meant to be prescriptive. In any case, I hope to have offered enough alternatives for individuals to choose their own routes. But the most important factor to bear in mind is that what follows – like this book in general – is intended simply as a set of starting points. If you use any of the items listed here (and in the bibliography), follow up the references that they give to investigate the topic further.

Points of departure

General outlines of early Christian history

Histories of early Christianity are not in short supply, and anyone looking for a general narrative introduction will not be starved of possibilities. That said, however, confessional allegiances loom large, not simply in terms of what is said, but in terms of the sorts of topics which are deemed important. Traditionally, studies have tended to reflect their authors' avowed Christianity: such is the case with (e.g.) H. Chadwick 1967 and 2001, Frend 1982 and 1984, and Hall 1991. Books like this concentrate on the affairs of the institutional church, emphasizing topics such as the role played by bishops or the so-called struggle of orthodoxy and heresy. They are sometimes criticized as being too credulous of information contained in Christian sources (cf. K. Hopkins 1999: 352, note 67). That is certainly a problem, but then nobody writes without some form of bias. For all the criticisms sometimes levelled against them, however, authors raised in the Christian tradition often have a sympathy for and sensitivity to their material that can be profoundly enlightening. In particular, they seem more alert than agnostic or atheist writers to the existence of beliefs and spiritual passions that can motivate human actions, and are less likely to reduce all actions to practical expediency.

Among more recent studies that have self-consciously sought to present a less confessional version of the story, there has been a marked tendency to try to place the rise of Christianity in the context of pagan religiousness and ancient culture. It is only fair to point out that it is with this approach that my personal allegiances lie. Of recent forays into the field, few have been more popular, and at the same time more notorious, than the late Keith Hopkins' *A World Full of Gods* (1999). Hopkins' approach is unconventional – for example, his descriptions of pagan religion are described by time-travellers to ancient Pompeii, Egypt, Syria, and Asia Minor – and for such reasons, the book has drawn some criticism. Nevertheless, it provides a daring, engaging, and riotously entertaining *entrée* to the whole topic.

For those who might find Hopkins' approach a little too unorthodox, I would recommend something rather more straightforward, but no less readable. Robin Lane Fox's *Pagans and Christians* (1986) provides a detailed investigation of many of the topics that I have covered in earlier chapters. For some, however, Lane Fox might be too detailed and discursive (it is nearly 800 pages long!): this might be the case especially for students (and particularly those with essay deadlines!) who want their material served up to them concisely. There are many briefer introductions available. Grant 1986 covers similar topics to Lane Fox in about a quarter of the space, though with less subtlety and panache. Among older accounts, Markus 1974 is still useful and illuminating, and is illustrated besides. Two recent syntheses can be recommended without hesitation. Rousseau 2002 provides a survey of the topic into late antiquity, and it includes useful chapter bibliographies and suggested starting points for further reading. On the interface between Christianity and Roman society, Clark 2004 is an outstanding treatment. Finally, for those who seek to understand the rise of Christianity within the context of Roman religious history, there can be no better place to begin than chapters 6 (on religious diversity in the Roman empire) and 8.1 (on Constantine) in the first volume of Beard, North, and Price 1998. All told, Beard, North, and Price's book represents a quantum leap in the quality and range of studies of Roman religion; the second volume of source materials (archaeological and textual) is fully cross-referenced from the first.

Handbooks and works of reference

Not everyone can remember everything, and sometimes in the course of studying a topic you will need to look up a name or a basic account of a particular matter or event. Here is where handbooks, dictionaries and encyclopaedias come in useful. Closely related to the broad surveys discussed above are those volumes of collected essays that cover many basic aspects of early Christian history. Hazlett 1991 is handy and brief, with essays on background context, on themes in early Christian history, and on the sources and their interpretation. Rather grander and more up-to-date are the two volumes of Esler 2000. Handsomely produced, these volumes contain introductions to a wide range of topics, encompassing social history, theology, institutional development, and archaeology. When it appears, Harvey and Hunter (forthcoming) promises to be the standard work in the field.

Briefer articles may be found in a wide range of encyclopaedias and dictionaries where the entries are arranged alphabetically rather than thematically, as is the case with Hazlett and Esler. The *Oxford Dictionary of the Christian Church* (revised edition, Oxford: Oxford University Press, 1997) edited by F. L. Cross and E. A. Livingstone, now in its third edition, is a basic tool for those working on any period of Christian history. It contains short articles, complete with rudimentary bibliography, on personalities and movements from all periods of Christian history, with early Christianity being quite well represented. For background material, but also some Christian items too, there is simply no better and more comprehensive guide than the third edition of the *Oxford Classical Dictionary* (Oxford: Oxford University Press, 1996), edited by Simon Hornblower and Anthony Spawforth; its format of short entries followed by summary bibliographies is almost identical to that of the *Oxford Dictionary of the Christian Church*. The *OCD* – as the *Oxford Classical Dictionary* is usually abbreviated – is now also available on CD-ROM. Cambridge University Press is producing its own classical encyclopaedia, tentatively called the *Cambridge Dictionary of Classical Civilization*, edited by Lin Foxhall, David Mattingly, Graham Shipley, and John Vanderspoel. It is intended to be livelier and less technical than the *OCD*, and is aimed deliberately at a less academic-oriented audience, but the date and format of its publication are not yet certain.

On early Christianity itself, there are now two very useful encyclopaedic collections: E. Ferguson (ed.), *Encyclopedia of Early Christianity* (Chicago and London: St James Press, 1992); and (translated from an Italian original) A. Di Berardino (ed.), *Encyclopaedia of the Early Church*, 2 vols (Cambridge: James Clarke and Co., 1992). Another useful resource is the English version of G. Kittel (ed.) *Theological Dictionary of the New Testament*, 10 vols (Grand Rapids, MI: Eerdmans, 1964–76): a mine of information on a range of subjects (classical and Jewish as well as early Christian); note, however, that the headwords for articles are in Greek.

Anyone whose linguistic ability ranges beyond English might find much that is useful in a number of European encyclopaedias. For those who can read French, the fifteen volumes of the *Dictionnaire d'archéologie chrétienne et de liturgie* (*Dictionary of Christian Archaeology and Liturgy*) (Paris: Letouzey et Ané, 1907–53), commonly abbreviated as *DACL*, is a fascinating repository of information on a wide range of topics. Its scope ranges beyond antiquity to the middle ages, and is considerably broader than its title might suggest. Useful discussions of material will be found on particular places and on motifs used in Christian art; much of it is illustrated with beautiful engravings, which make leafing through it one of the great pleasures of studying early Christianity. Its age, however, means that several recent and important excavations are not mentioned. A comparable encyclopaedia, but covering more than just early Christianity, is the *Dictionnaire d'histoire et de géographie ecclésiastiques* (Paris: Letouzey et Ané: 1912–), abbreviated as *DHGE*: entries in the more recent volumes are well-worth reading. The *Reallexikon für Antike und Christentum* (*Specialist Dictionary for Antiquity and Christianity*) (Stuttgart: Hieresmann, 1950–), usually abbreviated as *RAC*, contains articles in German; but illustrations are often included, and each article is accompanied by a very thorough bibliography. However, the length of time it has taken to produce *RAC* means that some of the material in the earlier volumes is now out of date. Other encyclopaedias include *Paulys Real-Encyclopädie der classischen Altertumswissenschaft* (*Pauly's Specialist Encyclopaedia on the Study of Classical Antiquity*), abbreviated as *RE*, was originally published 1894–1967. A new edition *Der Neue Pauly: Enzyklopädie der Antike* was published between 1996 and 2003 and is appearing in an English translation (Leiden: E. J. Brill, 2002–). However, the first edition is still worth consulting, not least because many of its entries are much more detailed than those in the second edition.

There are some multi-volume compendia of essays that contain much that is valuable for the study of early Christianity. Most important is the new edition of *The Cambridge Ancient History* (Cambridge: Cambridge University Press, 1996–2000). Volumes 10–11 cover the first and second centuries, and volumes 13–14 the period after Constantine. The second edition of volume 12 (on the third century) is promised soon. Rather more erratic in terms of organization, but including much that is directly relevant to early Christianity, is *Aufstieg und Niedergang der römischen Welt* (*The Rise and Decline of the Roman World*) (Berlin and New York: De Gruyter, 1972–), commonly abbreviated as *ANRW*.

Source materials

Biblical texts

Recommending versions of biblical texts for the student of early Christianity is a thankless task. A primary reason is that the text of the Bible was subject to change during the early Christian centuries (see p. 67), making it well nigh impossible to recommend a modern version that corresponds to what people in antiquity would have known. In addition, not all modern Christians agree which books are canonical, so that the bibles they use will often contain different collections of books; likewise, many can be so devoted to a particular translation of their scriptures that suggesting that they should try another runs the risk of giving offence. What I list here, then, reflects my personal tastes as much as anything else. I regret that I have little time for many modern translations. I recommend the excellent study version of the New Revised Standard Version (NRSV) prepared under the general editorship of Wayne A. Meeks (1993): it includes succinct but insightful introductions and commentaries on individual books. A recent trend has been to publish New Testament texts side-by-side with other early Christian writings (especially those of the 'apostolic fathers'): excellent recent specimens are Ehrman 1998, and Mason and Robinson 2004.

Early Christian literature outside the Bible

Apostolic materials can be found in the works of Ehrman and Mason and Robinson just cited. For apocrypha, see Schneemelcher 1992. For other texts, such as those from Nag Hammadi (chapter 5), see Layton 1987 and Robinson 1988.

A number of long-established series present English translations of a broad range of early Christian sources. The most important are:

> *The Ante-Nicene Fathers* (abbreviated as *ANF*). Originally published in the nineteenth century, this series has been reprinted by Eerdmans (Grand Rapids, MI, 1973–). It includes many Christian writers from the period before the council of Nicaea in 325. The translations, however, are often based on inferior texts, and their archaic style is often difficult for students to understand. For authors after Nicaea, there is a complementary series, *The Nicene and Post-Nicene Fathers*, again a nineteenth-century work being reprinted by Eerdmans. It is divided into two series: the first is devoted to Augustine and John Chrysostom; the second includes, amongst other things, the ecclesiastical histories by Eusebius, Socrates, and Sozomen.

> *Ancient Christian Writers* (abbreviated as *ACW*), published by the Newman Press (Westminster, MD; later New York

and Mahwah, NJ, 1949–). Translations are often supported by detailed commentaries of various apostolic authors, and second- and third-century writers such as Athenagoras, Minucius Felix, Origen, Cyprian, and Arnobius.

Fathers of the Church (abbreviated as *FC*), published by the Catholic University of America Press (Washington, DC, 1947–). This series provides alternative translations of several works found also in *ACW* (e.g. Minucius Felix, Cyprian). Many other works are translated, but the quality of commentary is not as good as *ACW*.

The *Hermeneia* series of biblical commentaries contains also several volumes of some very early non-scriptural texts: the *Apostolic Tradition* (Bradshaw, Johnson, and Philips 2002); Hermas' *Shepherd* (Osiek 1999); and Ignatius of Antioch (Schoedel 1985).

For those who can read French, *Sources Chrétiennes* (Paris: Editions du Cerf, 1943–) provides detailed introductions, translations, and commentaries, but above all new editions of many of the texts in their original languages.

Other useful series include *Translated Texts for Historians* (Liverpool: Liverpool University Press), which generally focuses on a later period than that covered by this volume, but includes translations of Lactantius' *Divine Institutes* and some texts relevant to the Donatist schism of the fourth century; and *Oxford Early Christian Texts*, providing original texts with introductions, translations, and commentaries. Some early Christian texts are also published in the handy Penguin Classics and Loeb Classical Library series.

Some modern translations of early Christian texts are masterpieces in their own right. On Cyprian of Carthage, Clarke 1984–9 is outstanding, as is Clarke 1974 on Minucius Felix's *Octavius*. On Lactantius see especially Creed 1984 for *On the Deaths of the Persecutors*, and Garnsey and Bowen 2004 on the

Divine Institutes. For Irenaeus' *Against Heresies*, there is the excellent Grant 1997. Eusebius of Caesarea is well served by a number of translators. His *Life of Constantine* is given thorough treatment by Cameron and Hall 1999. For the *Tricennial Orations*, see Drake 1976. Much older, but still worth consulting, is Lawlor and Oulton 1927–8: a treasure trove of information on the *Ecclesiastical History* and the *Martyrs of Palestine*.

Non-Christian literary sources

Many of the most important classical sources (Tacitus, Suetonius, Pliny) are available in the Loeb Classical Library (Harvard University Press), giving text and translation; translations only are provided in paperback series such as Penguin Classics and Oxford World's Classics. These series include also some Jewish works such as Josephus (Loeb; *Jewish War* also in Penguin) and Philo (Loeb). For Jewish apocrypha and pseudepigrapha, see Charlesworth 1983–5. The Dead Sea Scrolls are available in Vermes 1997.

Documentary sources: inscriptions and papyri

Access to documentary sources can be difficult (or intimidating) for beginners, since it often means delving into large and dusty volumes. There is a useful introduction in Snyder 1985: 119–62. Perhaps the easiest way in for beginners is via the various source-books now available, although many of these contain extracts from literary sources too. For the period covered in this book, the time-honoured compendium is Stevenson 1987. Also useful (although the translations are often gathered from old-fashioned versions) is Novak 2001. For the pagan background, see the second volume of Beard, North, and Price 1998. Also useful here is Klauck 2000b, although he is guilty of imposing a Christianizing interpretative framework on the pagan evidence.

Archaeology

The range of archaeological material available for early Christianity is always going to increase, but there already exist a number of useful collections of raw data. Snyder 1985 presents a useful manual. Most items discussed are also illustrated in some fashion, while documents are presented in both their original language and translation. Material is divided into pictorial representations, architecture, and physical documents (inscriptions, graffiti, and papyri). Although this makes types of early Christian remains clear, it also means that different categories of evidence from one site are often discussed in different parts of the volume: thus the early Christian building at Dura Europos is described separately from the graffiti found on its walls (Snyder 1985: 68–71, 147–8). For architecture, the second volume of White 1996–97 presents a wide range of Christian material set side-by-side with that for Judaism and the pagan cult of Mithras. It compiles the raw data on which the conclusions of the first volume are based. For the Roman (and other) catacombs see Stevenson 1978 and Rutgers 2000. Other aspects of the material record are analysed in Finney 1988 and 1994, and Elsner 2003. Finally, for the background to earliest Christianity (discussed in chapter 4 above), much of the material that is pertinent may be found described, discussed, and sometimes illustrated in Jerome Murphy-O'Connor's deservedly successful archaeological guidebook to the Holy Land, now in its fourth edition (Murphy-O'Connor 1998). Also on the archaeology of the New Testament see Charlesworth 1988 and Reed 2000. Some of the encyclopaedias and dictionaries listed above will also contain descriptions of archaeological material.

Specialist journals

Many new discoveries or methodological advances in any field do not at first result in the publication of books but are reported in specialist journals. Indeed, it is in such journals that much of the most vigorous debate on any academic discipline will occur.

Moreover, such journals often give outlines or critical reviews of new books published in the field. As such, they are essential tools for advanced study of a particular topic, and this is as true for early Christianity as for any other area of enquiry. And yet, academic journals often fill the uninitiated reader with apprehension. Journals are often found only in university libraries, and even then they tend to be read more frequently by academic staff and research postgraduates than by the undergraduates who make up the greater mass of any university's population. But because journals are the main venues for academic debate, anyone interested in a particular academic discipline should be encouraged to consult and read them. Recognizing that journals can be intimidating creatures, my aim here is to demystify them. I aim to indicate which ones are most important for the student of the early Christian world, and give an outline of their scope and the sort of articles that they contain. At the risk of being accused of cultural myopia, I have limited my selection to journals that publish articles in English (whether exclusively, frequently, or occasionally). For this my only apology is that this book is meant primarily for beginners and is intended to whet their appetite: that is not something that a densely argued article in technical German is likely to do. I will also note the abbreviations used to refer to them by scholars. Scholars like abbreviations, and not just for periodicals: it is so much easier to type out, or even say, something like *ANRW* rather than *Aufstieg und Niedergang der römischen Welt*. For ease of reference, it seemed best to me to list these journals alphabetically.

Church History (*CH*): covers a variety of topics in Christian history, from the ancient world to the modern period; it also includes book reviews.

Harvard Theological Review (*HTR* or *HThR*): published under the auspices of the Faculty of Divinity, Harvard University, this is one of the leading American journals. The range of articles is quite wide, but early Christian topics frequently receive coverage.

Jahrbuch für Antike und Christentum (*JAC* or *JbAC*): publishes articles on a wide range of early Christian topics, as well as some more broadly on the ancient world. Many of these articles cover archaeological material. Most of the contributions are published in German, though a number are published in other languages, including English.

Journal of Early Christian Studies (*JECS*): one of the newest journals in the field, and in many respects the most daring. *JECS* is a product of what might be deemed the 'secularization' of early Christian studies, as investigation of the subject has been colonized by non-clerical scholars whose approaches to the subject are informed by feminism, sociology, and anthropology. The journal also publishes book reviews and lists of newly published books.

Journal of Ecclesiastical History (*JEH*): now over half a century old, the *JEH* is clearly established as one of the leading journals for church history. Articles range from antiquity to the present day, and there are comprehensive reviews and lists of new books.

Journal of Roman Studies (*JRS*): the leading international journal for the study of Roman history and literature. It has published numerous important articles on Roman religion and on other religious groups, such as Jews and Christians, in the Roman world. Each volume includes book reviews, which often cover early Christianity.

Journal of Theological Studies (*JTS* or *JThS*): undoubtedly the most distinguished journal on religious subjects published in Britain, if not, indeed, in the Anglophone world. Topics range across Old Testament, New Testament, and early Christianity. There are also extensive book reviews, and lists of newly published items.

Studia Patristica (*SP* or *StudPatr*): this is not, technically speaking, a journal; rather it publishes the papers read at the regular patristic conferences that have met in Oxford every four years since 1951. The publication history of these volumes is somewhat convoluted, which means that they are not always shelved together in university libraries, thus necessitating a bit of sleuthing in the catalogues (and among the bookstacks). At first, the volumes were published in the German series *Texte und Untersuchungen zur Geschichte der altchristlichen Literatur* (abbreviated as *TU*; for discussion, see pp. 59–60). The eighth conference, however, was published at Oxford; the ninth and later conferences have been published by the Belgian publisher Peeters based in Leuven (in Flemish, or Louvain in French).

Vigiliae Christianae (*VChr* or *VigChr*): the leading international journal for the study of early Christian life and thought, together with book reviews; articles are mainly in English.

In addition, topics germane to the study of early Christianity appear in a number of biblical and Jewish studies periodicals. Some of the ones worth dipping into are: *Biblical Archaeologist* (*BA*); *Journal for the Study of Judaism in the Persian, Hellenistic, and Roman Period* (*JSJ*); *Journal of Jewish Studies* (*JJS*); *Journal for the Study of the New Testament* (*JSNT*); *Journal for the Study of the Pseudepigrapha*; and *Novum Testamentum* (*NT* or *NovT*).

Bibliographical guides to chapters 3–6

In what follows I give suggestions for those wishing to begin their investigations into the topics treated in this book; students should also consult the various general histories listed earlier in this chapter. For more detailed analyses of individual topics, readers are directed to the references given in each chapter. I have not given details for chapters 1 and 2: further reading can be found in the various references cited in them.

Chapter 3

For accessible sources, see pp. 230–3. On the New Testament, the best place to start is one of the many excellent introductory guides now available. Some can be written in a theological language that students of Classics and Ancient History might find intimidating. Accessible introductions, however, can be found in Burkett 2002, Ehrman 1997, Johnson 1999, and Schnelle 1998. For the complex processes underlying the formation of the New Testament canon, see Ehrman 1993, Metzger 1987, and Stanton 2004. The importance of Q is hotly debated: Tuckett 1996 is a useful introduction to its positive virtues, but compare the negative verdict on Q made by Stanton 2004: 2–4. The complexity of the issues can be grasped rather swiftly from a quick glance at the rather bewildering pages of Robinson, Hoffman, and Kloppenborg 2000.

General histories, notably H. Chadwick 2001, devote much space to examining early Christian literature outside the New Testament. There are useful essays in Hazlett 1991. For a detailed description, see especially Quasten 1950–60; this should now be supplemented by Young, Ayres and Louth 2004. A helpful introduction to themes is B. Ramsay 1985. Various of the translations referred to above contain good introductions. Useful historical studies of a number of early Christian writers are available, such as E. J. Hunt 2003 on Tatian; Barnes 1971 on Tertullian; Trigg 1983 on Origen; and Barnes 1981 on Eusebius of Caesarea.

For Jewish literature, wide-ranging but accessible introductions may be found in Jonge 1985 and Nickelsburg 2003. Charlesworth 1985 examines the relevance of the pseudepigrapha for the New Testament and Christian origins. Most translations of the Dead Sea Scrolls provide an introduction to the problems presented by the Qumran texts; for more detail, see Davies, Brooke, and Callaway 2002 (beautifully illustrated), Stegemann 1998, and Vermes 1999. Williamson 1989 is a helpful introduction to Philo and his works. For Josephus, see Rajak 2003.

Chapter 4

Judaism, and the relationship of early Christianity to it, has prompted a vast amount of scholarship. For general orientation on Judaism in this period, Horbury, Davies, and Sturdy 1999 is up-to-date. Other useful surveys are Smallwood 1976, especially for political history, and, covering a vast range of material in immense detail, the modern revised edition of Schürer 1973–87. Lieu, North, and Rajak 1992 assemble an extremely valuable set of essays.

For Jesus' immediate historical context, the bibliography is similarly enormous, but useful starting points are provided by Vermes 1981 and 2000 (among many works by him), Rowland 1985, Sanders 1993, Fredriksen 2000. For Galilee, see Freyne 1988 and Reed 2000. The question of banditry is treated in detail by Horsley 1987. The topic of messianic expectation is elucidated by Nickelsburg 2003, and in useful collections of essays edited by Charlesworth 1992, and Neusner, Green, and Frerichs 1987. Horsley 1992 is a penetrating analysis of messianism in connection with banditry in the age of Jesus.

For the relationship of emerging Christianity to Judaism, particularly the question of the 'parting of the ways', see Georgi 1995, Lieu 1996 (and many other works by her), Dunn 1999. The concept of a dialogue, whereby Judaism was as much influenced by Christianity as vice versa, can be approached via the works of Boyarin 1999 and 2004, and, on the origins of missionary ideology, Goodman 1994.

Descriptions of Christian expansion in the Roman world are given in MacMullen 1984 and Lane Fox 1986. The sociological model was advanced by K. Hopkins 1998 and Stark 1996; for critique of Stark see Castelli 1998 and Klutz 1998, with a trenchant response in Stark 1998. The extent to which Christianity might have appealed in times of duress is examined from a cross-cultural perspective in Reff 2005. Early Christianity at Rome, before 200, is examined in immense detail by Lampe 2003.

Paul's missionary journeys are analysed with typical insight by Clarke 1996. Meeks 1983, a classic study, is essential for the background of the Pauline communities. The implications of the Delphi inscription were first raised by Brassac 1913: if you can read French, this is a fascinating piece of detective work that is still worth reading. For the text of the inscription, see Oliver 1971; Murphy-O'Connor 1992: 137–60 provides a succinct analysis of the issues. The link between Paul, Sergius Paullus and Antioch in Pisidia is discussed in detail by Mitchell 1993: II, 3–10. The thrill of the discovery of the inscriptions from Antioch in Pisidia is palpable in Cheesman 1913, Jacquier 1916, and W. M. Ramsay 1926 – all of them fine pieces of pioneering scholarship. The link between the preaching of the gospel and emperor worship in Asia Minor, first put forward by Deissmann 1910, has been the subject of recent analyses by Oakes 2001 and Stanton 2004: 9–62. For emperor worship in Asia, see Price 1984.

Chapter 5

The council of Nicaea and the debates that followed it are analysed by Barnes 1981, H. Chadwick 1960, and (in great detail) Hanson 1988. The making of the creeds can be explored in Young 1991 and J. N. D. Kelly 1972. For the term 'ecumenical council', see H. Chadwick 1972.

For Cyprian's episcopal career, see Amidon 1983 and Rives 1995: 285–307 (this latter particularly good on seeing Cyprian in the context of civic life in Roman Carthage). Grant 1997 is a good introduction to Irenaeus. For Ignatius of Antioch, see Schoedel 1985. For the emergence of a Christian community and leadership see Burtchaell 1992, Campbell 1994, and Kee 1995. Developments in the face of schism and heresy are analysed by Brent 1995, Lampe 2003, and Thomassen 2004. On the role of women, from the New Testament period onwards, there is an immense bibliography: to start with, see Fiorenza 1983, Witherington 1988, and Eisen 2000. On councils, Hess 2002 is more broad-ranging than its title promises. For ritual diversity, see especially Bradshaw

1992. The curious Easter practices in Asia are investigated by Stewart-Sykes 1998.

For the conflict between orthodoxy and heresy, Bauer 1972 is fundamental; see also R. Williams 1989; Logan 1996. Frend 1985 provides a lively introduction to the whole topic of schism and heresy. For Montanus see Trevett 1996. The relationship between doctrine and text can be approached via Metzger 1987, Ehrman 1993, Gamble 1995, and Stanton 2004.

There is a huge bibliography on Nag Hammadi and Gnosticism, so I will be very selective. The texts themselves are most easily accessible in Layton 1987 and Robinson 1988 – the latter is much to be preferred because it presents the tracts in the order in which they occur in the codices. Layton rearranges them thematically, something which gives the misleading impression that they constitute a coherent collection. General surveys of the issues may be found in Rudolph 1983, and in various readable studies by Elaine Pagels (1979, 1988, 2003). On the provenance of the texts, see Goehring 2001, while Harmless 2004: 160–3 provides a useful survey of the supposed link with the monastery of Pachomius. For the problems of defining Gnosticism, see M. H. Williams 1996 and King 2003. Implications for the canon are discussed in Ehrman 2003. For a further indication of how the reading of ancient texts can be seen to be influenced by modern agendas, see Lamberigts 1989.

Chapter 6

For general works on the interaction between the Christians and the Roman empire, see Markus 1974, MacMullen 1984, Lane Fox 1986, and Clark 2004. For a view of Christianity in the context of Roman paganism, see Beard, North, and Price 1998.

The persecutions have probably been responsible for the spilling of more ink than blood. Much older work (and some recent work too, alas) is hamstrung by being excessively partisan and accepting of hagiographical traditions. The classic treatment remains Frend 1965, but cf. Boyarin 1999: 127–30 for some objections. An important debate on the topic was played out in the pages of the journal *Past and Present* in the early 1960s: see Ste Croix 1963, with the criticism of Sherwin-White 1964, and Ste Croix's own response in 1964. These essays are conveniently available together in Finley 1974. Bowersock 1995 provides a recent synthesis, and Boyarin 1999 sets the topic in the context of contemporary Judaism.

Pagan attitudes to Christianity are analysed by Wilken 2003. The basis for our knowledge of anti-Christian legislation is subjected to scrutiny by Barnes 1968. For individual persecutions, see Salisbury 1998 on Perpetua and Rives 1999 on Decius. The 'great persecution' of Diocletian receives detailed treatment in any history of the age, e.g. Barnes 1981 and Drake 2000; Twomey and Humphries (forthcoming) will present a series of essays on various aspects of this persecution. For the texts of the martyr acts, Musurillo 1972 is unreliable (also in its translation), but a new edition is promised.

The question of alienation and accommodation between Christianity and the Roman empire is examined in various of the works already mentioned. Note, however, Brown 1988, excellent on attitudes towards sexuality and the body; and Edwards, Goodman, and Price 1999, an important collection of essays that sets Christian apologetic in a broader pagan and Jewish context.

The fortunes of Christianity in the period after Constantine are traced in many general surveys, notably Rousseau 2002 and Clark 2004. E. D. Hunt 1998 analyses the emergence of the church as an institution of the empire. Cameron 1991 examines the development of a Christian discourse. For Christianity at the end of antiquity, see Markus 1990.

For Pliny and Trajan, the starting point is Sherwin-White's massive commentary on Pliny's *Letters* (Sherwin-White 1966). A short but incisive analysis may be found in Wilken 2003: 1–30. The role of the emperor can be elucidated by reference to Millar 1992 and Talbert 1984. The situation in Asia Minor can be examined via Sherwin-White's commentary, or through Magie 1950. Various essays in *The Cambridge Ancient History*, second edition, volume XI (2000) provide more up-to-date surveys of issues relevant to provincial administration in the age of Trajan. For the letters themselves, see Radice 1969.

Notes

1 What is early Christianity and why does it deserve study?

1 This is not to say that there was, in the pre-Constantinan period, a total absence of efforts to achieve an overarching administrative structure. Even so, its effects were limited to regional episcopal hierarchies, such as those claimed by the bishops of Rome over central and southern Italy, or the bishops of Carthage over north Africa: Amidon 1983; cf. more generally Hess 2002.

2 There is much too large a bibliography on this subject to cite here; but a useful introduction may be found in Bowersock 1986.

3 For use of the plural 'Christianities', see (e.g.) the title of Ehrman 2003. The problem of defining the boundaries of Christianity is well explored in Boyarin 1999 and 2004.

4 See, for example, the travel writer Colin Thubron's account of his participation in an Orthodox Church procession at Omsk in western Siberia in the late 1990s, where a veteran of the Second World War explained how Christian beliefs had been preserved under Communism: 'For me it was my mother. We lived in a remote region near Voronezh – not a town at all, you understand, just a country village. No church for hundreds of miles. My mother was illiterate, but she remembered all the prayers from the old days, and taught me them' (Colin Thubron, *In Siberia*, London: Chatto & Windus, 1999, p. 58).

5 The realities of such trends were brought home to me when I visited Split in Croatia at Easter 2000. The engaging elderly man from whom I rented a room made much of my Irishness, stressing that the Croats, like the Irish, were Catholics. Then he remembered that there was a large Protestant population in Northern Ireland: 'Protestants', he hissed, 'are like Serbs.' The role of religion in the ethnic divisions of the post-Cold War Balkans was chillingly predicted (it seems to me now) by Stella Alexander in an essay published in 1982. She wrote that '[r]eligion in Yugoslavia is a divisive, not a unifying force', and that '[t]he Yugoslav communists have reason to fear the disintegrative force of unfettered nationalism, and as long as the churches are associated with this, the regime will continue to attack them' (Alexander 1982: 591 and 607). Indeed, the anthropologist Clifford Geertz has noted of the regime of Croatian president Franjo Tudjman (1990–9) that it would not have been able 'to stir up Croats against the large Serbian minority in Zagreb by plastering the town with "God Protects Croatia" posters, if there wasn't something already there to be stirred up' (Geertz 2000: 173).

6 On the topic of 'new religions', see the various essays in Wilson and Cresswell 1999.

7 Although it has been suggested by some sections of the news media that the popularity of the film in North America owed much to the appetite among some young males for images of extreme violence. The re-release of the film for Easter 2005 saw many of the more extreme scenes of violence excised.

2 Tradition and revelation: the historical quest for early Christianity

1 It was precisely for this reason that ecclesiastical authorities in the north Italian city of Ravenna were troubled by the early history of their bishopric penned by the ninth-century priest Agnellus. A staunch defender of the prerogatives of the Ravenna church, Agnellus highlighted the independence from Rome that Ravenna had enjoyed in earlier centuries. In a civilization that had for centuries subscribed to the notion of papal supremacy, and even more so in the sensitive atmosphere of Catholic Europe after the Protestant Reformation, accounts of such challenges to the authority of the bishop of Rome could be considered dangerous. Hence a succession of humanist scholars were

denied access to Agnellus' work at Ravenna's episcopal library (Momigliano 1990: 133).

2 The statement comes in the introductory diatribe against 'the theories of certain Protestant archaeologists' (Marucchi 1929: 1–29). The tenor of Marucchi's opinions can be divined from the opening sentence that recounts how 'the majestic unity of Christendom in the West was destroyed, thanks to Luther' (1929: 1). Of course, Protestant scholars were equally guilty of such biases, as the examples of Gilbert Burnet and Conyers Middleton (see p. 57) show. The influence of such views has been long lasting. Consider, for example, the *Origines ecclesiastici: the antiquities of the Christian church* (published 1708–22) of Joseph Bingham (1668–1723). This work – like those of Burnet and Middleton – was concerned to show the purity of the primitive church prior to its corruption in the Catholic 'Dark Ages'. Yet its influence has been considerable: it was used as a textbook in Anglican universities until the early twentieth century; comparatively recently it has been described as 'unsurpassed' by Lane Fox 1986: 9. For a recent discussion, see O'Loughlin 2001: 124–8 (a useful study marred, however, by the mistaken impression that Bingham wrote in the late nineteenth century).

3 The search for early Christianity: sources and their interpretation

1 On this and other examples from the author called Luke (who also probably wrote *Acts*), see Frederiksen 2000: 31.

2 An eighth-century manuscript preserved at Milan contains a description, known after its first editor Ludovico Antonio Muratori as the Muratorian canon, of the contents of the New Testament. The date of the original text that was copied into the manuscript is hotly debated: some date it as early as the second century; others see it as belonging to a much later period. For a brief discussion of the issues (with further references to the large bibliography on the topic) see Metzger 1987: 191–201 (favouring a later date) and Stanton 2004: 68–71 (arguing for the earlier date).

3 For further examples, related to teachings of sexual and dietary abstinence, see Pagels 1988: 16–25.

4 I do not have space to discuss these here, but the problems are highlighted in any of the guides to New Testament writings listed in chapter 7 (e.g. Schnelle 1998: 365–433).

5 For example, the inauthentic status of the pastoral epistles is disputed by Murphy-O'Connor 1996. For a review of the debates about their authenticity, see Prior 1989: 13–60.
6 From such discrepancies it is often argued that the gospels were composed for different audiences. This is a matter of considerable debate among contemporary New Testament scholars: for a guide to the issues, see Stanton 2004: 63–91.
7 Most general works on the Scrolls and translations of them contain accounts of their discovery and protracted publication history: e.g. Stegemann 1998: 1–11; Vermes 1999: 1–21.
8 This point is well made by Reed 2000. For a recent example, see Witherington 1998, which illustrates the world of the *Acts of the Apostles* with images of appropriately first-century artefacts that are explained by captions like 'Paul, Priscilla, and Aquila *may* have practised their trade in a shop *like* this' and 'A *typical* small first-century sailing vessel of the sort that Paul, Barnabas, and Mark *would likely* have sailed in to Cyprus or Paul and Luke to Mitylene' (pp. 546 and 782: emphases added).

4 Messiahs and missions: contexts for the origins and spread of Christianity

1 Good discussions of the issues relating to the film can be found in Corley and Webb 2004. Various of their contributors emphasize the extent to which Gibson's film distorts the details found in the gospels and relies heavily on the visions of Christ's passion experienced by the German nun Anne Catherine Emmerich (1774–1824).
2 For example, Frend 1984, 11–52; Ferguson 1993: 373–546; J. K. Aitken, 'Jewish tradition and culture', in Esler 2000: I, 80–110.
3 There are too many works to mention more than a small sample. Horsley 1987 provides a thorough analysis, but the idea has been incorporated into more general studies of Jesus: e.g. Crossan 1991: 168–224; Fredriksen 2000: 79–81, 90–1.
4 Useful guides to the issues may be found in the various essays collected in Dunn 1999.
5 Certainly, we know of forced conversion of Jews at a later date, such as that which occurred to the entire Jewish population on the island of Minorca in 418: Bradbury 1996.

5 Doctrine and power: orthodoxy and organization in early Christianity

1 Interestingly, one of the books is by Bart D. Ehrman, chair of the Department of Religious Studies at the University of North Carolina, Chapel Hill, and a respected scholar of the place of texts in the debate between orthodoxy and heresy in early Christianity (Ehrman 2004). Some other responses have been unusually intemperate (and are directed not so much against the novel's use of the Nag Hammadi texts, as against its perceived broader anti-Catholic agenda). Among them is *The Da Vinci Hoax: Exposing the Errors in The Da Vinci Code* (Chicago: Ignatius Press, 2004) by Carl Olson and Sandra Miesel, which contains a polemical foreword by the Cardinal Archbishop of Chicago.

2 For the later influence of 'Gnosticism', see Richard Smith, 'Afterword: The Modern Relevance of Gnosticism', in Robinson 1988: 532–49.

3 Some of the texts clearly have an origin outside of Gnosticism. Codex VI, for example, contains a Coptic translation of a couple of pages from Plato's *Republic*; indeed scholars generally agree that *none* of the texts in this codex can be defined as Gnostic in any way. Meanwhile, Codex XII contains a fragmentary Coptic version of a work called the *Sentences of Sextus*, a text that had originally been composed in Greek and was known also in translations into Latin, Syriac, Armenian, and Georgian. The *Sentences* consist of a series of moral maxims (e.g. number 165c: 'Untrue words are the evidence of evil persons'). Even if they contained statements about moral and spiritual rigour that might have appealed to Gnostics, their circulation in other contexts suggests that they enjoyed a broader popularity among communities of early Christians.

4 Plotinus' treatise is preserved scattered about his surviving *Enneads* (2.9, 3.8, 5.5, 5.8). It is perhaps worth mentioning that Plotinus came from Lycopolis in Egypt, not far from the site of Nag Hammadi.

5 See R. Collins, *Early Medieval Spain: Unity in Diversity 400–1000*, second edition, London: Macmillan, 1995, ch. 3. The 'location' of Arianism within the fourth century is explicit in the dates given in the title of Hanson 1988.

6 See the story 'The Lost Gospels' in *Time* magazine, vol. 162, no. 25 (22 December 2003), pp. 54ff.

6 Confronting Babylon: early Christianity and the Roman empire

1 For example, the 1994 paperback reprint of Sordi 1988 carried a colour reproduction of *The Last Prayer*. Robert Louis Wilken tells an amusing tale that highlights the gap between popular perceptions and what scholars would like to achieve:

> On the original book jacket [of the first edition of Wilken 2003, published in 1984] there is a scene of sacrifice from first-century Rome . . . [I] proposed it for the book jacket because it gave a positive depiction of religious devotion among the Romans. One of the aims of the book was to overcome the stereotype of Roman society as irreligious and immoral. But when I received the German translation I was chagrined to find that the publisher had concocted a picture of a Roman soldier about to thrust his spear into a group of Christian women and children cowering before the cruel and merciless might of Rome. So much for high-minded intentions.
>
> (Wilken 2003: ix)

Bibliography

It would be impossible here to provide anything close to a full bibliography of early Christianity. I have limited myself, therefore, to listing works referred to and cited in chapters 1–6, together with some other works that I have found useful: this is a guide to the book, not the subject. Certain reference works mentioned in chapter 7 do not appear. For guidance on such works, and on collections of sources, see chapter 7.

Alexander, S. (1982) 'Religion and national identity in Yugoslavia', in S. Mews (ed.) *Religion and national identity* (Studies in Church History 18), Oxford: Blackwell, 591–607.

Amidon, P. R. (1983) 'The procedure of St Cyprian's Synods', *Vigiliae Christianae* 37: 328–39.

Baarda, T. (2003) 'The Gospel of Thomas', *Proceedings of the Irish Biblical Association* 26: 46–65.

Backus, I. (1991) 'The early church in the Renaissance and Reformation', in Hazlett 1991: 291–303.

Ballhatchet, K. and H. (1990), 'Asia', in McManners 1990: 488–518.

Barclay, J. M. G. (1996) *Jews in the Mediterranean Diaspora from Alexander to Trajan (323 BCE–117 CE)*, Edinburgh: T. & T. Clark.

Barnes, T. D. (1968) 'Legislation against the Christians', *Journal of Roman Studies* 58: 32–50.

—— (1971) *Tertullian: a historical and literary study*, Oxford: Clarendon Press.

—— (1981) *Constantine and Eusebius*, Cambridge, MA: Harvard University Press.

—— (1995) 'Statistics and the conversion of the Roman aristocracy', *Journal of Roman Studies* 85: 135–47.

Bately, J. (ed.) (1980) *The Old English Orosius* (Early English Text Society, Supplementary Series 6), Oxford: Oxford University Press.

Bauckham, R. (1993) *The climax of prophecy: studies in the Book of Revelation*, Edinburgh: T. & T. Clark.

Bauer, W. (1972) *Orthodoxy and heresy in earliest Christianity*, Philadelphia: Fortress.

Beard, M. and Crawford, M. (1985) *Rome in the Late Republic: problems and interpretations*, London: Duckworth.

Beard, M., North, J., and Price, S. (1998) *Religions of Rome*, 2 vols, Cambridge: Cambridge University Press.

Berger, P. L. (1999) 'The desecularization of the world: a global overview', in P. L. Berger (ed.) *The desecularization of the world: resurgent religion and world politics*, Washington DC: Ethics and Public Policy Center/Grand Rapids, MI: Eerdmans, 1–18.

Bickerman, E. J. (1968) *Chronology of the ancient world*, London: Thames and Hudson.

Bolgar, R. R. (1954) *The classical heritage and its beneficiaries*, Cambridge: Cambridge University Press.

Bowersock, G. W. (1986) 'From emperor to bishop: the self-conscious transformation of political power in the fourth century AD', *Classical Philology* 81: 298–307.

—— (1995) *Martyrdom and Rome*, Cambridge: Cambridge University Press.

Boyarin, D. (1999) *Dying for God: martyrdom and the making of Christianity and Judaism*, Stanford: Stanford University Press.

—— (2004) *Borderlines: the partition of Judaeo-Christianity*, Philadelphia: University of Pennsylvania Press.

Bradbury, S. (ed.) (1996) *Severus of Minorca: Letter on the Conversion of the Jews of Minorca*, Oxford: Clarendon Press.

Bradshaw, P. F. (1992) *The search for the origins of Christian worship*, London: SPCK.

Bradshaw, P. F., Johnson, M. E., and Phillips, M. E. (2002) *The apostolic tradition: a commentary*, Minneapolis: Fortress Press.

Brakke, D. (1994) 'Canon formation and social conflict in fourth-century Egypt: Athanasius of Alexandria's thirty-ninth *Festal Letter*', *Harvard Theological Review* 87: 395–419.

—— (1995) *Athanasius and the politics of asceticism*, Oxford: Clarendon Press.

—— (2002) 'The early church in North America: late antiquity, theory, and early Christianity', *Church History* 71: 473–91.

Brassac, A. (1913) 'Une inscription de Delphes et la chronologie de Saint Paul', *Revue Biblique* 10: 36–53 and 207–17.

Braudel, F. (1972) *The Mediterranean and the Mediterranean world in the age of Philip II*, trans. S. Reynolds, 2 vols, London: Collins.

—— (2001) *The Mediterranean in the ancient world*, trans. S. Reynolds, London: Allen Lane.

Brent, A. (1995) *Hippolytus and the Roman church in the third century: communities in tension before the emergence of the monarch bishop*, Leiden: E. J. Brill.

Brown, P. (1978) *The making of late antiquity*, Cambridge, MA: Harvard University Press.

—— (1981) *The cult of the saints: its rise and function in Latin Christianity*, Chicago: University of Chicago Press.

—— (1988) *The body and society: men, women, and sexual renunciation in early Christianity*, New York: Columbia University Press.

Burkett, D. (2002) *An introduction to the New Testament and the origins of Christianity*, Cambridge: Cambridge University Press.

Burtchaell, J. T. (1992) *From synagogue to church: public services and offices in the earliest Christian communities*, Cambridge: Cambridge University Press.

Cameron, A. (1991) *Christianity and the rhetoric of empire: the development of Christian discourse*, Berkeley: University of California Press.

Cameron, A. and Garnsey, P. (eds) (1998) *The Cambridge ancient history*, vol. XIII: *The late empire AD 337–425*, Cambridge: Cambridge University Press.

Cameron, A. and Hall, S. G. (1999) *Eusebius: Life of Constantine*, Oxford: Clarendon Press.

Campbell, R. A. (1994) *The elders: seniority within earliest Christianity*, Edinburgh: T. & T. Clark.

Castelli, E. (1998), 'Gender, theory, and *The rise of Christianity*: a response to Rodney Stark', *Journal of Early Christian Studies* 6: 227–57.

Chadwick, H. (1953) *Origen: Contra Celsum*, Cambridge: Cambridge University Press.

—— (1960) 'Faith and Order at the Council of Nicaea', *Harvard Theological Review* 53: 171–95.

—— (1966) *Early Christianity and the classical tradition*, Oxford: Oxford University Press.

—— (1967) *The early church*, Harmondsworth: Penguin.

—— (1972) 'The origin of the title "Oecumenical Council"', *Journal of Theological Studies*, new series 23: 132–5.

—— (2001) *The church in ancient society from Galilee to Gregory the Great*, Oxford: Oxford University Press.

Chadwick, O. (1998) *A history of the popes 1830–1914*, Oxford: Oxford University Press.

Charlesworth, J. H. (ed.) (1983–5) *The Old Testament pseudepigrapha*, New York: Doubleday.

—— (1985) *The Old Testament pseudepigrapha and the New Testament*, Cambridge: Cambridge University Press.

—— (1988) *Jesus within Judaism: new light from exciting archaeological discoveries*, New York: Doubleday.

—— (ed.) (1992) *The Messiah: developments in earliest Judaism and Christianity*, Minneapolis: Fortress.

Cheesman, G. L. (1913) 'The family of the Caristanii at Antioch in Pisidia', *Journal of Roman Studies* 3: 253–66.

Clark, E. G. (2004) *Christianity and Roman society*, Cambridge: Cambridge University Press.

Clarke, G. W. (1974) *The Octavius of Marcus Minucius Felix*, New York and Mahwah, NJ: Newman Press/Paulist Press.

—— (1984–9) *The Letters of St Cyprian of Carthage*, 4 vols, New York and Mahwah, NJ: Newman Press/Paulist Press.

—— (1996), 'The origins and spread of Christianity', in *The Cambridge ancient history*, second edition, Cambridge: Cambridge University Press, vol. X, 848–72.

Coleman, K. (1990) 'Fatal charades: Roman executions staged as mythological enactments', *Journal of Roman Studies* 80: 44–73.

Conzelmann, H. (1987) *Acts of the Apostles*, Philadelphia: Fortress.

Cooper, K (1999) 'The martyr, the *matrona*, and the bishop: the matron Lucina and the politics of martyr cult in fifth- and sixth-century Rome', *Early Medieval Europe* 8: 297–317.

Corley, K. E. and Webb, R. L. (eds) (2004) *Jesus and Mel Gibson's The Passion of the Christ*, London and New York: Continuum.

Creed, J. L. (1984) *Lactantius: De Mortibus Persecutorum*, Oxford: Clarendon Press.

Croke, B. and Harries, J. (1982) *Religious conflict in fourth-Century Rome: a documentary study*, Sydney: Sydney University Press.

Crossan, J. D. (1991) *The historical Jesus: the life of a Mediterranean Jewish peasant*, Edinburgh: T. & T. Clark.

Davies, P. R., Brooke, G. J., and Callaway, P. R. (2002) *The complete world of the Dead Sea Scrolls*, London: Thames and Hudson.

Deissmann, A. (1910) *Light from the ancient East*, London: Hodder and Stoughton.

Ditchfield, S. (1995) *Liturgy, sanctity, and history in Tridentine Italy: Piero Maria Campi and the preservation of the particular*, Cambridge: Cambridge University Press.

Dodds, E. R. (1965) *Pagan and Christian in an age of anxiety*, Cambridge: Cambridge University Press.

Downing, F. G. (1995) 'Pliny's prosecutions of Christians: Revelation and 1 Peter', in S. E. Porter and C. S. Evans (eds) *The Johannine writings: a Sheffield reader*, Sheffield: Sheffield Academic Press, 232–49 (reprinted from *Journal for the Study of the New Testament* 34 (1988) 105–33).

Drake, H. A. (1976) *In praise of Constantine: a historical study and new translation of Eusebius' Tricennial Orations*, Berkeley and Los Angeles: University of California Press.

—— (2000) *Constantine and the bishops: the politics of intolerance*, Baltimore: Johns Hopkins University Press.

—— (forthcoming) 'Lessons from the Great Persecution', in Twomey and Humphries forthcoming.

Drijvers, H. J. (1992) 'Syrian Christianity and Judaism', in Lieu, North, and Rajak 1992: 124–43.

Duffy, E. (1977) 'Primitive Christianity revived: religious renewal in Augustan England', in D. Baker (ed.) *Renaissance and Renewal in Christian History* (Studies in Church History 14), Oxford: Basil Blackwell, 287–300.

Dunn, J. D. G. (ed.) (1999) *Jews and Christians: the parting of the ways AD 70 to 135*, revised edition, Grand Rapids, MI: Eerdmans.

Edwards, M. (2003) *Constantine and Christendom*, Liverpool: Liverpool University Press.

Edwards, M., Goodman, M., and Price, S. (eds) (1999) *Apologetics in the Roman Empire: Pagans, Jews, and Christians*, Oxford: Oxford University Press.

Ehrman, B. D. (1993) *The orthodox corruption of scripture: the effect of early Christological controversies on the text of the New Testament*, Oxford and New York: Oxford University Press.

—— (1997) *The New Testament: a historical introduction to the early Christian writings*, Oxford and New York: Oxford University Press.

—— (1998) *The New Testament and other early Christian writings: a reader*, Oxford and New York: Oxford University Press.

—— (2003) *Lost Christianities: the battles for scripture and the faiths we never knew*, Oxford and New York: Oxford University Press.

—— (2004) *Truth and fiction in The Da Vinci Code: a historian reveals what we really know about Jesus, Mary Magdalene, and Constantine*, Oxford and New York: Oxford University Press.

Eisen, U. E. (2000) *Women officeholders in early Christianity: epigraphical and literary studies*, Collegeville: Liturgical Press.

Elsner, J. (2003) 'Archaeologies and agendas: reflections on late ancient Jewish art and early Christian art', *Journal of Roman Studies* 93: 114–28.

Esler, P. F. (1994) *The first Christians in their social worlds: social-scientific approaches to New Testament interpretation*, London: Routledge.

—— (ed.) (1995) *Modelling early Christianity: social-scientific studies of the New Testament in its context*, London: Routledge.

—— (ed.) (2000) *The early Christian world*, 2 vols, London: Routledge.

Feeney, D. (1998) *Literature and religion at Rome: cultures, contexts, and beliefs*, Cambridge: Cambridge University Press.

Ferguson, E. (1993) *Backgrounds of early Christianity*, second edition, Grand Rapids, MI: Eerdmans.

Finley, M. I. (ed.) (1974) *Studies in ancient society*, London: Routledge and Kegan Paul.

Finney, P. C. (1988) 'Early Christian architecture: the beginnings', *Harvard Theological Review* 81: 319–39 (with correction at vol. 82 (1989) 343).

—— (1994) *The invisible God: the earliest Christians on art*, Oxford and New York: Oxford University Press.

Fiorenza, E. S. (1983) *In memory of her: a feminist theology reconstruction of Christian origins*, New York: Crossroads.

—— (2000) *Jesus and the politics of interpretation*, London and New York: Continuum.

Fortey, R. (1997) *Life: an unauthorised biography*, London: HarperCollins.

Fredriksen, P. (2000) *From Jesus to Christ: the origins of the New Testament image of Jesus*, revised edition, New Haven: Yale University Press.

Frend, W. H. C. (1952) *The Donatist church*, Oxford: Clarendon Press.

—— (1959) 'The failure of the persecution in the Roman empire', *Past and Present* 16: 10–30; reprinted in Finley 1974: 263–87.

—— (1964) 'A note on the influence of Greek immigrants on the spread of Christianity to the West', in Alfred Stuiber (ed.), *Mullus: Festschrift für Theodor Klauser*, Münster: Aschendorff, 125–9.

—— (1965) *Martyrdom and persecution in the early church*, Oxford: Blackwell.

—— (1982) *The early church: from the beginnings to 461*, revised edition, London: SCM.

—— (1984) *The rise of Christianity*, Philadelphia: Fortress Press.

—— (1985) *Saints and sinners in the early church*, London: Darton, Longman and Todd.

—— (1996) *The archaeology of early Christianity: a history*, London: Geoffrey Chapman.

—— (2003) *From dogma to history: how our understanding of the early church developed*, London: SCM.

Freyne, S. (1988) *Galilee, Jesus, and the gospels: literary approaches and historical investigations*, Philadelphia: Fortress Press.

Gamble, H. Y. (1995) *Books and readers in the early church: a history of early Christian texts*, New Haven: Yale University Press.

Garnsey, P. and Bowen (2004) *Lactantius: Divine Institutes*, Liverpool: Liverpool University Press.

Garnsey, P. and Saller, R. (1987) *The Roman empire: economy, society, and culture*, London: Duckworth.

Geanakoplos, D. J. (1976) *Interaction between 'sibling' Byzantine and Western cultures in the Middle Ages and the Italian Renaissance*, New Haven: Yale University Press.

Geary, P. J. (1994) *Living with the dead in the Middle Ages*, Ithaca, NY: Cornell University Press.

Geertz, C. (1973) *The interpretation of cultures*, New York: Basic Books.

—— (2000) *Available light: anthropological reflections on philosophical topics*, Princeton: Princeton University Press.

Georgi, D. (1995) 'The early church: internal Jewish migration or new religion?', *Harvard Theological Review* 88: 35–68.

Gibbon, E. (1776–88 [1994]) *The history of the decline and fall of the Roman Empire*, ed. D. Womersley, 3 vols, London: Allen Lane.

Goehring, J. E. (2001) 'The provenance of the Nag Hammadi codices once more', *Studia Patristica* 35: 234–53.

Goodman, M. (1994) *Mission and conversion: proselytizing in the religious history of the Roman empire*, Oxford: Oxford University Press.

Grant, R. M. (1986) *Gods and the One God: Christian theology in the Graeco-Roman world*, London: SPCK.

—— (1997) *Irenaeus of Lyons*, London: Routledge.

Griffin, M. (2000) 'Nerva to Hadrian', in *The Cambridge ancient history*, second edition, Cambridge: Cambridge University Press, vol. XI, 84–131.

Gryson, R. (1973) 'Les elections ecclésiastique au IIIe siècle', *Revue d'Histoire Ecclésiastique* 68: 353–404.

Hall, S. G. (1991) *Doctrine and practice in the early church*, London: SPCK.

Halton, T. (1985) *The church* (Message of the Fathers of the Church 4), Wilmington, DE: Michael Glazier.

Hanson, R. P. C. (1988) *The search for the Christian doctrine of God: the Arian controversy 318–381*, Edinburgh: T. & T. Clark.

Harmless, W. (2004) *Desert Christians: an introduction to the literature of early monasticism*, Oxford and New York: Oxford University Press.

Harries, J. (1991) 'Patristic historiography', in Hazlett 1991: 269–79.

Harvey, S. A. and Hunter, D. G. (eds) (forthcoming) *The Oxford handbook of early Christian studies*, Oxford: Oxford University Press, forthcoming.

Hawthorne, G. F. and Martin, R. P. (eds) (1993) *Dictionary of Paul and his Letters*, Downers Grove: InterVarsity Press

Hay, D. (1977) *Annalists and historians: western historiography from the eighth to the eighteenth centuries*, London: Methuen.

Hazlett, I. (ed.) (1991) *Early Christianity: origins and evolution to AD 600*, London: SPCK.

Heather, P. and Matthews, J. (1991) *The Goths in the fourth century*, Liverpool: Liverpool University Press.

Hess, H. (2002) *The early development of canon law and the Council of Serdica*, Oxford: Oxford University Press.

Hobsbawm, E. J. (1992) *Nations and nationalism since 1870: programme, myth, reality*, second edition, Cambridge: Cambridge University Press.

Hollerich, M. J. (1999) *Eusebius of Caesarea's* Commentary on Isaiah: *Christian exegesis in the age of Constantine*, Oxford: Oxford University Press.

Hopkins, C. (1979) *The discovery of Dura-Europos*, ed. B. Goldman, New Haven: Yale University Press.

Hopkins, K. (1998) 'Christian number and its implications', *Journal of Early Christian Studies* 6: 185–226.

—— (1999) *A world full of gods: pagans, Jews, and Christians in the Roman empire*, London: Weidenfeld and Nicolson.

Horbury, W., Davies, W., and Sturdy, J. (eds) (1999) *The Cambridge history of Judaism*, vol. III: *The early Roman period*, Cambridge: Cambridge University Press.

Hordern, P. and Purcell, N. (2000) *The corrupting sea: a study of Mediterranean history*, Oxford: Blackwell.

Horsley, R. A. (1987) *Jesus and the spiral of violence: popular Jewish resistance in Roman Palestine*, San Francisco: Harper and Row.

—— (1992) '"Messianic" figures and movements in first-century Palestine', in Charlesworth 1992: 276–95.

Humphries, M. (1998) 'Trading gods in northern Italy', in C. J. Smith and H. Parkins (eds) *Trade, traders, and the ancient city*, London: Routledge, 203–24.

—— (1999) *Communities of the blessed: social environment and religious change in northern Italy, AD 200–400*, Oxford: Oxford University Press.

—— (forthcoming a) Review of Salzman 2002, *Classics Ireland* forthcoming.

—— (forthcoming b) 'The West (1): Italy, Gaul, and Spain', in Harvey and Hunter (forthcoming).

—— (forthcoming c) '"The Gracious Favour of the Gods": the mind of the persecutors', in Twomey and Humphries forthcoming.

Hunt, E. D. (1982) *Holy Land pilgrimage in the later Roman empire AD 312–460*, Oxford: Clarendon Press.

—— (1998) 'The church as a public institution', in Cameron and Garnsey 1998: 238–76.

Hunt, E. J. (2003) *Christianity in the second century: the case of Tatian*, London: Routledge.

Jacquier, E. (1916) 'Le Nouveau Testament et les découvertes modernes', *Revue Biblique* 13: 239–49.

Jaeger, W. (1962) *Early Christianity and Greek paideia*, Cambridge, MA: Harvard University Press.

Jehovah's Witnesses (1990/2000) *How blood can save your life?* Online. Available http://www.watchtower.org/library/hb/toc.htm (4 July 2000).

Jenkins, K. (1991) *Re-thinking history*, London: Routledge.

Jenkins, P. (2002) *The next Christendom: the coming of global Christianity*, New York: Oxford University Press.

Johnson, L. T. (1999) *The writings of the New Testament: an interpretation*, revised edition, London: SCM.

Jones, B. W. (1992) *The Emperor Domitian*. London: Routledge.

Jonge, M. de (1985) *Outside the Old Testament*, Cambridge: Cambridge University Press.

Kee, H. C. (1995) *Who are the People of God? Early Christian models of community*, New Haven: Yale University Press.

Kee, H. C. and Cohick, L. H. (eds) (1999) *Evolution of the synagogue: problems and progress*, Valley Forge, PA: Trinity Press International.

Kelly, J. (1991) 'Why study early church history?', in Hazlett 1991: 3–13.

Kelly, J. N. D. (1972) *Early Christian creeds*, third edition, London: Longman.

—— (1975) *Jerome: his life, writings, and controversies*, London: Duckworth.

—— (1977) *Early Christian doctrines*, fifth edition, London: A. & C. Black.

Kepel, G. (1994) *The revenge of God: the resurgence of Islam, Christianity, and Judaism in the modern world*, trans. A. Braley, Cambridge: Polity Press.

King, K. L. (2003) *What is Gnosticism?* Cambridge, MA: Harvard-Belknap

Klauck, H.-J. (2000a) *Magic and paganism in early Christianity: the world of the Acts of the Apostles*, Edinburgh: T. & T. Clark.

—— (2000b) *The religious context of early Christianity*, London and New York: T. & T. Clark.

Klutz, T. (1998) 'The rhetoric of silence in *The Rise of Christianity*: a response to Rodney Stark's sociological account of Christianization', *Journal of Early Christian Studies* 6: 162–84.

Knibb, M. A. (1999) 'Eschatology and messianism in the Dead Sea Scrolls', in P. W. Flint and J. C. Vanderkam (eds) *The Dead Sea Scrolls after fifty years*, Leiden: E. J. Brill, vol. II, 379–402.

Knowles, D. (1959) 'Great historical enterprises II: the Maurists', *Transactions of the Royal Historical Society*, fifth series 9: 167–87.

Koester, H. (ed.) (1995) *Ephesos, metropolis of Asia: an interdisciplinary approach to its archaeology, religion, and culture*, Valley Forge, PA: Trinity Press International.

Lamberigts, M. (1989) 'Augustine, Julian of Aeclanum, and E. Pagels' *Adam, Eve, and the Serpent*', *Augustiniana* 39: 393–435.

Lampe, P. (2003) *From Paul to Valentinus: Christians at Rome in the first two centuries*, Minneapolis: Fortress.

Lane Fox, R. (1986), *Pagans and Christians*, Harmondsworth: Penguin.

Lawlor, H. J. and Oulton, J. E. L. (1927–8) *Eusebius: The Ecclesiastical History and The Martyrs of Palestine*, 2 vols, London: SPCK.

Layton, B. (1987) *The Gnostic scriptures*, New York: Doubleday, repr. 1995.

Lepelley, C. (1981) *Les Cités de l'Afrique romaine au Bas-Empire*, Paris: Études Augustiniennes.

Levick, B. (1990) *Claudius*, London: Batsford.

Levinskaya, I. (1996) *The Book of Acts in its Diaspora setting*, Grand Rapids, MI: Eerdmans.

Lieu, J. (1996) *Image and reality: the Jews in the world of the Christians in the second century*, Edinburgh: T. & T. Clark.

Lieu, J., North, J., and Rajak, T. (eds) (1992) *The Jews among Pagans and Christians in the Roman empire*, London: Routledge.

Logan, A. H. B. (1996) *Gnostic truth and Christian heresy*, Edinburgh: T. & T. Clark.

Lyman, R. (1999) *Early Christian traditions* (The New Church's Teaching Series 6), Boston, MA: Cowley Publications.

MacCormack, S. (1991) *Religion in the Andes: vision and imagination in early colonial Peru*, Princeton: Princeton University Press.

McLynn, N. (1994) *Ambrose of Milan: church and court in a Christian capital*, Berkeley and Los Angeles: University of California Press.

McManners, J. (ed.) (1990) *The Oxford illustrated history of Christianity*, Oxford: Oxford University Press.

MacMullen, R. (1981) *Paganism in the Roman empire*, New Haven: Yale University Press.

—— (1984) *Christianizing the Roman empire AD 100–400*, New Haven: Yale University Press.

—— (1997) *Christianity and Paganism in the fourth to eighth centuries*, New Haven: Yale University Press.

Magie, D. (1950) *Roman rule in Asia Minor*, 2 vols, Princeton: Princeton University Press.

Markus, R. A. (1974) *Christianity in the Roman world*, London: Thames and Hudson.

—— (1988) *Saeculum: history and society in the theology of St Augustine*, revised edition, Cambridge: Cambridge University Press.

—— (1990) *The end of ancient Christianity*, Cambridge: Cambridge University Press.

Marshall, I. H. (1980) *The Acts of the Apostles: an introduction and commentary*, Grand Rapids, MI: Eerdmans.

Marucchi, O. (1929) *The evidence of the Catacombs for the doctrines and organisation of the primitive church*, London: Sheed and Ward.

Mason, S. and Robinson, T. (2004) *Early Christian Reader*, Peabody, MA: Hendrickson.

Meeks, W. A. (1983) *The first urban Christians: the social world of the apostle Paul*, New Haven: Yale University Press.

Meer, F. van der and Mohrmann, C. (1959), *Atlas of the early Christian world*, London and Edinburgh: Nelson.

Metzger, B. M. (1987) *The canon of the New Testament: its origins, development, and significance*, Oxford: Clarendon Press.

—— (1992) *The text of the New Testament: its transmission, corruption, and restoration*, third edition, Oxford and New York: Oxford University Press.

Meyendorff, J. (1991) 'Patristics', in N. Lossky *et al.* (eds) *Dictionary of the ecumenical movement*, Geneva: World Council of Churches Publications, 781–4.

Millar, F. (1992) *The emperor in the Roman world (31BC–AD337)*, revised edition, London: Duckworth.

Mitchell, S. (1988) 'Maximinus and the Christians in AD 312: a new Latin inscription', *Journal of Roman Studies* 78: 105–24.

—— (1993) *Anatolia: land, men, and gods in Asia Minor*, 2 vols, Oxford: Oxford University Press.

—— (1999) 'The cult of Theos Hypsistos between pagans, Jews, and Christians', in P. Athanassiadi and M. Frede (eds) *Pagan monotheism in late antiquity*, Oxford: Clarendon Press, 81–148.

Momigliano, A. (1990) *The classical foundations of modern historiography*, Berkeley and Los Angeles: University of California Press.

Murphy-O'Connor, J. (1992) *St Paul's Corinth: texts and archaeology*, revised edition, Collegeville: Liturgical Press.

—— (1996) *Paul: a critical life*, Oxford: Oxford University Press.

—— (1998) *The Holy Land: an Oxford archaeological guide from earliest times to 1700*, fourth edition, Oxford: Oxford University Press.

Musurillo, H. (1972) *The Acts of the Christian martyrs*, Oxford: Clarendon Press.

Neusner, J., Green, W. S., and Frerichs, E. (eds) (1987) *Judaisms and their Messiahs at the turn of the Christian era*, Cambridge: Cambridge University Press.

Nickelsburg, G. W. E. (2003) *Ancient Judaism and Christian origins: diversity, continuity, and transformation*, Minneapolis: Fortress.

Nock, A. D. (1933) *Conversion*, Oxford: Clarendon Press.

Novak, R. M. (2001) *Christianity and the Roman empire: background texts*, Harrisburg: Trinity International Press.

Noy, D. (2000) *Foreigners at Rome: citizens and strangers*, London: Duckworth/Classical Press of Wales.

Oakes, P. (2001) *Philippians: from people to letter*, Cambridge: Cambridge University Press.

O'Daly, G. (1999) *Augustine's* City of God: *a reader's guide*, Oxford: Clarendon Press.

O'Loughlin, T. (2001) 'The Early Church', in D. Cohn-Sherbok and J. M. Court (eds), *Religious diversity in the Graeco-Roman World: a survey of recent scholarship*, Sheffield: Sheffield Academic Press, 124–42.

Oliver, J. H. (1971) 'The Epistle of Claudius which mentions the proconsul Junius Gallio', *Hesperia* 40: 239–40.

Osiek, C. (1999) *Shepherd of Hermas: a commentary*, Minneapolis: Fortress Press.

Pagels, E. (1979) *The Gnostic Gospels*, New York: Random House.

—— (1988) *Adam, Eve, and the serpent*, New York: Random House.

—— (2003) *Beyond belief: the secret Gospel of Thomas*, New York: Random House.

Park, C. C. (1994) *Sacred worlds: an introduction to geography and religion*, London: Routledge.

Parke, H. W. (1988) *Sibyls and Sibylline prophecy in classical antiquity*, ed. B. C. McGing, London: Routledge.

Pelikan, J. (1993) *Christianity and classical culture: the metamorphosis of natural theology in the Christian encounter with Hellenism*, New Haven: Yale University Press.

Peukert, D. J. K. (1994) 'The genesis of the "Final Solution" from the spirit of science', in D. F. Chew (ed.) *Nazism and German Society, 1933–1945*, London: Routledge, 274–99.

Pocock, J. G. A. (1999) *Barbarism and religion*, Cambridge: Cambridge University Press.

Price, S. R. F. (1984) *Rituals and power: the Roman imperial cult in Asia Minor*, Cambridge: Cambridge University Press.

Prior, M. (1989) *Paul the letter-writer and the Second Letter to Timothy*, Sheffield: Journal for the Society of the Old Testament Press.

Quasten, J. (1950–60) *Patrology*, 3 vols, Utrecht and Antwerp: Spectrum.

Radice, B. (1969) *Pliny: Letters and Panegyricus*, 2 vols, Cambridge, MA: Harvard University Press.

Rahner, K. (1964) *On heresy*, Freiburg: Herder.

Rajak, T. (2003) *Josephus: the historian and his society*, revised edition, London: Duckworth.

Ramsay, B. (1985) *Beginning to read the Fathers*, Mahwah, NJ: Paulist.

Ramsay, W. M. (1926) 'Studies in the Roman province of Galatia', *Journal of Roman Studies* 16: 201–15.

Reed, J. L. (2000) *Archaeology and the Galilean Jesus*, Harrisburg: Trinity Press International.

Reff, D. T. (2005) *Plagues, priests, and demons: sacred narratives and the rise of Christianity in the Old World and the New*, Cambridge: Cambridge University Press.

Reynolds, J. E. (1982) *Aphrodisias and Rome*, London: Society for the Promotion of Roman Studies.

Rives, J. B. (1995) *Religion and authority in Roman Carthage from Augustus to Constantine*, Oxford: Clarendon Press.

—— (1999) 'The decree of Decius and the religion of empire', *Journal of Roman Studies* 89: 135–54.

Robbins, K. (1975) 'Institutions and illusions: the dilemma of the modern ecclesiastical historian', in D. Baker (ed.) *The materials, sources, and methods of ecclesiastical history* (Studies in Church History 11), Oxford: Basil Blackwell, 355–65.

Robinson, J. M. (ed.) (1988) *The Nag Hammadi library in English*, second edition, Leiden: E. J. Brill.

Robinson, J. M., Hoffmann, P., and Kloppenborg, J. S. (2000) *The critical edition of Q*, Minneapolis: Fortress.

Rodgers, R. H. (ed.) (2004) *Frontinus: De Aqueductu Urbis Romae*, Cambridge: Cambridge University Press.

Rousseau, A. and Doutreleau, L. (eds) (1979) *Irénée de Lyon. Contre les heresies. Livre I* (Sources Chrétiennes 263–4), Paris: Editions du Cerf, vols I–II.

Rousseau, P. (1999) *Pachomius: the making of a community in fourth-century Egypt*, revised edition, Berkeley and Los Angeles: University of California Press.

—— (2002) *The early Christian centuries*, London: Longman.

Rowland, C. (1985) *Christian origins: an account of the setting and character of the most important messianic sect of Judaism*, London: SPCK.

Rudolph, K. (1983) *Gnosis: the nature and history of an ancient religion*, ed. R. McL. Wilson, Edinburgh: T. & T. Clark.

Rutgers, L. V. (2000) *Subterranean Rome: in search of the roots of Christianity in the catacombs of the Eternal City*, Leuven: Peeters.

Ste Croix, G. E. M. de (1963) 'Why were the early Christians persecuted?' *Past and Present* 26: 6–38; reprinted in Finley 1974: 210–49.

—— (1964) 'Why were the early Christians persecuted? A rejoinder', *Past and Present* 27: 28–33; reprinted in Finley 1974: 256–62.

Salisbury, J. E. (1998) *Perpetua's passion: the death and memory of a young Roman woman*, London: Routledge.

Salzman, M. R. (2002) *The making of a Christian aristocracy: social and religious change in the western Roman empire*, Cambridge, MA: Harvard University Press.

Sanders, E. P. (1977) *Paul and Palestinian Judaism: a comparison of patterns of religion*, London: SCM.

—— (1993) *The historical figure of Jesus*, London: Allen Lane.

Schnapp, A. (1996) *The discovery of the past: the origins of archaeology*, London: British Museum Press.

Schneemelcher, W. (1992) *New Testament Apocrypha*, English edition ed. R. McL. Wilson, 2 vols, Cambridge: James Clarke and Co./Louisville: Westminster/John Knox.

Schnelle, U. (1998) *The history and theology of the New Testament writings*, trans. M. E. Boring, London: SCM.

Schoedel, W. R. (1985) *Ignatius of Antioch: a commentary on the Letters of Ignatius of Antioch*, Philadelphia: Fortress Press.

Schürer, E. (1973–87) *The history of the Jewish people in the age of Jesus Christ (175 BC–AD 135)*, English edition ed. G. Vermes, F. Millar, and others, 3 vols, Edinburgh: T. & T. Clark.

Segal, A. F. (2002) *Two powers in heaven: early Rabbinic reports about Christianity and Gnosticism*, Leiden: E. J. Brill.

Sherk, R. K. (1969) *Roman documents from the Greek East*, Baltimore: Johns Hopkins University Press.

—— (1984) *Rome and the Greek East to the death of Augustus*, Cambridge: Cambridge University Press.

Sherwin-White, A. N. (1963) *Roman society and law in the New Testament*, Oxford: Clarendon Press.

—— (1964) 'Why were the early Christians persecuted? An amendment', *Past and Present* 27: 23–7; reprinted in Finley 1974: 250–5.

—— (1966) *The Letters of Pliny: a historical and social commentary*, Oxford: Clarendon Press.

Siker, J. S. (1991) *Disinheriting the Jews: Abraham in early Christian controversy*, Louisville: Westminster/John Knox Press.

Simon, M. (1986) *Verus Israel: a study of the relations between Christians and Jews in the Roman empire, AD 135–425*, Oxford: Oxford University Press/Littman Library of Jewish Civilization.

Smallwood, E. M. (1966) *Documents illustrating the Principates of Nerva, Trajan, and Hadrian*, Cambridge: Cambridge University Press.

—— (1967) *Documents illustrating the Principates of Caius, Claudius, and Nero*, Cambridge: Cambridge University Press.

—— (1976) *The Jews under Roman rule from Pompey to Diocletian*, Leiden: E. J. Brill.

Smith, J. Z. (1990) *Drudgery divine: on the comparison of early Christianities and the religions of late antiquity*, Chicago: University of Chicago Press.

Snyder, G. F. (1985) *Ante Pacem: archaeological evidence of church life before Constantine*, Macon, GA: Mercer University Press.

Sordi, M. (1988) *The Christians and the Roman Empire*, trans. A. Bedini, London: Croom Helm; paperback reprint London: Routledge, 1994.

Stanton, G. (2004) *Jesus and gospel*, Cambridge: Cambridge University Press.

Stark, R. (1996) *The rise of Christianity: a sociologist reconsiders history*, Princeton: Princeton University Press.

—— (1998) 'E Contrario', *Journal of Early Christian Studies* 6: 259–67.

Stegemann, H. (1998) *The library of Qumran: on the Essenes, Qumran, John the Baptist, and Jesus*, Leiden: E. J. Brill.

Stevenson, J. (1978) *The Catacombs: rediscovered monuments of early Christianity*, London: Thames and Hudson.

—— (1987) *A New Eusebius: documents illustrating the history of the church to AD 337*, revised edition by W. H. C. Frend, London: SPCK.

Stewart-Sykes, A. (1998) *The Lamb's High Feast: Melito,* Peri Pascha, *and the Quartodeciman paschal liturgy at Sardis*, Leiden: E. J. Brill.

Talbert, R. J. A. (1984) *The senate of imperial Rome*, Princeton: Princeton University Press.

Taylor, J. (1990) 'The future of Christianity', in McManners 1990: 628–65.

Taylor, L. J. (1995) *Occasions of faith: an anthropology of Irish Catholics*, Philadelphia: University of Pennsylvania Press.

Thomassen, E. (2004) 'Orthodoxy and heresy in second-century Rome', *Harvard Theological Review* 97: 241–56.

Tilley, M. A. (1997) *The Bible in Christian North Africa: the Donatist world*, Minneapolis: Fortress.

Trevett, C. (1996) *Montanism: gender, authority, and the new prophecy*, Cambridge: Cambridge University Press.

Trigg, J. W. (1983) *Origen: the Bible and philosophy in the third century church*, Atlanta: John Knox.

Tuckett, C. M. (1996) *Q and the history of early Christianity*, Edinburgh: T. & T. Clark.

Twomey, V. and Humphries, M. (eds) (forthcoming) *The great persecution, AD 303: a commemoration. Proceedings of the Fifth Maynooth Patristic Conference*, Dublin: Four Courts Press.

Urbainczyk, T. (1997) *Socrates of Constantinople: historian of church and state*, Ann Arbor: University of Michigan Press.

Vermes, G. (1981) *Jesus the Jew: a historian's reading of the gospels*, revised edition, Philadelphia: Fortress.

—— (1997) *The complete Dead Sea Scrolls in English*, London: Allen Lane.

—— (1999) *An introduction to the complete Dead Sea Scrolls*, London: SCM.

—— (2000) *The changing faces of Jesus*, London: Allen Lane.

Veyne, P. (1990) *Bread and circuses: historical sociology and political pluralism*, London: Allen Lane.

Walker, P. W. L. (1990) *Holy city, holy places? Christian attitudes to Jerusalem and the Holy Land in the fourth century*, Oxford: Clarendon Press.

Ward-Perkins, B. (1998) 'The cities', in Cameron and Garnsey 1998: 371–410.

Ward-Perkins, J. B. and Goodchild, R. G. (1953) 'The Christian antiquities of Tripolitania', *Archaeologia* 95: 1–84.

White, L. M. (1990) *Building God's house in the Roman world: architectural adaptation among pagans, Jews, and Christians*, Baltimore: Johns Hopkins University Press (= White 1996–7: I).

—— (1996–7) *The social origins of Christian architecture*, 2 vols, Valley Forge, PA: Trinity Press International (vol. I = White 1990).

Wiles, M. (1996) *Archetypal heresy: Arianism through the centuries*, Oxford: Clarendon Press.

Wilken, R. L. (1983) *John Chrysostom and the Jews: rhetoric and reality in the 4th century*, Berkeley and Los Angeles: University of California Press.

—— (2003) *The Christians as the Romans saw them*, revised edition, New Haven: Yale University Press.

Williams, M. A. (1996) *Rethinking 'Gnosticism': an argument for dismantling a dubious category*, Princeton: Princeton University Press.

Williams, R. (1989) 'Does it make sense to speak of pre-Nicene orthodoxy?', in R. Williams (ed.), *The making of orthodoxy*, Cambridge: Cambridge University Press, 1–23.

—— (2005) *Why study the past? The quest for the historical church*, London: Darton, Longman and Todd.

Williamson, R. (1989) *Jews in the Hellenistic world: Philo*, Cambridge: Cambridge University Press.

Wilson, B. (1990), 'New images of Christian community', in McManners 1990: 572–601.

Wilson, B. and Cresswell, J. (eds) (1999) *New religious movements: challenge and response*, London: Routledge.

Wilson, S. G. (2004) *Leaving the fold: apostates and defectors in antiquity*, Minneapolis: Fortress.

Witherington, B. (1988) *Women in the earliest churches*, Cambridge: Cambridge University Press.

—— (1998) *The Acts of the Apostles: a socio-rhetorical commentary*, Grand Rapids, MI: Eerdmans.

Womersley, D. (1988) *The transformation of The Decline and Fall of the Roman Empire*, Cambridge: Cambridge University Press.

Young, F. M. (1991) *The making of the creeds*, London: SCM.

Young, F. M., Ayres, L., and Louth, A. (eds) (2004) *The Cambridge history of early christian literature*, Cambridge: Cambridge University Press.

Index

Note: the following abbreviations have been used.
bp = bishop   emp. = emperor